LOVING'S LOVE

SMITHSONIAN HISTORY OF AVIATION SERIES
VON HARDESTY, SERIES EDITOR

This series of books is intended to contribute to the overall understanding of the history of aviation—its science and technology as well as the social, cultural, and political environment in which it developed and matured. While the series appeals to a broad audience of general readers and specialists in the field, its hallmark is strong scholarly content.

SMITHSONIAN STUDIES IN AVIATION HISTORY
Works that provide new and original knowledge

CLASSICS OF AVIATION HISTORY
Carefully selected out-of-print works that are considered essential scholarship

CONTRIBUTIONS TO AVIATION HISTORY
Previously unpublished documents, reports, symposia, and other materials

LOVING'S LOVE

A BLACK AMERICAN'S EXPERIENCE IN AVIATION

NEAL V. LOVING

SMITHSONIAN INSTITUTION PRESS
WASHINGTON AND LONDON

This book was edited by Initial Cap Editorial Services and designed by Linda McKnight.

Library of Congress Cataloging-in-Publication Data
Loving, Neal V., 1916–
    Loving's Love: a Black American's experience in aviation / Neal V. Loving.
    p. cm. — (Smithsonian history of aviation series)
    ISBN 1-56098-342-6
    1. Loving, Neal V., 1916– .   2. Air pilots—United States—
Biography.   3. Afro-Americans in aeronautics.   I. Title. II. Series.
TL540.L68A3   1994
629.13'092—dc20
[B]   93-24418

British Library Cataloguing-in-Publication Data is available.

Printed in the United States of America
10 9 8 7 6 5 4 3 2 1 99 98 97 96 95 94

⊛ The paper used in this publication meets the minimum requirements of the American National Standard for Permanence of Paper for Printed Library Materials Z39.48-1984.

For permission to reproduce individual illustrations appearing in this book, please correspond directly with the owners of the images, as stated in the picture captions. (The author owns the rights to the illustrations that do not list a source.) The Smithsonian Institution Press does not retain reproduction rights for these illustrations individually or maintain a file of addresses for photo sources.

Publisher's note: The descriptions of otherwise undocumented personal incidents and the recollections of episodes and persons are entirely the author's. Every effort has been made to verify details and ensure correctness; inaccuracy if it occurs is regretted.

TO CLARE THÉRÈSE

CONTENTS

CONTENTS

SERIES EDITOR'S NOTE

The "African American Pioneers in Aviation" books in the Smithsonian History of Aviation Series seek through the publication of memoirs and narrative histories to reveal the many contributions of African Americans to aviation. For blacks, careers—or even involvement—in aviation came only after considerable struggle. The achievements of black pioneers in this important sphere of technology mirrors the evolving character of American society with its built-in contradiction of opportunity and racial discrimination. The achievement of controlled powered flight was a unique American accomplishment. A unique American obsession was the establishment of laws and customs mandating because of race and color exclusion of a whole group of American citizens from equal participation in the social, political, economic, and technical life of the nation. The determination to restrict African Americans from participating freely in aviation blighted their ambitions and clearly limited the accomplishments of those whose love of flight was the dominating theme of their lives. For many others, the restrictions imposed on entry into aviation, as in many other fields, were enough to drive them away from the extreme efforts required to learn and practice the art and science of flight. But achieve and practice they did, and, considering the obstacles that had to be overcome, their accomplishments were magnificent, their lives significant, and America became a better place for everyone.

The personal histories included in this series provide insights into the individual characters of these pioneers who displayed perseverance, courage, strength, self-confidence, and a determination to succeed set against an American society hostile to black achievement.

THEODORE W. ROBINSON

FOREWORD

I first met Neal Loving in November 1953 when I visited him at City Airport in Detroit. I found we had many things in common, most notably an interest in designing and building airplanes.

I remember greeting Neal as he taxied his airplane up to the flight line at one of our early Experimental Aircraft Association (EAA) fly-in conventions in the 1950s. His smiling face symbolized the energy and enthusiasm Neal has for flying activities. It also characterized the interest he showed for others, their families and friends.

Neal has set an example we all seek to emulate. Rising from very humble beginnings, he has enjoyed a successful career as a pilot, aircraft designer, and builder. Reading his book is an education as well as an inspiration for all ages and interests.

Neal—like aviation itself—has touched many people from across the country and around the world. Many share his "can do" attitude that is exhibited each year at the EAA National Convention at Oshkosh, Wisconsin. They also share Neal's love for airplanes and, even more important, for the people who fly them. The story of Neal's life and his passion for aviation that is contained within these pages is well worth reading.

PAUL H. POBEREZNY, Founder and Chairman of the Board
Experimental Aircraft Association

PREFACE AND ACKNOWLEDGMENTS

A strology is not a subject in which I have much faith, but I believe my interest in aviation may be due in part to being born under what I call the "Sign of Lindbergh."

Charles A. Lindbergh, the first pilot to fly solo across the Atlantic, was born in Detroit, Michigan, on February 4, 1902. I was born in Detroit on February 4, 1916. His early years were spent in Minnesota (Little Falls) and mine in Minnesota (Duluth). His father was a professional (lawyer) and mine was a professional (doctor of optometry). I attended Cass Technical High School in Detroit while his mother was teaching there. Finally, our last names begin with the letter *L* and have two syllables.

What blessings I may have derived from these similarities are small compared to the blessings I have received from my family, relatives, and friends, particularly in support of my writing this autobiography. It was their prodding, encouragement, and support (plus the wonders of a word processor) that kept me working on it until completion.

This project lay dormant for years because my ego was never sufficient for me to feel that writing about my life would be of interest to anyone but myself and (possibly) my family. But it eventually occurred to me that if just one person would read this book and be persuaded that he or she was not handicapped because of race, sex, color, or physical disability, my efforts would be fully repaid.

In the case of most personal histories, there are occasionally people who would prefer not or should not be identified by name. I have used pseudonyms in three instances, Jerry Frazier, Marie Patterson, and Lt. Charles Phelps.

My gratitude goes to my entire family, which includes all of my relatives and friends, who never failed to provide support when my energy or ambition sagged. To each and all I express my humble thanks. I would be remiss, however, if I did not acknowledge the most important contributor to the successful completion of this book, my wife, Clare. She gave me the inspiration and daily assistance necessary to finish this arduous and time-consuming task. It is to her this book is lovingly dedicated.

I also wish to acknowledge the specific contributions of these individuals whose selfless and unstinting efforts have led to the publishing of this book. Without the initiative and dedication of Antoinette Amos, minority outreach officer at the National Air and Space Museum, Washington, D.C., this book would still be an unfulfilled dream. Carlton Spitzer, the president of Opportunity Skyway, Inc., voluntarily undertook the mammoth job of editing the entire original manuscript, the results of which are self-evident. Paul Poberezny took time from his busy schedule to write the kind words in the foreword. Thanks also to Duane Cole for permitting me to quote from his book, *This Is EAA,* and to June Holt, whose comments and recommendations were incorporated in the final version.

All of the above efforts would have been in vain if Felix Lowe, director of the Smithsonian Institution Press, had not approved my manuscript for publication. I thank him for this decision and for naming Theodore Robinson, aviation historian, as general editor. Ted spent many hours searching for errors and omissions, of which there were many. Last, and certainly not least, I wish to express my gratitude to Therese Boyd of Initial Cap Editorial Services. It was she who had the final responsibility, aided by Mr. Robinson, to raise the quality of my amateur autobiographical efforts as necessary to meet the high professional standards of the Smithsonian Institution Press.

HASTENING TO DISASTER

Sunday morning, July 30, 1944, I was scheduled to hold a training session for selected Civil Air Patrol (CAP) cadets at Wings Airport outside Detroit. To ensure that my glider, Wayne S-1 (NX27775), was airworthy, I went to my glider manufacturing facility, Wayne Aircraft Company (co-owned by long-time friend Earsly Taylor) the day before to complete the preflight inspection.

Upon finding a loose seat bracket I began the necessary repairs but was not able to finish before it became necessary to leave for the 3 P.M. shift at the Ford Motor Company. When I called Earsly, without hesitation she promised her brother Rudy would be able to complete the repairs that day. With that assurance I went to work in pleasant anticipation of a date the next day with my fiancée, Marie Patterson. The spring and summer had been unseasonably cool and this was our first opportunity for an outdoor activity. We had planned a picnic just for the two of us at Belle Isle after my morning CAP duties were completed. We looked forward to being together in the quiet, wooded picnic area, enjoying our lunch and watching the huge iron ore freighters move down the Detroit River.

Reporting for work on the Saturday afternoon shift, I asked my supervisor for permission to take Sunday off (due to the war Ford was working seven days a week) with the provision that if the weather was bad I would cancel my plans and report for work as usual. However, Sunday turned out to be a beautiful summer day which, in the course of events to follow, changed the shape of my life forever.

After leaving Ford's at midnight I drove straight to the shop to check on NX27775. The repairs had not been completed. Since it was too late to cancel the CAP training session, I worked furiously to repair the damaged seat structure. It was almost 5 A.M. when the job was completed and my body and mind were fatigued. Arriving home, I took a quick bath and went to bed for two hours of sleep.

At 8 A.M. I was back at the glider shop where the CAP cadets had been ordered to report. Earsly (our CAP commander), Rudy, and Marie were already there and joined the cadets in loading NX27775 onto the trailer. Since we had done this procedure many times, it was not long before we departed for Wings Airport, 18 miles north of Detroit.

After turning into the airport driveway, I stopped at the office to ask the manager about the condition of the field, which was being graded and was in poor condition except for the one sod runway. He suggested I check on the field condition by driving my car out on the field. Looking at my watch, I knew this would delay my planned picnic so I decided against it and walked directly to the fully assembled glider. My crew chief informed me that a critical portion of the glider tow rope had been inadvertently left at the shop, which would seriously reduce the altitude I could attain before completing my usual 180-degree turn and downwind landing. Again, ignoring proper safety procedures and precautions, I decided to proceed without delay.

A glance at the windsock showed the wind was blowing across the runway, which would mean a loss of precious altitude while compensating for drift. Even with this disturbing news there was no sense of alarm.

Climbing into the cockpit I checked the airspeed indicator, a chrome-plated, circular wind vane mounted in front of me on a vertical streamlined post. The vane rotated against a calibrated spring as airspeed increased. Readings from 0 to 50 MPH were printed on the outer edge. It was properly set at 0 MPH. In my hurry, however, I failed to note that the calibrated spring was not also set at 0, resulting in the airspeed indicator registering 10 MPH higher than actual airspeed. This meant my normal indicated gliding speed would be dangerously close to stalling speed. But full of confidence and anxious to get this training mission completed, I ordered the tow rope hooked up. Earsly raised the left wing until NX27775 was level on its single wheel and I signaled Rudy in the tow car to start the tow.

The morning air was cool and my yellow and blue creation, the S-1, climbed like the proverbial "homesick angel" after takeoff. Soon the tell-tale aerodynamic burble shaking the glider indicated that maximum attainable altitude had been reached. Pulling the tow-rope release knob, I soared away in the smooth morning air, enjoying the special beauty of silent flight. This brief exhilaration ended as I entered a gentle 180-degree turn to the left in preparation for my final approach. The lowered wing blocked sight of the runway until a major portion of the turn had been completed. When the runway came into view it was evident the crosswind had pushed me well to the right of the centerline. This meant a loss of precious altitude during the extra turn required to line up with the runway.

In my haste, I decided to land in the area adjacent to the runway which I had neglected to inspect. Turning on final approach I saw the graded area in front of me had a ridge of dirt piled about two feet high, making it dangerously unsuitable for landing. My airspeed indicator indicated a normal 35 MPH (which was actually only 25 MPH) so I increased my bank angle to get back to the runway. As the necessary control pressures were applied the glider stalled and immediately entered a left tailspin. The earth whirled furiously around as I plunged almost vertically toward the ground. My gentle, obedient little glider had turned against me like a family pet suddenly gone wild. Even though it seemed sure I would crash into the spinning earth of brown and green, I tried desperately to recover. Pushing the stick forward with ailerons neutral and full right rudder stopped the spin, but now the ground rushed up to meet me before the glider could level off. Diving into the ground, the nose of the glider collapsed into wood splinters, crushing both my feet while my head pitched forward against the metal instrument panel with tremendous force. In an instant I was transformed from a young man happily looking forward to a fun-filled afternoon to one in a state of blinding, overwhelming pain, followed by brief oblivion—prologue to a radically different, sometimes difficult, and always challenging new way of life.

CHAPTER ONE

DREAMS

The pilot of a silver-winged de Havilland DH-4 biplane flying over the west side of Detroit on a summer day in 1926 will never know the lasting impact his passage of flight had on me, a 10-year-old boy. At that moment I was engaged in a losing argument with my oldest brother, Bernard ("Barney"), regarding my right to build an outdoor radio antenna adjacent to his.

He had already successfully built several radios from plans printed in a monthly radio magazine, and I was envious. The sounds and smells that emanated from his relatively crude, battery-powered radios were so fascinating I wanted one of my own. Putting on a pair of earphones and listening to static-filled voices and music was magical indeed. However, to reach beyond the local stations an outside antenna at least 75 to 100 feet in length was required. It was considered quite a feat in those early days to get what was called "distance," that is, to pick up radio stations from such far-off places as WLW in Cincinnati, Ohio, or KDKA in Pittsburgh, Pennsylvania.

Barney had already laid out long, shiny copper strands of antenna wire on the ground, ready to string it from our house to the garage, when he raised objections to my proposed antenna, arguing it would interfere with his radio reception. At that moment the roar of the approaching airplane almost drowned out his words. As the low-flying

5

biplane passed overhead, my attention was drawn to the sky and the apparent magic of flight.

Barney's fellow radio enthusiast, Harold Madgett, looked up and stated with the sure confidence of a 14-year-old, "I know what kinda airplane that is, it's a DH-4 mail plane with a Liberty engine." Following Harold's gaze, I watched the silver and blue DH-4 until it disappeared into the haze-filled horizon of downtown Detroit. Noticing my curiosity, Barney seized the opportunity to suggest I change my interest from radio to aviation. In retrospect, my brother really did me a favor: his idea changed the direction of my life forever.

But I am not sure I was appreciative at the time. The more I thought about aviation the more exciting and attractive it became. I found my family's reaction, however, to be skeptical and derisive. My parents, Hardin Clay Loving and Alma Loving, were pessimistic since they knew there were no opportunities for blacks in aviation. My father had first-hand experience with the difficulties of being a pioneer. In 1925, he was the first black to pass the Michigan State Board of Examiners in the practice of optometry. He studied at Columbia Optical College in St. Paul, Minnesota, and had graduated in 1924 while supporting a wife and four children with a full-time job as conductor on the South Shore Railroad operating from Duluth to St. Paul.

In retrospect, I realize my father, a tall, fair-skinned man with gray eyes and dark wavy hair, must have been "passing" for white as blacks were at that time restricted to more menial positions, such as Pullman porters. His Caucasian appearance confused a white real estate salesman who came into his office at 911 Gratiot Avenue to sell him a home in an exclusive area where blacks were barred by restrictive covenants. Father immediately called out, "Alma, come into the office please." Mother came in, her brown face in pleasing contrast to her starched, white office uniform. Looking the salesman straight in the eye my father introduced her, "I want you to meet my wife, Mrs. Loving." Salvaging what dignity he could, the salesman beat a hasty retreat.

Looking eagerly for someone to share my newfound interests, I tried to talk aviation with my brother Robert and sister Ardine, but they wouldn't listen, much less partake in conversation. Despite the lack of support and skepticism at home, I searched for airplane information in nearby stores. Evidently there was little public interest in aviation, for I could not find a single aviation periodical, even at the newsstands.

Mother, an avid reader, suggested I visit the local branch of the Detroit Library, which turned out to be a treasure trove of information. The library services were free, a boon to my limited financial resources. The periodical section displayed current aviation magazines for in-library reading and maintained a reservoir of old issues. The aircraft book section provided a source of material for every aspect of aviation, from preliminary aircraft design to engine maintenance and flight instruction. It wasn't long before I had checked out every aviation book and magazine in their collection, many of them several times.

As my knowledge grew, so did my enthusiasm. Every time an airplane flew overhead I raced outside to watch until it was out of sight. During school hours teachers took a dim view of my sky-gazing at passing airplanes when I should have been concentrating on my studies. After hours of staring at the sky whenever airplanes flew over, I was able to distinguish the staccato bark of the fast pursuit planes based at nearby Selfridge Field from the smooth, throaty roar of the Ford Trimotors being flown from the factory located in Dearborn, a suburb of Detroit.

Mother marveled at my ability to identify airplanes by the sound of their engines without even looking up. However, there still remained little family support for my aviation activities. Their negative thinking was based on newspaper reports reflecting the dangers in aviation as well as their belief that no significant career opportunities in aviation existed for blacks. Father told me many times to stop playing with model airplanes and learn something at which I could earn a living. Also, among many blacks there was still the feeling that "we should stay in our place," and that place certainly didn't include aviation. There was even peer pressure from some of my family and friends who felt, since they were restricted to menial jobs, that I shouldn't try to be "better than they were." Despite the negative climate, my enthusiasm increased every day as I built more model airplanes and read more magazines.

My first career ambition was to be a smartly uniformed, military aviator and fly one of the speedy, nimble Curtiss Hawk pursuit planes I frequently saw darting about the Detroit skies. When one of my schoolteachers said I could obtain an application for the U.S. Air Corps from any U.S. post office, I quickly went to the nearest one and obtained a copy. On arriving home I went straight to my bedroom to read the requirements in privacy, knowing my family would laugh and taunt me for dreaming such an impossible dream.

One line on the application told me they were right: it clearly stated that the applicant had to be "a white, male citizen." But, with my unbounded enthusiasm at the age of 11, the facts of life were not all that important. I threw the application blank away and continued to dream impossible dreams.

On May 20, 1927, Charles A. Lindbergh took off from Long Island, New York, on his epic nonstop flight to Paris, creating new public interest in aviation. Any doubts I had about the seriousness of my interest were removed by that spectacular event. Airplane magazines became plentiful at all the newsstands and drugstores. Model airplane kits and supplies were available at specialty shops and major department stores, all taking advantage of the "Lindbergh Era." Every major newspaper had aviation cartoon strips, one of which included my favorite, "Tailspin Tommy."

I even stopped going to the Saturday movies with my brothers, saving what little money I could earn to buy magazines and model airplane material. At that time I had the nightly job of cleaning up the little restaurant my mother operated in the back of our home for Pullman porters from the nearby Michigan Central Railroad Station who were laying over in Detroit for the night. I was paid 75 cents a week for my services. I gave up all my usual spending activities, including my daily 5-cent school lunch, to pay for aviation magazines and model airplane material. I was understandably a skinny kid.

My first major model-airplane building project was a 24-inch flying scale model of the Curtiss Hawk P1-B, the airplane based at Selfridge Field I had dreamed of flying as a military aviator. In my eyes, it was the most beautiful airplane in the world with its red-starred, bright orange wings and olive drab fuselage. One look at a completed model of the Hawk in the model airplane shop created an instant desire to have one. The cost of the kit was three dollars, a tremendous amount of money in those days. Saving every penny of my 75-cents-a-week wage, it took a month to earn the required three dollars.

After opening the box and reading the instructions I was ready and eager to start work on my very own model Curtiss Hawk. The only table in our house big enough for this project was in the kitchen. Mother said it was mine to use each day provided I cleared it off in time for the family meal.

I worked several weeks to complete the fuselage, landing gear, and tail, teaching myself the necessary skills as I made mistakes along the way. One evening, as I started to assemble the wings, Mother asked me to clear the table for supper. Putting the fuselage and other completed parts on a kitchen chair, I started to remove the wing assembly from the table. At that moment my 9-year-old sister Ardine dashed into the house and without looking sat down on my model, crushing it flat. One month's wages and many weeks of concentrated effort were reduced to matchsticks. My typically boyish low regard for little sisters dropped to a new low. But in retrospect, that first disaster was good training for the many challenges that were to follow.

A major aviation event of the late 1920s was the Ford Reliability Tour, sponsored by the Stout Metal Airplane Company, a division of the Ford Company. Ford was engaged in building one of the leading transports of the day, the all-metal Ford Trimotor. The general public still had little faith in the airplane as a safe and reliable means of transportation. Daredevil barnstorming pilots deliberately exaggerated the dangers of flight to enhance their reputation and, hence, earn more money.

To bolster public confidence, the Ford Motor Company sponsored the Ford Annual National Air Tour to demonstrate the dependability and performance of all types of aircraft, from open-cockpit three-seater biplanes to huge ten-passenger monoplane transports. The 1928 tour originated at Ford Airport in Dearborn on June 30. Twenty-four airplanes started the 6,000-mile tour, which stopped at thirty-two cities in fifteen states, ending at Dearborn on July 28. The planes were judged on performance and reliability.

It may be more than simple coincidence that the Ford Trimotor won the last three air tours, taking permanent possession of the Ford Trophy. Waco biplanes had won the two previous tours, resulting in rule changes that evidently favored large passenger-carrying mono-planes such as the Ford Trimotor. Due to the size of the event, special bus service was available from downtown Detroit. Until that time I was unable to visit any of the local airports because they were located miles from public bus and streetcar routes. So I saved my money to ride the airport bus to my "special heaven" of the day, Ford Airport.

The sounds of revving airplane motors, the smell of engine exhaust and doped fabric, airplanes taking off and landing at frequent intervals all conveyed a sense of excitement that I still cannot adequately describe. Airplanes of all types, large and small, went through their flight trials. I stayed all day without lunch, a black kid alone in the milling crowd, but I certainly was not lonesome.

In addition to the hustle and bustle of the airplane activities, another prestigious event was scheduled: the Gordon Bennett International Balloon Race. Those manned hydrogen-filled balloons were a quiet contrast to the noisy tour aircraft. I watched with enthusiasm as teams from the United States and Europe took off in their respective colorful balloons in an effort to win the Gordon Bennett Trophy for their country. Despite my personal disappointment with the application form for the Army Air Corps, I was pleased to hear it won possession of the trophy that year.

The real highlight of the day for me was watching a brand new Ford Trimotor as it rolled out of the comparatively dark recesses of the factory hangar onto the bright sunshine of the ramp. Shiny aluminum wings and fuselage reflected the sun's rays like a giant, multifaceted jewel. Three 200-HP Wright J-5 Whirlwind engines (just like the one on Lindbergh's *Spirit of St. Louis*) turned the Hamilton-Standard steel propellers into mirror-like disks with a powerful roar.

But then a troubling thought came to my mind. As I looked at this magnificent technical masterpiece it occurred to me (at the age of

12) that this was the perfect airplane and therefore could not be improved upon. After all, it carried ten people in cabin comfort at the terrific speed of 95 MPH (my father insisted 35 MPH in his Maxwell was fast enough for anybody). Each passenger sat in a wicker seat by a window and, in addition to cabin heat, the plane even had a lavatory! I had no doubt that the ultimate airplane had already been built, hence there was no need for future airplane engineers. My budding career as an airplane designer seemed hopeless.

But again, my boundless enthusiasm and eternal optimism returned undiminished, and I went home eager to read about that day's events in the daily newspapers, already looking forward to buying airplane magazines reporting on the tour in technical detail.

My father was not only pessimistic about my aviation career opportunities, but he also had little confidence in my mental and physical capabilities. His argument, repeated many times, was: "Neal, if skilled aviators are getting killed almost every day, how can you expect to survive with your ordinary talent?" This certainly was a rational argument which I fully understood. But just the thought of flying in an airplane (which I had not yet experienced) outweighed whatever personal risks I might encounter. One day my father, who was in charge of the Pullman quarters at the time, met a porter, "Smitty" Smith from Cincinnati. Smitty had a part-time job at Lunken Airport in Cincinnati as an "aeroportah," carrying luggage to and from visiting aircraft. This placed him in close proximity to airplanes and gave him the frequent opportunity to meet skilled pilots.

I was green with envy. My father took this opportunity to test my knowledge by having Smitty ask me a few questions about aviation. I answered Smitty's query about the use of radio beams for navigation quite readily. His question about aircraft engine starting procedures was also quickly answered. This was one of the few moments Father actually showed pride in my aviation knowledge.

This elevated status with my father didn't last long. One of the more complex tasks associated with building a model airplane was carving the propeller. Each propeller had to be carved from a solid block of balsa about one inch square and six to eight inches long. I bought a supply of blocks from the nearest model airplane store and started carving with a razor blade, in my usual self-teaching mode. Father watched in silence as the pile of shavings on the floor increased steadily in size. After many attempts that day, my last one was completed with one blade going backward. I heard a soft but very sarcastic "I told you so" laugh from my father. I redoubled my efforts the next day and was soon carving serviceable props for my models. That laugh, I am sure, drove me on to success.

While Mother was not at all enthusiastic about my aviation interest (she considered it dangerous), she provided what little encouragement I received from my family. On Christmas Day 1928, she gave me a copy of Charles Lindbergh's autobiography, *We*, and an imitation leather helmet complete with goggles. There wasn't a happier 12-year-old boy in the neighborhood that day. I have long since lost the helmet and goggles but I still cherish my copy of *We*.

Another major aviation event of the year was the second annual All-American Air Show held April 6–14, 1929, at Convention Hall in downtown Detroit. Streetcar fare was only 6 cents so transportation was not a problem. It was a big show with over seventy airplanes on display and many smaller exhibits of aviation interest.

Arriving in the morning as the show opened I could not have been happier had I been entering the gates of heaven! The sounds, colors, and exotic smells overwhelmed my senses. Graceful, curved wings of monoplanes and biplanes blended with sleek fuselages in a brilliant panorama of color. Shiny steel propellers stood out in sharp contrast to the black engine cylinders and cowling. One airplane that caught my eye was a Bellanca cabin monoplane, custom finished and painted for a reigning movie star of the day, beautiful Ann Harding. It was painted two-tone green with cream striping to complement her blonde hair and green eyes. Just to be near these beautiful creations (not Ann Harding) was a dream come true.

As I walked up and down the rows of display aircraft it became clear to me that a 13-year-old black kid in clean but shabby clothes wasn't considered a likely prospect by airplane salesmen. Ignoring me, they handed out colorful and informative brochures, many of which were discarded by often disinterested air-show attendees. I followed right behind them, picking up their discarded brochures from the floor before they were stepped on.

One airplane in particular became my favorite, the Doyle Oriole, painted in authentic oriole colors of yellow and black. It was a high-wing, two-place, open-cockpit sport monoplane (in contrast to the more common biplanes of the day) with exceptionally smooth, graceful lines. I stood by this exhibit for at least an hour before someone finally threw away a Doyle brochure, which I quickly added to my collection.

In the weeks following the show I carefully examined my colorful brochures, especially my favorite, the Doyle. Also among my treasure of brochures were those for the Wacos, Stinsons, Ryans, Bellancas, Fokkers, and Fords I had carefully inspected during the show. I spent much of my spare time at home fantasizing about the wonderful and exciting flights I would make someday in these marvelous machines. As my model airplane skills increased I built detailed flying scale models of those same airplanes, adding a touch of reality to my fantasies of flight.

Another touch of reality was not so obvious to me in December 1928. I had already experienced the realities of racial discrimination in reading the cadet application for the U.S. Air Corps. However, discriminatory attitudes in commercial aviation were much more subtle. The exclusion of blacks from all aspects of aviation, including white flying schools (even when the applicant had sufficient funds), was not advertised, but no less rigidly practiced. The low regard for the intelligence and moral character of Negroes was evident in a joke printed in the aviation humor section of the December 1928 edition of *Aero Digest*. This magazine was the leading aviation periodical of that era and, by referring to blacks only in a derogatory manner, typified the prevailing negative racial attitudes, even at highly respectable levels of aviation. The humor page was entitled "Picked from the Air":

Colored man to pilot: "Say, Boss, give me one of dem $3 hops."
Just before taking off the colored man signals to the pilot: "Roll
her jes a little bit sos I can get dat drunken sensation.
Pilot: "How much rolling you want?"
Colored man: "Use yo own jedgement, you know $3 'ill buy a lot
o' gin."

I was only 12 years old at the time when I read this so-called humor
and was blissfully unaware of its implications. However, I soon learned
the whites-only practices in commercial aviation were no less rigid
than those of the U.S. Air Corps. But true dreams are not confined by
reality so I continued to look to the bright blue sky for my future.

Most memorable in 1929 was the official opening of Detroit City
Airport located at Gratiot and Conner avenues, well within the city
limits of Detroit. The Gratiot streetcar line went right by the airport
and the fare was still only 6 cents. This was the first airport I could
reach by regularly scheduled public transportation. French Road ran
parallel to the north-south runway across the middle of the frequently
used east-west runway. A policeman from the nearby Conners Station
patrolled the airport in his yellow Model A Ford roadster, stopping the
auto traffic as necessary to prevent auto/airplane collisions.

The only hangar on the field was operated by the 107th Army
Observation Squadron of the Michigan National Guard. During my
many visits the mechanics never spoke to me but did not seem to mind
as I quietly watched them perform their maintenance duties. For their
peace of mind I kept my hands in my pockets and never interfered
with their work. Occasionally I was especially rewarded when the flight
crews took off in their Liberty-powered Douglas 0-2H observation
biplanes on routine missions. The National Guard personnel must have
become comfortable with my presence for I was there as often as I
could afford the streetcar fare and no one questioned me.

The fall of 1929 was the beginning of my last year at Franklin Elementary School (eighth grade). Due to our family circumstances (poverty,

welfare, evictions) I had attended seven elementary schools prior to entering Franklin. But I managed to maintain a good scholastic record and was given the privilege of being a hall monitor, to check students in the hallway between classes to make sure they had an authorized pass. Since there was very little student traffic I started writing poetry to pass the time. My level of interest increased when my English teacher announced a poetry contest with an unidentified first prize. With this as inducement I wrote a poem titled "My Ambition." It was several verses long and ended with these lines:

> If my dreams for the future prevail,
> I shall be flying your daily mail.

There must have been very little competition for I won first prize, which I learned later was the unwanted honor of reciting my poem at the eighth-grade graduation ceremonies in January 1930. And even worse, my poetry efforts were to cause me serious problems when I entered Jefferson Intermediate School the following month.

Miss MacDonald was a very refined and cultured English teacher at Jefferson. She had dark, wavy red hair and always dressed in quiet good taste. I was very much impressed by her professional appearance and was proud to be in her class. Miss MacDonald was also editor of the school paper and occasionally invited members of her class to submit original material for possible publication. With confidence resulting from my winning the eighth-grade poetry competition at Franklin School, I submitted several of my poems for consideration.

A few days later, on entering my English class, it was obvious Miss MacDonald was upset. As soon as the door was shut she told us to close our books and announced she was going to read some literary material that had been submitted for publication in the school paper. No names would be mentioned since she wanted us to make an unbiased judgment as to whether or not a student in her class could write with such adult skills. It was clear she thought the work was plagiarized. Until then I thought I was an innocent bystander. But when she started to read one of my poems I knew I was in deep trouble. It didn't help knowing I was the only black kid in the class.

When Miss MacDonald finished reading the poem she asked the class to vote on the matter. Several of my classmates from Franklin School were in the class and recognized the poem as mine. When they expressed their belief that I had written it she became infuriated and ordered me to leave the class and report immediately to the principal's office.

In his private study, the principal told me attempted plagiarism was a very serious matter. After my denial he offered me an opportunity to prove my skills by allowing me the use of his walnut-paneled study, plus paper and pencil, so I could write an original literary work. As he closed the door I sat down in his chair in a state of panic. Staring blankly at the paper I was totally incapable of creative thought.

When he returned an hour later my paper was blank. After inquiring of my family background and finding no evidence of literary skills, the principal was assured of my guilt. He decided not to allow me to return to school until Mother came on my behalf. Although I was sure she had not convinced him of my innocence I was finally allowed to resume my English studies. Miss MacDonald refused to let me back into her class, however, and never spoke to me again. Years later, when free of raising children, Mother took an interest in creative writing and began a successful career as author, playwright, and publisher.

In retrospect, I have often wondered how a trained educator could give a 14-year-old boy pencil and paper, put him in an unfamiliar room under stressful conditions, and allow him an hour to "create" high-quality literature. It brought to an end my interest in writing poetry.

The one bright note during my one year at Jefferson Intermediate School was being elected president of the newly formed Jefferson Aeronautics Club even though I was the only black member. My election was probably by default since none of the student members had been studying aviation as long as I had and Mr. Merkobrad, our advisor and machine shop instructor, had very little aeronautical knowledge.

During my term of office I acted both as president and instructor. It was good experience for me since, in the process of teaching, I studied constantly and learned much more than I taught. It was also the first time I was able to share my interest in aviation with boys my own age.

One of my new friends was a chubby boy named Bob Summerfield. Both of us dreamed of owning an airplane but we realized our age and limited financial resources made it impossible. After much discussion we made a deal. I would design a ground trainer–type airplane and he would provide the funds for its construction. We took in another partner, Lester Leroue, who was to help with the construction. I completed my first design (based on the Curtiss Hawk, of course) to be powered by a one-cylinder air compressor that I planned to convert to a two-cycle gasoline engine.

After looking at my plans Bob immediately lost interest when he realized he was too big to get into the cockpit. The project was canceled by mutual agreement, but we remained friends and I would see Bob and Lester again when I entered high school.

May 5, 1930, is a date I remember as well as my birthday. I had saved up five dollars for my first airplane ride at Detroit City Airport. There, parked on the ramp on this warm spring day was an OX-5-powered Waco NC4045, an open-cockpit biplane, its yellow wings and green fuselage shining in the bright sunlight. The pilot, who was also the salesman, said the ride would cost only three dollars. With two dollars remaining from my five-dollar bill plus another one dollar I could raise during the week, I was already planning to come back the next Sunday for a second ride, even before I had my first. While these thoughts raced through my mind the pilot waited for another passenger to fill the other available front seat.

The longer I waited for my long-sought flight the more my youthful courage diminished. Overcome by fear, I finally went back to the pilot and asked him to return my money, but he refused. Realizing how scared I was, and with no other prospective customer in sight, he decided at long last to give me my ride. I climbed in the two-seated front cockpit and nervously strapped myself in. The engine started with a mighty roar and the airplane vibrated in response to the whirling prop. I began to shake with fright. While we taxied to the north end of the field along French Road, I noticed a young white boy about my age standing on the sidewalk signaling vigorously his desire to go

CHAPTER TWO

DESIGNS

When I entered Cass Technical High School in January 1931, the United States and many other nations of the world were in the grip of the Great Depression. As with millions of other families at that time, the Loving family's financial situation had reached a new low. Father had given up his practice of optometry but managed to eke out an existence by getting odd jobs using his skills in plumbing and carpentry. His income was sporadic, however, and we were forced to move quite often, sometimes even by eviction. Occasionally we moved to my maternal grandmother's house, where the relationship between my father and my grandmother was so strained they would not speak to each other, resulting in emotional stress in the Loving family, especially among the children. When we could not afford the price of a bushel of coal during cold weather, our water pipes would freeze, making our toilet unusable. By 1931 our circumstances were so desperate my mother applied for welfare assistance from the city (my father was too proud to do so himself). It was at this time, when my family was practically destitute, that I entered high school.

Cass Technical High School was, and is, a large facility, one city block long with seven full floors, located near downtown Detroit. The curricula offerings were equally impressive, with courses ranging from music, electrical theory and practice, and costume design to prenursing. I entered the auto/aero department, where naturally I chose to specialize in aeronautics. The two aeronautics courses, aircraft mechanics and aircraft engines, were offered in the senior year only. Cass Tech's school brochure emphasized that it was not a vocational school and all courses were college preparatory.

On entering Cass Tech I was overwhelmed by its physical size and the thousands of students moving randomly in the hallways on their way to class. This was quite a change from the regimented elementary school where students were required to walk in single file, under strict supervision, from class to class. In elementary school no student was allowed in the hallway during school hours unless he or she had a pass issued by a teacher. At Cass Tech, the faculty expected the students to act responsibly without strict adult surveillance.

The first problem I faced was financial. Up to the ninth grade, all books were provided to the students free of charge by the Detroit Board of Education. At the high school level, however, students were required to buy their assigned textbooks at the school bookstore. I managed to earn enough money to buy the paper supplies but books were financially out of the question. I partially resolved the problem by borrowing books from my Jefferson School friends, Bob Summerfield and Lester Leroue. They were happy to accommodate me since I promised to complete their homework assignments before I did my own. Lack of school books would cause me many problems but in one instance it was a blessing.

One day my freshman English teacher gave our class an assignment to read a famous French poem, "The Prisoner of Challon." I could not borrow a book and the next day was totally unprepared for class. On entering the room we were told to close our books and write a review of the poem. Knowing only the title and the time period in which it was written, I used my imagination to its fullest to write my review. I discussed at length the terrible condition of the French prisons and the political problems of the Napoleonic era.

At the next class session the teacher went over some of the reviews and expressed her special satisfaction with one. What made her particularly happy with this particular review was that it expressed original thoughts and did not parrot words directly from the poem. I was surprised and pleased that it was my work she was praising, for which I received an A-plus! Since I had not read the poem, how could I not be original? This is one of the few cases where I could say "Ignorance is bliss!"

Another memorable event for me in high school occurred about two weeks after I enrolled in the auto/aero department. The department head, A. D. Althouse, sent a note through my homeroom teacher asking me to see him in his office. Such a summons usually indicated serious trouble, but I could not think of what I might have done to warrant this request.

Trying to keep my fears under control, I went to his office at the appointed time. He was very pleasant and said that his only reason for wanting to see me was that he had just been informed there was a black student in the aero department. In his official capacity as my advisor, he wanted me to know there were no employment opportunities for me in aviation. He suggested I transfer to the auto department where my skills could be used to make a living among my own people.

Undeterred, I asked if I could remain in the aero department. He gave his permission without much enthusiasm but I left his office with a sense of relief and happiness. Not only was I not in trouble, but I could stay and graduate with the aeronautical knowledge and experience I had come to Cass Tech to obtain.

Meeting William "Bill" Madyck early in my freshman year began a friendship that I cherish to this day. He was a white teenager from a relatively affluent family. In spite of our widely different backgrounds he became a warm, caring friend. We shared a deep and passionate love for aviation at a level well above that of our classmates. I was especially impressed by Bill's background since he had already soloed and was practicing for his private pilot rating.

In one of our many conversations, he offered to sponsor my membership in the Cass Aero Club, of which he was already a member. With the pleasant memories of the Jefferson Aeronautics Club still fresh in my mind I agreed to apply for membership. At the next meeting of the Aero Club, Bill submitted my name. Much to his surprise (not mine), my application was rejected. Upon asking the club advisor for a reason, he was told that blacks were not eligible for membership. I think this action hurt his feelings far more than mine for this kind of racism was common in my life.

A few weeks later, Bill made the headlines of the Detroit newspapers when he failed to recover from an unintentional tailspin in a Fleet biplane. He was killed instantly in the ensuing crash near Detroit City Airport.

For the first time, the realities of the dangers involved in flying were brought home to me, but my enthusiasm was not diminished in any way. I was both surprised and pleased when I saw the school yearbook published at my graduation in 1934. It included a picture of Bill even though he had been dead for almost two years. I still have that yearbook.

The high point of my high school career was the aircraft mechanics course taught by George Tabraham. He was a World War I veteran, a skilled mechanic, and an experienced pilot. He was also a no-nonsense teacher who demanded mature behavior in class and set student performance standards that met the requirements for a government aircraft mechanic. This was my first opportunity to actually work on real airplanes and I was as happy as during my first airplane ride. The smell of aircraft dope, applied to tighten and waterproof the fabric covering of wings and fuselages, was like perfume! On one occasion, however, I created a serious problem because I didn't smell the dope before application.

Mr. Tabraham was unable to teach class for a few days and a substitute, Mr. Fisher, a chemistry teacher, took his place. Knowing nothing at all about aircraft mechanics he allowed the students to continue their projects on their own. However, when technical decisions had to be made, I was surprised when he came to me for help.

On Mr. Fisher's second day as teacher, when one of the students came asking for dope thinner, he referred him to me. I went into the supply room and found a five-gallon can labeled "aircraft dope thinner." I shook the can vigorously to make sure its viscosity was that of thinner, not the more viscous dope, and gave it to him to use.

He came to me later and said the thinner didn't seem right when he mixed it with the dope. After applying several coats to the wing he expressed concern that it did not produce the normal glossy sheen. After looking at it, I decided that high humidity was causing the dope to "blush," so I advised him to continue the application. I thought it was a minor problem that could be cured by applying a coat of pure thinner on a less humid day.

When Mr. Tabraham returned the next day I was sitting in the cockpit of an airplane installing an instrument. All of a sudden I heard him shouting loudly in uncharacteristic language. Clearly he was "madder than hell." Finally he came over and told me the problem. "Some lamebrain in this class," he confided, "has used aircraft gasoline instead of thinner which has ruined the covering on a complete set of wings." Knowing I was that "lamebrain," and being immobilized in the cockpit, I tried desperately to figure a safe way out of my dilemma. Realizing how angry he was, I was terrified at the thought of punishment. In a state of panic I couldn't think of a reasonable excuse for my mistake, so I confessed. He stared at me, his face almost livid with anger. Then he burst out laughing. He explained how he had marked three Xs on the thinner can with white chalk to identify it as gasoline. But only he knew of it. He did note, however, that if I had smelled the can I would have known it was gasoline, not thinner. Admitting it was partially his error, he never mentioned it again.

On his last day of class, Mr. Fisher asked me to meet him in the parking lot at the end of the school day. When I met him there, he invited me into his car and drove to his home. His teenage nephew had just moved out, leaving a supply of clothing which, fortunately for me, was my size. Mr. Fisher invited me to take whatever I wanted. I picked a beautiful dark oxford gray suit complete with matching accessories, including shirt and tie. Mr. Fisher then gave me carfare to get home. It was an act of generosity and thoughtfulness from a gentleman I would never see again.

Koehler Airlines initiated airline passenger service between the water-front cities of Milwaukee, Detroit, and Cleveland, using six-passenger Loening Amphibians that took off from downtown waterfront areas, eliminating long car trips to the airport. The passenger facility was set up near the Ambassador Bridge, a short distance west of downtown Detroit. Fortunately for me, it was within walking distance of my house and I was a frequent visitor. The red and black Loenings made an impressive sight as they taxied out in a cloud of spray and took off to the thunder of their 575-HP Wright Cyclone engines.

I built a three-foot exact scale model of the Loening, fitted it with six miniature seats and painted it in Koehler Airline colors. It represented months of work and several valuable dollars in materials. In a moment of financial desperation I placed it on sale at a variety store on busy Michigan Avenue, hoping it would bring a good price as promised by the store owner. I was crestfallen when he told me he had sold it for five dollars and gave me three dollars for my efforts. I was sure he had sold it for more than five dollars, so I made up my mind to increase my knowledge of the business world as well as aviation.

During the fall of 1932 my father, with the encouragement and support of the Detroit Welfare Department, opened an office of optometry catering especially to welfare patients. Again, his practice was unsuccessful due to insufficient clientele. But during the time his office was open, a young, eager black salesman, Don Pearl Simmons, came by selling "Airplane Brand Sausage." Intrigued by the name of the sausage, my father asked for additional information. Don told him he was president of the Ace Flying Club, an all-black organization devoted to teaching blacks to fly. The money raised by selling the sausage was to be used to help buy an airplane for that purpose. My father immediately told him of my interest in aviation and suggested that I be invited to join. I received the invitation from Don by phone the next day.

The first meeting of the Ace Flying Club I attended was in February 1933, in an abandoned storefront on Davison Avenue in northeast

Detroit. Shortly after my arrival a member came in who attracted the attention of all the males present. Earsly Taylor, the club's secretary, a tall and slender young woman with gray eyes and reddish blond hair, was quiet, modest, and soft-spoken. Her devotion to aviation was on a par with mine. It was the beginning of a lifelong friendship and shared aviation careers.

At this meeting I learned the club had purchased an OX-5-powered Alexander Eaglerock biplane that was complete in every respect except for the wings. An experimental set of wings had been purchased which were quite different from those originally installed on the Eaglerock. Therefore, considerable design and modification work were required before the airplane would be ready for flight. Since I was in Mr. Tabraham's aircraft mechanics course at the time, it was decided I should be in charge of the modification project. Knowing I could rely on Mr. Tabraham for whatever technical support I needed, I accepted this adult responsibility at the tender age of 17.

I went to the large garage where the airplane was located, taking detailed measurements necessary for the wing modifications. I took these data to Mr. Tabraham for his analysis and design recommendations. Since this would be a lengthy process I recommended that club members start building the upper wing centersection before starting other projects in planned sequence. During this time, the rusted wing fittings were to be either repaired or replaced. Although the garage was unheated and the weather chilly in March, the Eaglerock conversion project started with enthusiasm.

With our common aviation interests, Earsly and I became an inseparable team. Our lack of finances also was mutual. Usually we had only enough money for streetcar fare. One morning we had worked quite hard up to lunch hour and began to feel the pangs of hunger. We pooled our financial resources and found, after streetcar fare, we had five pennies between us. After much serious thought we decided to buy a nickel package of Cheese Tid-Bits instead of a candy bar. These were small, very salty, cheese-flavored crackers. We figured the salt would make us so thirsty that we would be glad to drink a lot of water, which would help fill our stomachs. This scheme took care of our thirst and hunger pains, too.

During the spring months I continued to supervise the airplane rebuilding project as well as work on some of the parts at Cass Tech with Mr. Tabraham's permission. In mid-May a severe throat infection kept me out of school for several weeks. During my absence Earsly proceeded with the project, and after a few days came to my house with disturbing news. It seemed Don Simmons had obtained a contract to use the club airplane for advertising purposes in early June. To meet this deadline he had to ignore many of the time-consuming procedures I had recommended to make the plane airworthy. At Earsly's suggestion, I went out to look at the airplane even though my doctor said I wasn't supposed to leave home.

I made sure that most of the members were present, including Don Simmons, at the time of my visit. I was appalled by the poor quality workmanship and the engineering shortcuts that were being taken to save time. Rusty fittings that should have been replaced were sanded and painted for reuse. Instead of making a completely new set of wing/fuselage attachment fittings, the group used the existing Eaglerock fittings. This placed the airplane's center of gravity well beyond safe limits, which was certain to cause serious control problems. I concluded the airplane was definitely unairworthy.

This portion of the work was being supervised by a member whose sole aviation education consisted of a short correspondence-school course. But he was so confident he offered to financially guarantee his work. Don asked if I was willing to do likewise. My reply was, "Yes, if the work was completed to proper airworthiness standards and an accomplished pilot hired to do the test flying." Don decided this would take too much time and money, so my offer was rejected. I left the shop immediately without further discussion, but I still had serious doubts about the success of the airplane rebuilding project. Little did I realize the magnitude of the disaster that was to follow.

Two weeks later, while still convalescing, I went downstairs to pick up my grandmother's *Detroit Free Press,* which I liked to read while eating breakfast. On unfolding the paper I saw the front-page headline in bold, black letters, "LOCAL PILOT AND WIFE KILLED IN AIRPLANE ACCIDENT." Without further reading, I knew it was Don Simmons and his wife, Kathleen. The newspaper story was so technically garbled, however, that I had to call Earsly for an accurate account of what happened.

Don and other club members had taken the airplane out to Burns Airport on the west side of Detroit for final assembly. The airport manager took one look at the assembled airplane and immediately declared it unairworthy. He not only ordered Don to cancel any test-flight plans but to remove the airplane from the airport as soon as possible.

Don waited until the manager went home for supper and then rolled the plane out for takeoff. This was to be not only the first flight for the airplane but Don's first solo flight as well. This was both an illegal and foolishly immature decision. He managed to get it off the ground successfully and after a short flight landed safely at the airport.

The club member who had supervised the work climbed in the passenger cockpit for the second flight, in total violation of all government regulations and common sense. Don's wife, Kathleen, objected, saying Don promised she would be the first passenger. Don acquiesced and she climbed in to replace the club member. On this second flight, with the extra weight of Kathleen making the airplane noseheavy, Don was unable to clear the telephone wires at the end of the field. The landing gear struck the wires, rolling the airplane upside-down and pulling the adjacent telephone poles directly across the cockpit. Don was killed immediately. His wife died two hours later. The aspirations and goals of the Ace Flying Club died with Don Pearl Simmons and his wife, Kathleen.

One of the annual events of the aircraft mechanics course under Mr. Tabraham was a field trip to Selfridge Field, one of the earliest bases established by the U.S. Air Corps. It was the home of the 94th Pursuit Squadron, made famous by Capt. "Eddie" Rickenbacker, America's leading ace in World War I. Despite my disappointment in the "whites only" Air Corps application form, I was happy to get near enough to touch a real military airplane. We also had opportunity to talk to the pilots themselves. We were awed by the power and speed of the Curtiss P6-Es and Boeing P-12-Es at a special air show flown for us. As they

29

flashed across the field at top speeds near 180 MPH, I felt like I had when I saw my first Ford Trimotor: they surely represented the absolute limit of airplane design and performance! I am sure Mr. Tabraham noticed how our grades improved as the result of our renewed enthusiasm from our trip to Selfridge Field.

Graduation ceremonies were held twice a year at Cass Tech, in January and June. My graduation day was in January 1934, on a particularly cold, wintry day. I had managed to save enough money to rent a cap and gown but my shoes were both socially inappropriate and totally inadequate for the cold winter weather. The only available solution was to borrow my father's shoes. He was about six feet tall, weighing close to 200 pounds, while I was about five and a half feet tall and weighed only about 130 pounds. His shoes fit me like loose tents and I feared getting them tangled in my graduation gown and possibly falling down on stage during the ceremonies. By exercising extreme caution I received my diploma without embarrassing myself. I was the first of the children in my family to graduate from high school so it was with some measure of pride that I walked home and showed my family my brand-new diploma in aeronautics.

Mr. Tabraham continued to encourage me after graduation by allowing me to come back to school unofficially to gain additional experience to meet government standards for an aircraft and mechanic's license. Because of his unstinting support and encouragement, Earsly and I often referred to him privately as the "Great White Father," in the popularly assumed tradition of the American Indians (as portrayed by Hollywood) in referring to the president of the United States. This term, though bestowed with great affection and respect, was never used in his presence.

On February 5, 1934, I went to work for the Detroit Welfare Department (today they call it "workfare") cleaning alleys and streets. When I arose early in the morning of February 9 the temperature had dropped to a record −16°F. Even though I had doubts about the adequacy of my clothing I walked about three miles to report for work. An hour later my white coworker looked intently at my face and told me it was turning white.

I thought it was a racist remark and started to get angry. When he said it was probably due to frostbite I realized he could be right. My hands and face had been painfully cold, but now they felt warm and comfortable, which I learned later was due to numbness. I went into the basement of a nearby apartment house where I was sensible enough not to expose my hands and face to the direct flames of the furnace. On taking off my gloves and seeing my grayish white fingers I realized my friend had been right and I offered him my sincere apologies. Without his quick thinking my injuries could have been much worse.

I walked several miles to Receiving Hospital, operated by the City of Detroit for indigent patients, for treatment. My face and all of my fingers had suffered severe frostbite, which turned out to be very painful and took several months to heal. During that time I lost all of my fingernails, two of which became infected. It was late April before I was ready to report for work again. This one incident made me resolve to pursue my aviation career so I would not be required to do outside manual labor to earn a living. When the weather was warm again and my hands and face had healed I went back to my welfare job. But in my spare time I was out looking for a better job.

In the summer of 1934 I worked for Mr. Tabraham at Cass Tech without pay to gain the necessary additional experience required for a aircraft mechanic's license. I invited a friend, King Walter Johnson, to come with me, as he had shown a mild interest in aviation in the past. Walter became quite enthused as we worked on the rebuilding of a bright red Waco biplane that the owner/pilot used primarily for banner towing in the Detroit area. The project was completed during summer vacation and we were quite proud of our handiwork.

The Waco was moved to Gratiot Airport (six miles beyond Detroit City Airport) where it was rigged and successfully test-flown. The owner told Mr. Tabraham he would give Walter and me a ride if we arrived at the airport before he shut the engine off from one of his banner-towing jobs.

On a nice day we thought he would be flying, we started our drive to the airport early enough to make sure we would arrive before he landed. As we crossed Eight Mile Road with the airport still two miles away we saw the red Waco pass overhead. We put the "pedal to the metal" but since my 1928 Chevrolet could only manage to reach 35 MPH, by the time we arrived the Waco had already landed and the engine was shut off. The pilot must have seen the disappointment on our faces for he smiled and told us to climb in the front cockpit for our promised ride.

This was Walter's first flight so I was able to explain the starting procedures and what to expect when we were airborne. He enjoyed the flight until the pilot throttled the engine back to begin our glide back to the airport. Walter thought the engine had quit. Once he was safely on the ground, however, his enthusiasm for flying seemed to be as great as mine. Walter's aviation career culminated in his learning to fly at the Tuskegee Army Air Field (TAAF) in 1944, an all-black flight training facility for prospective fighter pilots. The first graduates from this school formed the famous all-black 99th Fighter Squadron, which served with distinction in the European Theater during World War II.

Popular Mechanics and *Modern Mechanix* magazines followed the aviation trend of that era and featured articles on airplane-type ground trainers for children. These trainers had wing spans of about 10 feet, and one version was even powered by a one-cylinder gasoline engine from a Maytag washing machine. Although the trainers could not fly, children could learn the rudiments of airplane construction and even sit in the cockpit and let their imaginations run wild.

With these articles as inspiration, I designed and built one in the summer of 1934, using plywood from a large furniture packing crate. I bought a single-cylinder air compressor and used my own design to convert it to a gasoline engine. It was fun to sit in and pretend to fly it, although I was never able to get the engine to run. I sent a picture of it to *Mechanix Illustrated* and I was given a "Project of the Month Award" and a check for five dollars. The following year I was invited by the Junior Birdmen of America (sponsored by Hearst Newspapers) to put it on display at the Annual All-American Air Show. H. S.

Walesby, director of the *Detroit Times* chapter, helped me transport it to the huge main hangar at Detroit City Airport. I was now a full-fledged exhibitor along with the Wacos and Fords, just seven years after attending my first air show!

With the experience I gained in building the ground trainer I decided to embark on the design and construction of a full-size training glider. Due to my limited finances, this seemed the only way I could afford to learn to fly. Even if I had the necessary finances, no flying school in the Detroit area would accept a black student.

I started the preliminary design work in the fall of 1935 after reviewing the flight performance and construction details of various gliders in the primary training category. The drafting materials necessary to complete the design work were relatively inexpensive so that part of the project proceeded at a rapid pace.

Since space was at a premium in the basement of our house, I designed the all-wood, 30-foot wing in three components, a 6-foot centersection and two 12-foot outer wing panels. The fuselage was also of wood construction with an enclosed cockpit for better streamlining. To reduce costs and weight I used wire bracing to transfer wing flight loads to the fuselage. Other cost-cutting measures included using ordinary white pine instead of spruce for the structure, and substituting unbleached muslin from Sears Roebuck for aircraft fabric.

With all design work completed and the cost of materials reduced to a minimum, I faced the daunting task of raising the necessary funds. With millions of unemployed people looking for work during the Depression, finding a job was a nearly hopeless task. And being black, I found my job opportunities to be almost nonexistent.

CHAPTER THREE

LEARNING TO FLY

During President Franklin Delano Roosevelt's first administration, Congress passed many social welfare programs intended to provide federally funded jobs for the unemployed. One of the largest and most successful was the Works Progress Administration (WPA), which created projects to provide skilled and unskilled jobs. Projects receiving the most public attention employed artisans and artists of all kinds, using their talents to beautify local areas. Many of these works of art are still fulfilling their purpose today.

While looking for employment in 1936 I learned the WPA was hiring employees to work with the Detroit Department of Recreation at various community centers. Since I had extensive experience in model airplane design and construction, I applied for a job teaching these subjects. The local WPA officials I first contacted made it very clear they were not interested in hiring blacks for anything but unskilled labor. Because this job offered both a higher salary than unskilled labor and an enjoyable line of work, I decided to fight for it.

I first contacted Lebron Simmons, attorney and president of the Detroit chapter of the Urban League. He was very sympathetic to my story and promised to use all available legal means to get me hired. I then went to see Rev. Horace White, pastor of Plymouth Congregational Church and an outstanding civil rights leader. Their combined efforts resulted in my being hired but not before the WPA officials could arrange predominantly black classes for me to teach. This was standard policy for the Department of Recreation and, as I was to learn several years later, the Department of Education as well.

My first assignment was in the Boys Work Department of the all-black St. Antoine branch of the YMCA, located in the ghetto area near downtown Detroit, popularly known as "Paradise Valley." The dismal surroundings belied the name. But for me the name was particularly appropriate, for being paid to teach eager kids to build model airplanes was a veritable paradise. Because my new position required dependable transportation, I traded in my slow and not-so-trusty 1928 Chevrolet for a shiny black 1930 Ford Model A Coupe. The selling price was $100 and with my trade-in the balance was $90, paid in six monthly payments plus finance charges.

At the age of 20 I was now a full-fledged member of the WPA skilled work force, earning the princely sum of $85 per month. I gave Mother 75 percent for support of the household which, as she frequently told me, provided the first steady income she had received in years.

My WPA supervisor was Art Vhay, a gentleman whose leadership and friendship I enjoyed immensely over the five years I worked for him. One of his favorite city-wide events was the military model airplane contest held every year at the Statler Hotel in downtown Detroit. Although prominent, successful businessmen were invited to act as judges, they knew very little about model airplanes. Art Vhay named me technical assistant to assist them in making their decisions. I sat next to them at the large banquet table where the models were on display, providing the technical advice they needed.

At midday waiters cleared one of the tables in preparation for lunch. The judges were invited to the table for a elegant luncheon, but the manager told me I could not eat with them. It seemed odd, since I had been sitting at their side all morning in a cordial atmosphere, that I could not now sit with them during mealtime. To soothe my feelings the hotel manager offered me five dollars to buy a meal elsewhere. After lunch I sat next to the judges as usual. I was happy to use my lunch money to buy another airplane ride!

When my Model A Ford was finally paid for I had money available to start construction of my first glider, NLG-1, in my shop in the basement of our home. I made rapid progress using the skills I had learned at Cass Tech. It took months of patient, and sometimes frustrating, effort to fabricate the steel fittings, build thirty-two wing ribs, construct, assemble, and cover all major components with fabric and then apply dope to waterproof the fabric and shrink it so it was tight. With the glider now ready for final assembly I took all the finished component parts to a barn behind King Walter Johnson's house just one block away. The final assembly of the glider was completed without difficulty and I was thrilled to sit in the cockpit of my own airplane for the first time.

However, as I checked the control system for proper response, I suffered my first major setback. Moving the stick from side to side I found the aileron movements were opposite to what they should be. The wings were already completely covered so I had to devise a way to modify the aileron system which I hoped would not require removal of large parts of the fabric cover. It took several days of redesign before I resolved the problem.

When the glider was finished I applied to the Bureau of Air Commerce for a registration number and was assigned NX15750. When I told my good friend and *Detroit Times* editor Mr. H. S. Walesby that my glider was finally completed he decided to write a story about my project. At his request I assembled my glider in nearby Rose Park for a photo session and interview. To my surprise (and my family's, too), the story and picture appeared on the front page of the second section of the Sunday *Detroit Times!* When my father saw his son receiving this kind of attention from outsiders, his skepticism began to break down. He even accompanied me to the next All-American Air Show held at Detroit City Airport. I really enjoyed showing him around the airplanes. Judging by the smile on his face, he was happy to be with me.

The St. Antoine branch sponsored an annual all-week open house program to which parents were invited to see the activities their sons were engaged in. The Boys Work secretary, Ramon Scruggs, asked if I would put my glider on display during the open house. A full-size airplane was sure to attract a lot of attention. However, I was worried about possible damage to the glider during my absence occasioned by my need to be at my other classes at Brewster, Kronk, and Birdhurst community centers.

To alleviate my concern, he assured me there would be a full-time person assigned to protect my airplane. With this assurance I brought it to the Y and assembled it in the lobby of the Boys Department. It was quite a sensation. Unfortunately, the promised protection was not provided and the resulting full-time assault by large numbers of hyperactive boys virtually destroyed NX15750.

I am sure the U.S. Bureau of Air Commerce could not have devised a more destructive test. I finally scrapped the glider without ever taking it to the airport. In retrospect, that was probably a good thing. Since I had no flight training whatsoever, I would probably have killed myself trying to test-fly it. Obviously, I did not remember the tragedy of Don Pearl Simmons who attempted to test an airplane without sufficient experience. Still undaunted and with fresh enthusiasm, I began planning glider number 2.

As a convenience to the boys in my classes I kept a supply of model airplane materials available to them at costs well below market prices. I customarily bought dope and thinner in five-gallon lots for my full-size airplane projects at a relatively low cost, bottling some of it in two-ounce glass containers for sale to my students.

Before going home one weekend, I decided to take a quart of thinner home for bottling purposes. Not having a clean quart container on hand I went into the alley behind the YMCA where there was an ample supply of quart-size whiskey bottles left by the "winos." After picking the cleanest one and washing it out, I filled it with aircraft thinner from a five-gallon can. Dope thinner, coincidentally, had the amber color of whiskey. I did not bother to remove the label from the whiskey bottle.

On arriving home I saw a strange car in front of the house but assuming it was one of my brother's friends I walked in without further thought. On entering the living room I saw the visitor was the pastor of our church! He smiled pleasantly, glancing briefly at my whiskey bottle. I was so embarrassed I could not think of a plausible way to explain to him that it was aircraft thinner in the bottle, not whiskey. I even thought of inviting him to smell it. Sensing this was not a good idea, I just said, "Hello, Reverend," and made as graceful an exit as I could to my bedroom. He must have been very discreet about it for neither he nor anyone in my family ever mentioned the incident in my presence.

One of my favorite model airplane students was a young teenager, Jerry Frazier, who seemed mature beyond his years. He never mentioned his family so I guessed his home life was less than ideal. I became sort of a father figure to him during the many hours we spent together, and I was equally happy to treat him as a son.

One day he asked if he could talk to me in private after classes were over. The Y closed at 9:00 P.M., so we went into my office for our chat. After a few pleasantries Jerry, in a very hesitant, shy manner, mentioned that he had never heard me discuss any women in my life except my mother and sister. I explained to him that I had a natural interest in having a girlfriend but had neither time nor money to spend on such activities.

With a serious look on his face, he told me he would be happy to provide, at no cost, a woman companion for me any evening of my choice. Before I could protest, he went on to explain that he had a variety of women to choose from and surely one would meet my needs.

Realizing Jerry was being generous with the only gift he had to offer I thanked him sincerely. He was very disappointed by my refusal. It was then I realized Jerry Frazier was a "pimp" for a ring of prostitutes, and why he seemed mature well beyond his years. Although I surely did not intend to, I must have hurt Jerry's feelings, for he never came back to my model airplane class again.

In December 1937, I met Clinton Thomas Walker, the first black in the state of Michigan to obtain a private pilot rating. He was a very quiet, slow-talking person and rather difficult to get to know. When he found how serious I was about learning to fly, he offered to take me out to Erin Airport, about 12 miles from Detroit, to meet his instructor. A common problem for blacks in those days was that white flying schools would not accept them as students, presumably to protect their social standards.

But Clinton's instructor, Paul Hinds (a captain in the Army Air Corps Reserve), was fair-minded enough to teach serious-minded black students to fly without regard for the racial sensibilities of his white students. I was very impressed with Paul Hinds, especially when I found out he was qualified to fly the latest version of my beloved Curtiss Hawk, the P6-E. After a serious talk he offered to give me four hours of dual flight instruction ($12 per hour) for the price of three, provided I paid cash in advance. I told him I would definitely be back.

Before leaving the airport one Sunday in December 1937, Clinton offered to take me for my first free airplane ride. The snow was fairly deep and covered by a layer of ice, making takeoff difficult. It was necessary to drive a car up and down the runway to clear a path. Paul then took Clinton up for a short check ride. There was a strong crosswind and, unfortunately, Clinton allowed the blue and red Rearwin Sportster to drift off the runway into the deep snow and ice. His attempts to taxi out of the snow were futile, so the mechanic and I drove out and pulled the stranded airplane back onto the runway.

After receiving additional advice from his instructor, Clinton invited me into the cockpit and we were soon airborne in the crisp, clear December air. Although not dressed for winter flying, I was so filled with the exhilaration of flying I didn't notice the cold.

On landing, Clinton again drifted off the runway and stuck in the snow. I climbed out and struggled through the snow to the tail of the airplane and pushed while Clinton gunned the engine and finally got the airplane moving. Blinded by the propwash-driven snow, I stumbled back to the airplane and climbed in. Snow in my low-cut oxfords made my feet feel frozen. Once back in the warmth of the airport lounge my discomfort was forgotten. On the way home I thanked Clinton profusely for what I considered a wonderful Christmas gift.

It was May of 1938 before I had raised the required advance payment for my first four hours of flight instruction. Due to scheduling difficulties and weather delays, my first training flight was not scheduled until June 4. On the appointed day, while driving my Model A Ford Coupe down Groesbeck Highway to Erin Airport, I became so excited I had trouble remembering the flight manual material I had carefully studied in preparation for this momentous event.

On approaching the airport I could see my training airplane, the bright-red cabin Rearwin Sportster NC15896, parked near the grassy runway, ready for takeoff. It was difficult to pay attention to Paul's instructions as I gazed at the wonders and complexities of the instrument panel. Finally the preflight preparations were over and I was seated in the front of this tandem two-seater. Clark Wales, the mechanic, pulled the shiny wooden prop through slowly several times, then called "Contact." He swung the propeller vigorously and the five-cylinder, air-cooled Leblond engine came to life. The Rearwin vibrated with the engine impulses; my body shook in unison from excitement and anticipation. My first lesson in flying was about to begin!

Paul Hinds performed the takeoff but instructed me to keep my hands lightly on the controls so I could feel his movements. Once in the air I found I did not have time to enjoy the scenery as I usually did when riding as a passenger. My mind was fully occupied trying to learn the coordination between control-stick movement and airplane response. I practiced turns, climbs, glides, and other basic maneuvers. All too soon my hour was up. After landing we went to the airport lounge for a postflight briefing. Paul assured me my progress was satisfactory and suggested I come back for my next lesson as soon as possible. My Ford and I were on "cloud nine" all the way home.

I used up my paid-up flight time on my fourth dual flight with Paul Hinds on July 26. Filled with optimism, I promised him I would return within a week for my next lesson. Unfortunately, my father died on August 1, 1938, after a lengthy illness. Due to the hospital and funeral expenses, I had no money for further flight training for the rest of the year.

When I went back to Erin Airport in March 1939 to resume flight instruction, Paul Hinds had left. The new instructor, Steve Stanislaw, a sandy-haired man of medium height with a wisp of a mustache, greeted me with a firm handshake, posed a few questions about my career goals, and invited me to start flying again.

My first flight with Steve was March 29, 1939, in a bright-yellow Piper J-3 Cub, NC21563, powered by a 50-HP Franklin engine. Evidently, my long layoff from flying and the opposite seating arrangement from that of the Rearwin (in a Piper Cub the student sits in the back seat with the instructor up front) did not impede my progress.

My lessons went very well except on one memorable flight before solo when Steve got angry enough to say a few cusswords. Because our 50-HP Cub was definitely underpowered with two people on board, it was considered safe practice to drop the nose to level flight before starting the first turn after takeoff. After I forgot this procedure several times, Steve turned around to me and said angrily, "Dammit, Neal, drop the nose before starting your turn!" I never forgot again. After four hours of dual instruction with Steve (eight hours total) he decided I was ready for solo.

The date was April 20, 1939. I had just completed 66 minutes of dual flight. Smiling confidently as he climbed out of the front seat, Steve patted me on the back and told me to take off and land near where he was standing. Although I had been doing most of the flying during the lesson and was reasonably sure I was near soloing, I was still surprised.

With only my 135 pounds on board, the yellow Cub leaped off the ground almost before I was ready. Flying the traffic pattern as practiced many times before, I lined up on final approach to the runway. Leaning slightly to the right of the cockpit and looking out the open window I could see the little figure of the man I knew to be my instructor. The thought occurred to me that despite his proximity, he could be of no assistance if I ran into difficulties. Overcoming my misgivings I landed quite smoothly and taxied up to Steve. Shaking my hand in congratulation, he told me to do several more takeoffs and landings. After I flew solo for 30 minutes Steve climbed back in the cockpit and we taxied back to the hangar.

I sponsored the usual Coke party, highlighted by Steve's cutting off my shirt tail, a time-honored ritual associated with a first solo. Driving home, I recalled every detail of my flight. But the reality of my dream come true was still difficult to believe. My head was in the clouds for weeks.

Earsly was the first person I told about my solo flight. After I described the thrills of being alone in the sky she couldn't wait to start flying herself. I promised to take her to the airport the next time I scheduled a flight. Just three days later I was showing her the Cub and introducing her to my instructor. Steve was impressed by her knowledge and enthusiasm and welcomed her as his newest student. Earsly flew several hours with Steve during the spring but soon ran out of money and had to wait until summer before resuming her flying. While visiting her aunt in Chicago, Earsly was soloed by a black instructor at Harlem Airport. My last flight at Erin Airport was on August 1, 1940, after completing almost 12 hours of solo flying. I never saw Steve Stanislaw again after Erin Airport was purchased by the wealthy William P. Joy family of Detroit and renamed Joy Airport. Unfortunately for Earsly and me, there was no joy in it for us for the traditional restrictions against black students were resumed. We again lacked a local airport where we could fly.

During the summer of 1939 I met a very kind and generous man by the name of Ward Stone. He owned a small glider company, but it was a losing venture because he loved people and airplanes more than profit. Well aware of my limited finances, he offered to sell me a second-hand primary training glider for $150. He also wrote a letter appointing me purchasing officer for the Stone Aircraft Company. Not having enough money to buy the glider alone, I organized the St. Antoine YMCA Glider Club, open to boys 14 years or older, the minimum age government regulations required for soloing a glider. For powered airplanes the minimum age was 16. We finally raised enough money for a downpayment and took proud possession of our glider.

We selected a large vacant field on the outskirts of Detroit for our first test flight. We had regularly used this field for our model airplane flying. On this Sunday in August, the weather was perfect. We loaded the glider on a trailer and drove out to the field. This being our first experience, it took us a long time to locate all the parts and begin assembly. In our excitement we did not notice the clouds forming and an approaching thunderstorm. At the first sound of thunder I ordered the boys to start taking the glider apart. A few moments later a bolt of lightning struck nearby, causing one of the boys to feel a shock. I told everyone to move away from the glider without taking the time to tie the glider securely to the ground. We sat in the car and watched in utter helplessness as strong winds picked the glider up and flipped it on its back. Our pride and joy was destroyed before our first flight. Ward Stone, gentleman that he was, never asked us to finish our payments.

Still anxious to own and fly a glider, I started the design and construction of my second glider, which I designated the Wayne S-1, in my YMCA classroom. It was smaller than NX15750, thereby reducing material costs. Registered as NX27775, it had a 25-foot span, was 17 feet long, and when completed weighed only 160 pounds. With my previous experience at building the ground trainer and glider NX15750 I was able to build NX27775 in record time. However, a nearly disastrous event took place during the covering and doping process that frightened me out of my wits.

It was a cold day in February 1940 when I gave specific work assignments to designated boys in my class before I went off to another class at Kronk Recreation Center. The wings were ready for doping and, in spite of the cold weather, I gave strict instructions that the doors and windows were to be open at all times for ventilation.

Upon leaving, I promised the boys I would return by 10 P.M. Returning to the Y, I walked down the dark hallway to the lighted room we were using as a shop and saw all the doors and windows closed. As I opened the door the pungent smell of dope was overpowering. In spite of my specific orders, all the windows had been kept tightly shut during my absence.

After opening every window in the room I asked for an explanation. One boy told me he had heard that dope fumes made you feel "dopey" if inhaled too much. They all wanted to experience the "high" feeling. I then noticed that one student, George Graves, was missing. I went into the pitch-black lobby (the Y was closed) looking for him. There was enough light coming in the window for me to see him on a seat bench, flat on his back, apparently unconscious.

I was panic-stricken. After fumbling in the dark I found a water glass, filled it with cold water from the drinking fountain, and poured it on his upturned face. He woke up quickly with a dazed look and started wiping his face. Temporarily relieved, I took George home and explained the whole incident to his parents. They reiterated their full confidence in me and promised that they would deal with George in their own way. The next day George showed up for class very happy, showing no aftereffects. Clearly, my trauma had been worse than his.

With my students' continued help, I was able to finish S-1, NX27775, and paint it a bright yellow and blue before my WPA job with the Detroit Department of Recreation ended in the spring of 1940.

Storing my glider temporarily, I went job hunting again. To increase my skills I enrolled in a six-month accelerated engineering drafting course at Highland Park Junior College during which I completed engineering drawings for the S-1 to aircraft factory standards.

Looking for an opportunity to utilize my new skills I responded to a large advertisement in the *Detroit Times* by the Excello Company inviting prospective employees to apply for openings in its drafting department. Wasting no time, I applied for a job. But on meeting the interviewer I was told that in spite of the ad there were no jobs available. Not willing to believe him, I asked to see the employment manager. In the privacy of his office he explained that if he hired me every man in his all-white drafting room would quit. Saying his company could not afford the risk to his company's production schedule (which was based on this country's support of the Anglo/French war effort against Germany), he ushered me out of his office.

Meanwhile I heard of the National Youth Administration (NYA), a federally funded project specially designed to aid young people. The program goal was to provide job training for young men and women of high school age and older. Having just completed an advanced drafting course I felt confident I could teach elementary drafting. I filled out an application at the Detroit Board of Education, which was responsible for managing the NYA program. A few days later I received a call from Mr. Tabraham asking me to see him at the newly opened Aero Mechanics High School located at the north end of Detroit City Airport.

I had not seen my friend and mentor in six years. For a few minutes it was like a happy family reunion. He was now the principal of Aero Mechanics High School and wanted me to work for him. He had seen my application at the Board of Education, and on his own initiative changed my teaching subject from drafting to aircraft mechanics. He had also submitted an application on my behalf for the required teaching certificate to the Michigan State Board of Vocational Education, which was quickly approved.

Naturally I was overjoyed at this good news, especially when he told me my class was already formed and waiting for me. My starting salary was $76 per week with a promised raise to $100 per week. What a princely sum to be paid for doing something I dearly loved to do. Once again Mr. Tabraham had earned the title Earsly and I had bestowed on him years before, the "Great White Father."

I waited impatiently for a call to report for work from Mr. Garrity, the Detroit Board of Education employment officer in charge of processing my application. After a week of waiting, I went to his office. When I introduced myself he seemed very cordial and helpful but spoke of the large amount of paperwork involved and asked for my patience. After two such interviews I went back to Mr. Tabraham and asked for his assistance. His secretary told me later that he immediately called Mr. Garrity and asked for an explanation. He was told it was official Detroit Board of Education policy that black teachers were not to be hired to teach predominantly white classes. Upon hearing this Mr. Tabraham nearly exploded with anger and blistered the phone with strong language.

Mr. Garrity called the next day and told me to report for work on Monday, July 28, 1941.

My pretty yellow and blue glider, S-1, was ready for first flight in July 1941. With almost 20 hours of flight experience I felt qualified to be a test pilot. On July 23, with the aid of my good friend and ex-pugilist Bill Hampton I loaded NX27775 onto a trailer and headed for Stinson Field on the west side of Detroit. Assembly was quickly completed and we stretched out about 150 feet of tow rope on the ground.

The glider had a jaunty look as it sat on its single wheel with one wing tip resting on the ground and the other pointed toward the beckoning sky. The wind was light so I decided to have Bill tow me up and down the runway, with and against the prevailing wind. My plan was to start at 10 MPH and increase the tow speed of each run in 5-MPH increments. After a thorough preflight inspection I hooked up the rope and started my first tow. Other than poor lateral control at low speeds the initial ground tests went smoothly. After several of these runs Bill came over with my goggles and suggested that I put them on. When I told him I didn't think I needed them yet he angrily stomped off, muttering loud enough for me to hear, "If you didn't want the damn goggles you should have left them at home!"

On the next tow, NX27775 took to the air—much to my surprise, for I did not realize that on this run I was headed into the increasing wind. The control responses were perfectly normal so I started a shallow climb. Suddenly I was totally blind! I had not noticed the dust layer rising from the dry ground behind the car during the ground tows, since I had remained well below it. But now I was in the middle of the dust layer and unable to see. As I panicked, my mother's words before I left home came instantly to mind, "Neal, don't go out and hurt yourself now that you have such a good job with the Board of Education." Instinctively easing the stick gently forward to lower the nose and still blinded, I pulled the release knob, allowing the tow rope to drop away. With no further control inputs from me, the glider touched down smoothly and rolled to a stop. Bill rushed out to congratulate me on my successful first test flight and a perfect landing. I was elated but I had to tell him, "I take credit for the takeoff but God alone made the landing." I sheepishly asked for my goggles, which I wore for the next two flights. Further testing had to be canceled when I damaged the single landing gear wheel on my third landing of the day.

I reported for work at Aero Mechanics High School the following Monday morning and met my NYA supervisor, Art Sawtell. He greeted me cordially but I wasn't sure he was in full agreement with my being hired. I was given my class schedule and introduced to my tool crib boy, a young, blond teenager by the name of Ed Sarnowski. The next day I met my class of thirty boys and eagerly started my job as an instructor of aircraft mechanics. My students and I got along very well with no hint of racial problems. In fact, I became so popular that the girls in the school went to Mr. Sawtell and asked to join my class. He gave them vague excuses and did nothing about their request. They persisted, however, and went to Mr. Tabraham for help. He immediately called Mr. Sawtell and asked why the girls were not being transferred to my class. His excuse was that he did not feel a black instructor should be teaching white girls. After a few blistering words from Mr. Tabraham, Art Sawtell changed his policy and the girls entered my class.

The girls were a mischievous group. Their ringleader was blonde teenager Virginia Krolikowski. Knowing I was a dedicated bachelor they decided to play a trick on me. Gathering around the pay phone on the hangar floor, the girls listened in as Virginia called my Aunt Bertha with whom I was rooming at the time and asked her to call me at the school and pretend to be my wife with four children. Minutes later I was called to the office by loudspeaker from my class on the shop floor. Mr. Tabraham's secretary handed me the phone while a bunch of giggling girls looked on from the hallway. Aunt Bertha fooled me by disguising her voice and proceeded to ask embarrassing questions about when I was going to come home and take care of my family. I stammered a lot and did my best to discreetly get rid of her. Finally it was over and I couldn't wait to go home for lunch and tell Aunt Bertha my tale of woe. She was able to hold a straight face for a while but soon burst out laughing. I didn't know whether to blame her or the girls for this embarrassing episode. In the long run I think I enjoyed the prank more than they did.

My last glider flight of 1941 was on November 29. I was now flying at Triangle Airport, which was dedicated exclusively to glider flying. The manager, genial Johnny Nowak, was a national authority on gliding and was a very good friend. I had finished two very successful auto-tow flights and was about to climb into the cockpit for a third when Johnny called to me. Leaving the glider in charge of two of my students I walked over to talk to him. He complimented me on my flying and offered the use of the winch tow on my next flight.

The heart of the winch system was a large circular metal drum powered by an auto engine. About 2,000 feet of rope was wound on the drum, allowing the winch-towed glider to reach nearly 1,000-feet altitude before rope release. This was well above the 300 feet I had been able to achieve with my 450 feet of rope on auto tow. During our discussion the wind turned suddenly gusty and strong. When I heard the boys scream I looked around and saw my glider rise slowly into the air and roll inverted before falling back to the ground. Obviously, my ground crew had not been paying attention. Their repentance did little to relieve my feelings of frustration. We took the battered glider back to the YMCA. After weeks of intensive activity repairing broken wing ribs and other damage, the S-1 was ready to fly again.

When Pearl Harbor was attacked a week later, war was declared and all private flying ceased immediately. Only airports providing 24-hour armed guard service were allowed to reopen. Very few privately owned airports could afford such costly protection. Large municipal airports such as Detroit City Airport were opened without much delay. But war emergency rules enacted by federal and local agencies placed so many restrictions on privately owned airplanes that many were, in effect, grounded. Gasoline was rationed and special pilot identification cards were required by the Civil Aeronautics Administration (CAA). All flights (including local) required flight plans. Glider NX27775 did not take to the air again until 1944.

them of its unsuitability. In my response I offered to build a larger version suitable for military training and a civilian counterpart for sale on the commercial market. One particular advantage of my glider was its almost exclusively wood structure, saving scarce and expensive strategic metallic materials for important military purposes.

I discussed this manufacturing venture with Earsly. After considering all the possibilities, we joined in partnership to form the Wayne Aircraft Company and rented a large empty store at 642 Hastings Street near downtown Detroit. Earsly's office/reception area was located in the front of the store with my drafting room behind it. The large remaining space to the rear became the manufacturing facility. Using NX27775, the S-1, as a prototype, I started design of a larger and refined production version, the S-2. Earsly's brother Rudy joined our team and performed most of the shopwork, including building assembly jigs and small component parts.

Since each of us had full-time jobs, progress at Wayne Aircraft Company was dismally slow. But we continued our efforts and the S-2 soon began to take shape. We were determined that ours, the first black aircraft factory, would become a success. In preparation for the civilian market we prepared a glossy informational brochure and advertised in *Air Trails* magazine, one of the leading aviation publications of that era.

Entering the shop floor at Aero Mechanics one morning I noticed Mr. Tabraham working on a yellow and black Waco biplane, NC4711, powered by a 125-HP, German-made Siemens-Halske engine. The nine-cylinder air-cooled radial powerplant was equipped with a shiny Hamilton Standard metal propeller. It was a beautiful airplane and I quickly went over to find out who had brought it in.

Mr. Tabraham informed me that he had just bought the Waco and after minor work was going to place it on sale for only $300. I asked him not to sell it until I could contact Earsly. After a very short discussion we agreed to join in partnership and buy the Waco. Using all the money we had on hand and borrowing the rest, we purchased our first powered airplane, thus joining the elite company of Waco owners.

After completing minor repairs and painting it yellow and blue, I rolled the Waco out on the ramp for an engine runup. Satisfied with the results, I taxied down to the main hangar at the other end of Detroit City Airport to apply for hangar space. The assistant manager, Wesley O. Walker, was very polite; he accepted my application but regretfully informed me the hangar was full despite the large expanse of vacant hangar space clearly visible. When I called this to his attention, he insisted the airplanes were on cross-country flights and would return. Discouraged, I taxied back and told my story to Mr. Tabraham. He thought a moment and then asked me to sell the Waco to him for one dollar. Without giving it a second thought I agreed to the transfer.

The next day Mr. Tabraham taxied the Waco down to the main hangar and parked it in front of the airport office. He was warmly greeted by the airport manager and after requesting hangar space was told that attendants would park the Waco in a choice spot in the hangar. After a few pleasantries Mr. Tabraham arranged an auto ride back to the school and called me into his office. He sold it back to me for one dollar and gave me a receipt for the first-month hangar rent. Mission accomplished by the "Great White Father"!

On December 1, 1941, the U.S. Army Air Forces formed the Civil Air Patrol (CAP), an all-volunteer branch to provide premilitary training for young men and women. Airplane owners also joined and were utilized for preflight training and air-sea rescue missions. After the war began, these aircraft also performed submarine-hunting missions off both the Atlantic and Pacific coasts. Each state established a wing with groups and squadrons at the local level.

With our Waco and glider available for duty, Earsly and I applied for CAP membership the summer of 1942. As expected, none of the white squadrons in the Detroit area would accept our applications. Not willing to give up, we wrote to wing headquarters and requested permission to form an all-black squadron. Several months later we were given authorization and formed Squadron 639-5, which meant we were assigned to the 63rd Wing, Group 9, and designated as Squadron 5. Major Robert "Bob" Lunceford, an outwardly gruff but fairminded officer, was our group commander. Earsly was appointed commanding officer of our squadron and I was her executive officer. We wore standard Army Air Forces uniforms and insignia of rank. However, our epaulets were uniquely red and we wore distinctive CAP emblems on our caps and uniforms.

We had no trouble recruiting cadets and soon were fully immersed in military drill, learning everything from military courtesy to theory of flight. All cadets, especially the women, enjoyed the experience of working with real aircraft in their training program. They performed preflight inspections and engine runups on the Waco and learned how to assemble the glider. As our specialty, we gave training in parachute jumping and became informally known as the Parachute Squadron.

In May of 1943 Marie Patterson became the first black female student in my class at Aero Mechanics High School. She was a very outgoing, personable, and friendly young woman with a sprinkle of freckles on her brownskin face. Marie was short, barely five feet tall, with beautiful, straight black hair, hinting of possible American Indian ancestry. Her interest in aviation was sparked by her first airplane ride in her home-town of Marion, Indiana. The pilot, Lewis Jackson, later became director of primary flight training at Tuskegee Institute's Division of Aeronautics. I was to know him later as Dr. Jackson, Ph.D., president of Central State University, Wilberforce, Ohio, and a fellow builder of experimental aircraft.

Marie and I soon became good friends and sometimes shared our lunch hour. One day she surprised me by preparing a lunch for both of us featuring shrimp salad sandwiches. This was my first experience with such exotic fare. Our relationship, however, remained well within the social boundaries of student and teacher.

Two events in the spring of 1943 remain pleasant memories. On my return to Detroit City Airport after a short local flight in the Waco, when I was on final approach chief tower operator Bill Giddings called me in his usual flippant manner, "If you are feeling lucky Waco 711, you are cleared to land on Runway 25." This reference to my being lucky was due to 4711's nasty tendency to "groundloop" after touch-down. This rapid, uncontrolled, circular movement on landing rollout rarely damaged the airplane, but definitely damaged the pilot's reputation. I was lucky that day. After a perfect three-point landing I taxied up to the ramp with confidence. Climbing out of the cockpit I saw three black military pilots standing on the flight line in their impressive officers' uniforms, watching the civilian airplane traffic.

Walking over and introducing myself, I expressed my pleasure in meeting black military pilots. They had just graduated from Tuskegee and were stationed at Selfridge Field for transitional training in Curtiss Hawk P-40 fighters. I could scarcely contain my envy as I looked at the silver pilot wings pinned on their officer jackets. They asked about my Waco and I told them it was a nice airplane but scared me on takeoff when the engine occasionally coughed and briefly lost RPMs before resuming full power. They just grinned and said, "If the 1200-HP Allison powering our Curtiss P-40 doesn't cough a couple of times on takeoff we figure there must be something wrong!" We continued to talk flying for an hour before they departed with a brisk military stride. At that moment I felt deeply proud.

Later that month, one of the pioneer black pilots from the Chicago area, Col. John Robinson, popularly known as the "Brown Condor," landed his gull-wing Stinson monoplane at Detroit City Airport. Because of his flying and leadership skills he had been appointed chief of the Ethiopian Air Force by Emperor Haile Selassie, and given the rank of colonel. This was at the time when Italy, seeking territorial expansion, invaded Ethiopia. Without adequate personnel and military aircraft, the Ethiopians were quickly defeated and Colonel Robinson returned to Chicago. There he obtained a job as personal pilot for Mrs. Malone, a wealthy black woman, founder of Poro College, a successful school of beauty culture for black women. Colonel Robinson was given authority to select and buy a suitable airplane and arrange for its full maintenance. He had chosen a Stinson Reliant, NC16161, made in nearby Wayne, Michigan.

It was a five-place, high-wing cabin monoplane, beautifully uphol-stered in velour and leather, a real luxury airplane of the day. The courtesies he received from the airport personnel were quite different from my experience with the Waco. Colonel Robinson was a command-ing figure but very modest and soft-spoken. Earsly and I could not have been more proud if we had met Colonel Lindbergh. Before taking off for Chicago he gave us a ride in his beautiful pearl gray and red Stinson. His visit gave us a real sense of racial pride.

On Thursday morning, June 21, 1943, I said goodbye to my mother as usual and drove through our quiet east Detroit neighborhood to Aero Mechanics High School. I was surprised to hear on my arrival of a race riot that had started at Belle Isle (located in the middle of the Detroit River) the day before. It began when a fistfight between two males, one black and one white, escalated into a melee involving several hundreds and spread quickly into several racially segregated areas of Detroit. The violence became so out of control that President Roosevelt declared a state of emergency and sent in troops to quell the disturbance. Before it was over, thirty-four people were dead (twenty-five black) and thousands of dollars of property destroyed. But I had been unaware of the extent of the mounting racial tensions in Detroit which had led to this race riot, the deadliest of World War II.

Obviously I was no stranger to racial slurs and the bigotry that existed in Detroit. From my school years to the recent struggle I had had with the Detroit Board of Education, the wall of racial prejudice seemed at times impenetrable. But with the support and encouragement of respected members of the black community, as well as influential whites such as Mr. Tabraham, I managed to achieve a measure of success many thought impossible. Working every day with airplanes in the racially unbiased Aero Mechanics High School created by Mr. Tabraham was a labor of love. This probably insulated me from the feelings of anger and frustration which led to the riot. Even today, I cannot recall specific racial incidents or tensions that might have led to this climactic event. However, my subsequent experiences with racial discrimination while trying to attain new career goals in the racially segregated world of aviation gave evidence that my own battle for black equality was far from over.

By July 1943, with the winning of the war apparently assured, many wartime projects were either slowed down or canceled. As a result, my teaching assignment at Aero Mechanics was terminated. Although still busy with the Civil Air Patrol, Wayne Aircraft Company, and flying and maintaining the Waco, I needed a full-time job. Ford Motor Company was still building the eighteen-cylinder R-2800, 2000-HP air-cooled engine under license from Pratt & Whitney Corporation for installation in such diverse aircraft as the P-47 Thunderbolt fighter and the Martin B-26 Marauder bomber.

Armed with my credentials from Aero Mechanics, I applied for a job in the engineering department. Despite my extensive aviation background, Ford's employment office would only offer me a job as an engine assembler at entry level. I accepted the job on the promise of a transfer to the drafting department as soon as there was an opening. I soon discovered some of my coworkers didn't even know what a cylinder was and were making twice my salary! This was my first experience with labor unions and the power of seniority. I continued to work based on the naive assumption my stay as a lowly engine assembler would be brief.

Shortly after reporting for work I received my draft notice. Being an active pilot with an appropriate medical certificate I was absolutely sure I would be called to active duty. With that as a certainty, I wanted to complete all of the aerodynamic and structural analysis of the S-2 before I left for military service. Earsly and Rudy could handle every aspect of our production effort but not the engineering design work. I increased my engineering design activities to get our Wayne Aircraft S-2 off the drawing table and on the production line. This was in addition to maintaining the Waco, working seven days a week at Ford, and fulfilling my CAP duties. I was able to get very little sleep and, some nights, none at all. This lack of sleep eventually resulted in long-term fatigue, which later would have near-fatal consequences.

Now that I was no longer working at Aero Mechanics I felt free to let my friendship with Marie Patterson become more serious. This was my first experience at dating even though I was 27 years old. She accepted my awkwardness with good humor and our mutual affection grew at every meeting. Mother, seeing my interest in a girl for the first time, was anxious to meet her. When I did bring Marie home to meet my mother it was evident they were favorably impressed with each other. Mother was so impressed, in fact, that when I returned home she said in mock sternness, "Neal, if you don't ask Marie to marry you I will put you out of the house!" Being the ever-obedient son (and because I wanted to anyway), I proposed to Marie and she accepted.

My engagement to Marie was a surprise to many people, including my mother, who in spite of her recent advice on Marie always thought Earsly and I would someday be married. But the relationship between Earsly and me was based on our mutual love of aviation. Romance never intruded. After I introduced petite, outgoing Marie to tall, reserved Earsly, I was pleased when they apparently became good friends, despite their contrasting statures and personalities. One day I took a picture as they sat in the Waco and placed it in my photo album with the following words:

Oh, would that I were a Waco blue,
Then I also could hold Marie and Earsly too!

Several weeks later I drove down to Marie's hometown of Marion, Indiana, to meet her family. Her mother, a wonderful woman, was a devout Seventh-Day Adventist. Marie's father, a Methodist Sunday school teacher, welcomed me warmly as a prospective son-in-law. The Pattersons had eleven living children; at 23, Marie was the oldest daughter. I thoroughly enjoyed my visit and looked forward to becoming a permanent member of the family. Soon after, I drove my mother and sister to Marion for separate visits with the Pattersons and they were equally impressed. Due to the uncertainties of the war and my problem getting promoted to the drafting department at Ford, we decided to delay our wedding plans.

My long-awaited draft call came in February 1944. I was ordered to report to the induction center for a physical. Having consistently passed my pilots' medical exam for six years, there was no doubt in my mind that I would be called into service. I redoubled my efforts at Wayne Aircraft to complete the engineering work before going off to war. We had completed the major structural components of the S-2 but there was much time-consuming work to be done before final assembly and preparation for flight test. These extra hours of activity and attendant loss of sleep continued until the morning I reported for my draft physical.

After the preliminary paperwork was completed I went through all the physical exams and interviews with flying colors. The last exam was in the cardiology department. After several minutes of prodding and poking, the doctor told me to step out of line and wait in his office. As I sat there wondering what the problem was, the doctor came in and said with a tone of finality, "You have a bad heart and therefore I am placing you in the 4-F category." I protested and even showed him my pilot's license and medical certificate, but the doctor was unmoved. I asked for limited service (noncombat duty) and was again refused. I was disappointed, but Earsly and Rudy were happy to have me back at Wayne Aircraft Company. A few months later Earsly was to recall my heart problem under very different and distressing circumstances.

By the spring of 1944 it was clear I was not going to be promoted to the engineering department of the Ford Motor Company as promised, so I appealed to the War Manpower Commission (WMC) for a Statement of Availability (SA). During the war an SA was required before an employee could leave to seek another job. On July 14 the answer came, "Statement of Availability granted to enable utilization of the worker's highest skills as a draftsman. Seniority rights protected." With my SA granted I immediately started planning to enroll for the fall 1944 semester at Wayne State University in Detroit. Having already saved enough money for tuition, I decided to work on my 1941 Buick to make sure it was in good condition for the school years to follow. But as Robert Burns said, "The best laid schemes of mice and men oft go astray."

On Saturday, July 15, 1944, I took my glider out to Wings Airport, Utica, Michigan, 18 miles north of Detroit, to practice for a flight demonstration I was scheduled to give the next day. A war bond drive was being held at Adrian Airport, Adrian, Michigan, and it was my first public performance. I completed eight practice flights that day, renewing skills that had deteriorated since my last glider flight in November 1941.

A sizable crowd gathered at Adrian Airport the next day, July 16, watching with curiosity as I assembled the glider in preparation for my flight demonstration. To make sure the spectators had a good view I started my takeoff directly in front of the temporary bleacher seats. Using almost 400 feet of tow rope I achieved sufficient altitude to execute a 180-degree turn and land downwind almost at my point of takeoff. The audience enthusiastically applauded my performance. I suspect there was an element of surprise with my flight for the prevailing view of the general public was that without engine power an airplane would fall out of the sky like a brick. NX27775 landed light as a feather.

Two weeks later, on Sunday, July 30, 1944, I took off on what should have been a routine CAP training mission. It ended in a disastrous crash, excruciating pain, and instant unconsciousness—and would change my life forever.

The blessed oblivion of unconsciousness lasted just long enough for Earsly and crew to remove me from the glider and lay me on my back on the cool, damp earth. The pain was beyond belief, with no boundaries. I looked at my feet, which should have been pointing upward, and found they had twisted 90 degrees and were laying flat on the ground. With my left eye I could see my right eye had come out of its socket and was laying on my cheekbone. Blood was streaming profusely from a severe cut just above my eyes which extended across my entire forehead. In the midst of all of this pain I became angry with myself for all the mistakes I had made in my haste prior to the accident. I started scooping dirt from the ground with my right hand and throwing it in the air in frustration. Earsly held my hand firmly and advised me to save my strength.

After what seemed to be an interminable delay, the Utica Township fire/medical truck arrived in response to the emergency call and I was quickly loaded onto a stretcher and was on my way to St. Joseph Hospital in Mt. Clemens, nine miles away. The driver sped over the rough country roads as fast as possible to reach the hospital in minimum time, causing my broken legs to bounce uncontrollably, adding to my terrible pain. Telling the driver to slow down, Earsly and Marie prevented my legs from bouncing by placing them in their laps and holding them. Their red-trimmed khaki uniforms were soon covered with dark red blood.

As we drove up to the hospital emergency entrance we were met by a large medical team who were prepared to treat numerous survivors of the reported crash of a huge Army transport airplane. Evidently when the alert came in, the caller described the large number of people in Army Air Forces uniform at the scene of the accident and assumed many people were injured. Every available doctor and nurse had reported to the hospital for immediate duty. I don't know if they were disappointed with having just one scrawny, 135-pound patient, but I was blessed by having the head surgeon and the head nurse report for duty for this presumed disaster.

While I was being prepared for surgery in the emergency room, one of the nurses, a Catholic nun, asked me to hold my arm out so she could take blood samples. My arm sagged as she selected the necessary instruments and, noticing this, she spoke rather sharply, "Keep your arm up where I told you, young man." I responded weakly, "Sister, even when I am healthy I can't keep my arm up like that very long and right now I am not feeling that good." With an apologetic smile she cradled my arm and took her blood samples. This was followed by a general anesthetic and soon my agonizing pain disappeared into merciful, deep sleep.

Several hours later Earsly saw the head surgeon, Dr. Thompson. He stood in the hallway, looking quite tired in his blood-splattered operating room gown. Her voice trembling with emotion, Earsly asked about my condition and the prognosis. He admitted my condition was extremely critical but he was sure my heart was strong enough to pull me through. Earsly recalled with dismay I had failed my draft physical due to a bad heart!

CHAPTER FIVE

HOSPITAL DAYS

I t was the next morning before I began to emerge from my dream-state into the reality of the living world. In a way it reminded me of a familiar religious ceremony during Easter time when members entered their darkened church and, one by one, lit their candles. Gradually shadows would appear and shapes become visible in the gathering light.

Lying there, unable to move, I became aware of figures moving about and heard hushed voices I did not recognize. Slowly beginning to regain consciousness I tried to move my arms and head and found I was completely helpless. Although I was not hungry, a nurse was sitting by my bed gently holding my head and slowly placing spoonfuls of warm oatmeal in my mouth.

Again I struggled to raise my arms to perform the simple task of feeding myself but they remained motionless. It was very frustrating and humiliating—an adult unable to do such a simple thing as lift a teaspoon. The nurse at my bedside was understanding and with words of encouragement continued to place cereal into my mouth. As my energy returned I was able to focus my eyes and see the doctor and nurses in the room. Almost like a person looking on, I tried to determine what they were doing and for what purpose. It slowly dawned on me that all of their efforts were on my behalf.

Being heavily sedated I had little sense of pain. My right leg was elevated in traction. A surgical pin in my heel was attached to a wire that ran over a pulley mounted on the bedstead to a lead weight. I couldn't see my left leg lying flat on the bed but it felt normal, with the exception of a slight tingling sensation.

An intravenous feeding needle had been inserted into my right arm. Oxygen was provided by a cylindrical storage tank through a small plastic tube inserted in my nostril. I was in private room 306, but with all the activity going on it wasn't very private. In today's hospital terminology, my room would be called an intensive care unit. Blood samples were taken, medicines dispensed, questions asked, and my arms injected with various solutions. In spite of the high level of activity and noise in my room I frequently drifted off to sleep.

During my semi-awake moments I sometimes thought I heard familiar voices in this strange environment. I did not realize the hospital had called Earsly and asked for volunteers to donate four pints of blood for transfusion to compensate for my loss of blood. Earsly was the first donor, followed by Marie, my sister, Ardine, and my brother Bob's wife, Lottie. Each of them briefly visited my room but I was too sedated to be aware of their presence.

Late one night a student nurse came into my room and discovered my oxygen tank was nearly empty. Unfamiliar with the procedures for changing the tank she went to the floor above and asked the senior nurse on duty, Helen Starkweather, for assistance. Helen, a student nurse in her senior year of training, was familiar with the procedure. She came into the semi-darkened room and with professional skill completed the task with a pleasant smile. I thanked her and returned the smile. Many years later, Helen remembered my smile as awkward, strange, and "lumpy." My face was unevenly swollen from continued internal bleeding under sutured facial lacerations. From that exchange of smiles evolved a loving friendship which continues to this day.

When I woke up the next afternoon in the midst of visiting hours, the first person I recognized was my mother. She spoke as soon as my eyes opened, her voice filled with sadness, "Neal, I am so sorry you have lost your leg." Still unaware of the amputation I made a feeble attempt to humor her, "Mother, you must be in the wrong room." Realizing she was the first to inform me, Mother changed the subject and talked of more pleasant matters. Earsly joined in the conversation but did not mention the accident. Talking made me very tired. They said their goodbyes, and I thanked Earsly for driving my mother out to visit me at the hospital, a 20-mile drive from Detroit.

As my strength increased with each passing day, discomfort and pain also increased. Since my right leg was in traction, I was forced to lay flat on my back for a total of seven weeks. Moving any part of my body other than my arms increased the pain level. Using the bedpan was particularly agonizing. But with all these problems, I fully appreciated the kind, thoughtful, and supportive care the nurses and doctors were giving me.

For the first few weeks, when my condition was critical, only graduate nurses were allowed to provide primary care and administer medications. Mrs. Lucy Raemeyer, the head nurse, and Sister Florian, in charge of the third floor, gave unstintingly of their precious time. My slow but sure progress was due as much to their caring efforts as to the prescribed medical and surgical procedures.

It is not generally known that when a patient loses a limb there is no immediate, innate sense of physical loss. The nerves leading from the stump to the brain continue to send normal messages. Everything seems normal. Only when the stump becomes visible does the patient realize the loss. During this period of waiting no one brought up the subject of my amputation, other than my mother (I did not believe her at the time), and it became quite a game between my nurses and visitors to determine when I would make the discovery. In preparation for the expected, and usually highly visible, traumatic reaction when I did become aware of the procedure, Dr. Thompson left a standing order for a strong sedative at the first signs of emotional stress.

When Earsly, Marie, and friends came to the hospital they would stop first at the nurses' station to find out if I had acknowledged my loss. On their departure the nurses would stop them and ask the same question. I don't remember the moment when I found out. However, I did not experience the outward trauma they had predicted. I never required the sedation Dr. Thompson had prescribed.

Inwardly I was, of course, deeply disturbed not only by the amputation, but by the negative effect it would have on my career as a pilot. There were times of quiet despair, often difficult and sometimes impossible to overcome. But I kept these feelings to myself. I did not discuss them with anyone, especially the possibility I might never pilot an airplane again.

As soon as I had sufficiently recovered, two Civil Aeronautics Administration (CAA) investigators came to my room to discuss the accident. The CAA (now the Federal Aviation Administration [FAA]) was required to investigate every airplane accident in which serious injury is involved. I recalled in full detail every mistake I made leading to the accident, described the flight itself, and the flight control movements I made to avoid the crash.

They listened attentively and asked no questions. They smiled as I finished. One spoke up, "We cannot say we admire your judgment or your skills as a pilot but you are a helluva honest man. You are the first pilot we have talked to in years who placed the blame for an accident squarely where it belonged, on the pilot himself." His remarks made me feel both proud and humble. Their report, entitled "Investigation of an Accident Involving Aircraft During a Practice Flight," read as follows:

> Student pilot Neal Loving 28, of Detroit, Michigan was severely injured July 30, 1944 at Wings Airport, Utica, Michigan, when the homemade glider he was flying stalled and fell to the ground soon after he released the tow line.
>
> The pilot had accumulated 27 solo hours in powered aircraft and had made 45 solo glider flights prior to the accident. He had majored in aerodynamics at high school, was a student at an aircraft engine mechanic's school and had studied aircraft drafting and design at a junior college. The glider, NX 27775, built and owned by Loving was extensively damaged. About noon July 30, Loving piloted the glider while it was given a preliminary automobile tow southwest across the airport. Returning to the starting point by tow, he was again towed southwest into the air. The wind was 10 m.p.h. from the west and somewhat gusty. At a height of about 175 feet Loving leveled off and cast loose, then started a left turn of medium bank. After turning about 90 degrees downwind the glider was stalled. The pilot tried to regain control and had accomplished partial

recovery when the glider struck the ground laterally level but 45 degrees nose down.

The probable cause of this accident was a stall at low altitude during a downwind turn from which recovery was not effected.

BY THE BOARD

/s/ Fred A. Toombs, Secretary

One of the early visitors to my hospital room was a slightly overweight young salesman from a local artificial limb company. He had read the account of my accident in the newspaper and noted that one of my legs had been amputated. He was out of breath as he greeted me. I invited him to sit down. He had climbed three floors to reach my room without realizing an elevator was available. When I teased him about his weight being a factor he laughed and said the real problem was he had one artificial limb.

What an inspirational surprise that was. In spite of all the assurances from hospital staff about my ability to walk again, this was far more convincing proof. He showed me his prosthesis and gave a sales talk. I poured out my questions: would I drive a car again, or climb a ladder? I was afraid to ask if I might fly again. Assuring me I could live a reasonably normal life with his company's prostheses he gave me his business card and renewed confidence in the future. I promised to contact him when I left the hospital.

His visit reinforced the hope I had developed from reading about the exploits of the legendary, legless English combat fighter pilot, Douglas Bader, in his Rolls-Royce Merlin–powered Spitfire during World War II. Bader continued to be my role model and inspiration whenever I started dreaming of flying again.

Almost all of the student nurses at St. Joseph Hospital were enrolled in a U.S. government–sponsored nurses cadet training program administered by the Sisters of Charity, founders of the hospital. The young cadet nurses came from the many small towns in the area: Imlay City, Romeo, Emmett, and Memphis among them. Most were in their teens, full of fun and youthful energy. Some of their energy radiated into my body whenever they came into my room and lifted my spirits. Soon they knew my background and particularly wanted to meet my fiancée, Marie. I described her appearance and promised I would point her out when she came to visit. They agreed that one of them would find an excuse to come into my room at that time. Marie, who did not have a car, came with Earsly and a few CAP cadets the following Sunday afternoon. As promised, several of the nurses found an excuse to come into my room and each time I nodded toward Marie. When my visitors had departed a delegation of student nurses came in my room to give me their unanimous opinion she was not for me. I was surprised at their quick judgment but subsequent events supported their feminine intuition.

My mother observed, as did others, that Marie always left the room in the company of other visitors. It was clear my fiancée did not want to be in the room alone with me and at no time did she display any outward signs of affection. Mother finally called Marie and tactfully suggested she show signs of her love, especially at this time when I needed it most, even if her feelings had changed and she had to pretend.

That same night Marie called me from what I recognized as the Flame Show Bar, judging by the voices and music in the background. It was the largest, most popular black nightclub in Detroit. She expressed her displeasure with my mother's call and without further explanation told me she was breaking our engagement. Inwardly I was still trying to adjust to the loss of my leg. Now I had the additional problem of losing my first love, Marie. I concluded the nurses learned more about her in one meeting than I had over a period of months. When they found out about Marie canceling our engagement, the nurses gave even more generously of their affection, as well as their continued medical care. Their support helped sustain me through this difficult period.

One morning Dr. Thompson came in my room accompanied by Mrs. Raemeyer. Without the usual morning pleasantries he opened a small, black leather bag and started laying out shiny metal instruments on a small table. Mrs. Raemeyer bathed my foot in a fluid that smelled of hospital alcohol. Doctor then told her to wet a washcloth, fold it, and place it in my mouth. Without saying a word he started cutting away gangrenous tissue without any apparent concern for my feelings. Whenever he cut through and reached healthy tissue the pain was almost unbearable, especially since they had purposely withheld the use of anesthetic. When I clenched my teeth in pain I was thankful for the wet washcloth in my mouth.

When the operation was complete Dr. Thompson wiped his hands and, without even glancing at me, left the room. When my brother Bernard came to see me that evening I told him my doctor was really an uncaring butcher. I later learned he was very emotionally involved in my case and believed showing his feelings would constitute unprofessional conduct. The reason for the lack of anesthesia, when explained to me, was obvious. The only way he could tell when all the bad tissue had been removed was my reaction as he cut through to the healthy tissue. With that understanding I began to admire him more both as a doctor and a person. We soon became good friends and when he found we shared a mutual interest in opera he generously gave me a membership in the Metropolitan Opera Guild. Our friendship continued long after I left the hospital, until his death years later.

Late one afternoon Sister Florian came into my room and began to rearrange my well-furnished room so my bed could be placed near the window. She evidently heard of my desire to be able to look out the window and decided to do the job herself. She was a vigorous person and moving furniture was well within her physical capabilities. When finished she sat down in the comfortable chair and we had an enjoyable conversation. On rising to leave she looked at me and confessed, "In all my years of nursing this is the first time I have ever stayed in a patient's room after I had finished my medical duties." For those words, I admired her more than ever. I was also grateful for my view of the outside world through the window and the constantly changing scenery.

Months later, while looking out the window, I saw an old man on a cane struggling through the snow. How happy I would be, I thought, if I could ever walk as well as that old man.

During the first seven weeks of my stay at St. Joseph Hospital I had to remain flat on my back, unable to move because my right leg was in traction. The requirement to remain motionless for such an extended period of time was at times so unbearable that tranquilizers were prescribed to reduce emotional stress.

After the seventh week, Dr. Thompson decided to take my right leg out of traction and put it into a cast. The operation was performed in the morning and it was late afternoon before I began to recover from the general anesthetic. The first persons to come into my room after the operation were my mother and Earsly and although I wasn't very responsive I felt better just knowing they were there. After a short visit Mother excused herself from the room, followed in a few minutes by Earsly. Moments later they were back and, without sitting down, told me they were going home. They apologized for the short visit but I told them not to worry. I had discovered I could roll over just enough to get slightly off my back and the feeling was as soothing as a shot of morphine. I promised I would be asleep by the time they reached the elevator. Easing slowly on my side, sleep came almost immediately, and I did not realize I had said goodbye to my mother for the last time.

Although the leg pains had not diminished, I was thrilled by my new freedom in getting in and out of bed. Up to this time I had no idea what the hospital looked like, inside or out, except for the picture postcard of St. Joseph Hospital I received from Earsly. Even the adjacent hallway was new territory to explore. I waited impatiently for Dr. Thompson's permission to get out of bed and use a wheelchair.

After what seemed an eternity (two days actually), the nurses came in with a wheelchair and vied for the privilege of taking me out of the room for the first time. I was like a little child going out to see Santa Claus. Wheeling out into the hallway I saw the nurses' station, the labs, and the X-ray department, which I had envisioned during the weeks while bedridden.

The biggest thrill came when I rolled down the hallway and out on to the open patio overlooking the rear of the hospital. I was overwhelmed by the smell of fresh air for the first time in nearly two months. It was a heady perfume and I enjoyed every breath. The fall season had just arrived and the leaves were beginning to change to vivid colors. All too quickly the nurses wheeled me down the hallway and back to my room. They were worried, I guessed, that I might have a heart attack from all the excitement. But the excitement, plus the fresh air, combined to give me my most restful night since entering the hospital.

The next day, Sister Florian decided I needed more living space and possible companionship. So she removed the furniture from the sunroom at the end of a hallway and furnished it to meet my needs. There was space for an additional bed, which was brought in and made ready for use. It was a bright, sunny room with large windows, which helped to raise my sometimes sagging spirits. Sister Florian broke another strict hospital tradition when she told my friends, the student nurses, they could visit my room, day or night, whether I needed medical services or not. Since constant pain kept me awake much of the night, and these very young student nurses were often very lonely, it was good therapy for all of us. My room, which was number 328, became "Club 328."

On the morning of September 23, while sitting in my wheelchair listening to the radio, reading the newspaper, and keeping a watchful eye on activities in the hall, I saw Dr. Thompson and Mrs. Raemeyer coming toward my room. They had not scheduled a visit so I was somewhat puzzled about their intentions. Coming into the room, looking very somber, they quietly closed the glass-framed doors. Dr. Thompson leaned over and put his arm around my shoulder as he said in a quiet voice, "Your brother Bernard called this morning to tell me your mother passed away last night." His caring support was very helpful as I tried to adjust to this tragic news, my third personal loss in less than two months.

Mrs. Raemeyer comforted me also, providing the maternal support I so desperately needed. When the news of my mother's death reached the hospital she insisted that no one break the news to me other than she and Dr. Thompson. After staying much longer than professional courtesy required, Dr. Thompson offered a sedative, which I refused. I was deeply grateful that the head surgeon and head nurse would take time out of their busy morning to be with me at this time of need. Watching them walk down the hallway I felt a bright ray of hope in this moment of despair. Somehow, I reflected, this must be the low point of my life and therefore whatever lay ahead had to be for the better. The sum total of all the events that have occurred in my life since that fateful morning have proven that assumption correct.

One of the student nurses, Mae Dyet, was a student pilot at Pontiac Airport. We often talked about our experiences learning to fly. She was always eager to wheel me down the hallways for my daily sightseeing tours during which we communicated in pilots' language. Wanting to turn at a particular hallway I would say, "Navigator to pilot, 90 degree turn to the right at the next intersection." Mae would respond, "Pilot to navigator, roger wilco." We laughed quietly at our own special brand of humor. A cranky old lady patient complained to Sister Florian one day about the laughter in the hallway which she felt was an unnecessary disturbance. Sister told her in no uncertain terms the hospital could use more laughter, not less, and if she didn't like it she could close her door. The old lady never complained again.

My special support team of student nurses planned my next outing with care and thoughtfulness. With the fall colors at their peak they wanted to take me on a tour of the neighborhood, giving me my first look at the exterior of St. Joseph Hospital. They had already surveyed the sidewalks and curbs for the smoothest route. Suitable clothing had to be obtained, for the summer CAP uniform I was wearing when I crashed had been cut away from my body on admittance.

After several days of preparation they bundled me up in borrowed clothing and wheeled me outside for my adventure. The air was cool and crisp. Bright sun magnified the autumn colors. The one constant negative factor was the fact that every time we rolled over the slightest bump my right leg, although encased in a plaster cast, moved enough to cause me extreme pain. Unaware of my discomfort, my escorts eagerly pointed out all the sights of interest. On returning to my room I thought of myself as being twice blessed, blessed when I went outside and blessed when I came back in.

About once a month I was scheduled for the operating room to change the cast on my leg. I asked Dr. Thompson one day how I could predict when my visits to the operating room would be scheduled. With an unprofessional, impish smile he responded, "When I come to your door and wave through the glass without coming in, you know it will be the next morning." My leg still had a large open wound under the cast and after four weeks of drainage the unpleasant odor was unmistakable. When it got so bad he wouldn't even come into my room I knew the operation was scheduled.

One evening after he had waved to me from the door, I was invited over to the mineral bath house next door, also operated by the Sisters of Charity. The smelly, sulfurous waters piped in from underground sources were alleged to have therapeutic properties. Their clientele were offered a free first-run movie which was shown in the lobby twice a week. My invitation to attend the showing was clouded by the strong offensive odor emanating from my leg.

Sister Florian thought she could solve the problem by borrowing a bottle of "My Sin" perfume from one of the nurses. Sister, who was clearly unfamiliar with such worldly things, doused it liberally over the blanket covering my legs. The resulting aroma of sweet perfume blending with the noxious smell of my leg was nauseating. As the student nurse wheeled me into the lobby I replaced the movie as the center of attention for the assembled guests. Out of consideration for others, I offered to return to my room immediately but Sister Florian ruled otherwise. I am sure if there had been a ticket counter, the paying guests would have requested their money back.

In this era prior to Vatican II, the Sisters of Charity maintained a strict code of moral values, demonstrated on an occasion when I was able to attend a movie without giving an offending odor. It was a light comedy titled *Home in Indiana,* starring blonde and beautiful June Haver. In one lakeside beach scene she came out of the bathhouse clad in a swimsuit that was considered quite daring for its day. One of the sisters always sat next to the movie projector to act as official censor. When this scene appeared she stood up in front of the projector, blacking out the screen. She had to cover the projector several times to make sure the morally objectionable scene was over. If one of those sisters was censoring a movie of the present generation she would get an extraordinary amount of exercise jumping up to block the projector every time a sexually explicit scene appeared.

In 1944, even Roman Catholic hospitals observed the unwritten rule that white patients were not to be placed in the same room with blacks. But one day a 17-year-old white youth was brought into my room with a bandaged right arm. His parents told me a discussion they had with Sister Florian convinced them their son should share a room with me in spite of the racial biases of the time.

This teenage farm boy and I immediately took a strong liking to each other and became good friends. During one of our many conversations he explained how his hand and lower arm had been caught in a cornhusker machine on his father's farm. Although badly bruised, he was expected to recover rapidly. His parents expressed the hope that this injury would keep their son from being drafted. But as days went by his condition began to deteriorate to the extent it became necessary to amputate his arm. He died a few days later.

The father, talking to his son's doctor afterwards, casually mentioned he had lost several horses on his farm in recent years to lockjaw. On hearing this the startled doctor became extremely angry. The boy had died of chronic lockjaw! Had the father mentioned the presence of lockjaw on the farm when his son was admitted, medical procedures would have been taken beyond the standard tetanus shots. After the funeral the parents came to my room and gave me a beautiful bouquet of flowers and a memento of their son. I was deeply honored.

One Sunday morning a tall, red-headed young man rolled into my room in his wheelchair to deliver the weekly Catholic newspaper, *The Sunday Visitor.* With a boyish grin he said, "You must be Neal," and I replied, "And you are Red Rapp." The nurse who had changed my oxygen tank in the middle of the night, Helen Starkweather, had told Red about me and suggested a visit. Elwyn F. Rapp was a very outgoing person who met no strangers. We talked, among other things, about the circumstances that led to our being in the hospital. He was a paraplegic; a motorcycle accident in July 1937 severed his spinal cord. During his seven years in the hospital he learned the watch repair trade and set up a shop in the hospital basement. We made quite a sight as we wheeled down the hallways, Red was very tall, redheaded, and fair, while I was African American, comparatively short, and brown-skinned. We were a virtual Damon and Pythias team.

Another friend of Red's, David Van Wallace, joined our team of rolling wheels. Van was a quadriplegic who came to the hospital for care when his father passed away. His mother, Rosalie, was busy with funeral arrangements and did not have time to provide the daily care her only son required since his accident. Van had broken his neck during his first year at Notre Dame while diving into the shallow end of a swimming pool on a dare. He was completely paralyzed from the neck down, with no feeling or use of his arms or legs. Van had to be hand-fed at mealtimes. But he was probably the most pleasant, considerate, and optimistic person I had ever met. His sense of humor was legendary.

He loved to read and to travel whenever possible. He especially enjoyed going to Notre Dame football games where a special place was reserved for him on the 50-yard line. Among his many other travels he even made a pilgrimage to Lourdes. To support himself and his mother, Van sold insurance from his home, using a custom-made telephone system. His mother did the paperwork. The local Notre Dame Club furnished Van with a specially equipped station wagon. He had a small, eager army of volunteer drivers, including police, firemen, nurses, and friends from all walks of life. Van Wallace was a living institution in Mt. Clemens and had the admiration and respect of everyone who knew him.

One day during Van's stay at the hospital Red, Van, and I met in my spacious Club 328 for an informal discussion in which we concluded we were not only lucky to be alive but happier than some of our so-called unhandicapped brethren. That no one appeared to envy us was merely an indication they didn't know the situation as well as we did. Following our chat we moved out into the hallway, Red and I in our wheelchairs and Van pushed along in his specially made cot by an eager student nurse.

Dr. Thompson, on seeing this strange procession moving by the nurses' station one day, humorously referred to us as the "Panzer Division," a famous motorized division of the Nazi Army. That title remained with us for the duration. More important, the bond we formed at St. Joseph Hospital was an everlasting source of joy to each of us.

CHAPTER SIX

BACK IN THE AIR

One morning in early December, I entered the operating theater for my fifth medical procedure and after returning to my room remained in a deep, anesthesia-induced sleep until the next morning. The sun's rays streaming in my room finally woke me to a wonderful surprise: the constant pain I had endured for months had all but disappeared. I couldn't wait to tell the good news to Dr. Thompson and congratulate him on his surgical skills.

When he came to my room for his morning visit I was surprised by the glum expression on his face. I immediately decided to cheer him up by telling him how successful the operation had been and my new relief from pain. He listened patiently and then told me the bad news. During the operation, while he was scraping debris from around the ankle joint, my shin bone fractured completely just inches above the ankle joint. The only choice was to remove the broken bone. Now the only connection between my foot and ankle was cartilage and tissue. This was also the reason for the lack of pain, which had been caused by friction between the fractured bones. The only reasonable solution, he explained, was to amputate my right leg. My soaring hopes, which the relief from pain had brought, were crushed. The reality of becoming a double amputee now had to be faced.

Dr. Thompson discussed all the possibilities and suggested I send the X-rays of my foot to doctors of my choice for a second opinion. And to raise my sagging spirits, he offered to let me go home for Christmas. This, he hoped, would increase my appetite for I had been steadily losing both weight and strength. There would be considerable risk involved in the amputation. He wanted me to be at my best both mentally and physically. He estimated I had a 50-50 chance of survival.

To bolster my confidence he told me the operation would be scheduled on his day off so he would be free of obligations the entire day. Mrs. Raemeyer changed her schedule for the same reason. The operation was scheduled the first week of January, 1945. My Christmas and New Year's Day celebrations would now be clouded by this next medical crisis.

The first problem with my spending Christmas at home was that no one had lived there since Mother's death in September. Despite Dr. Thompson's permission, the sisters absolutely refused to let me go home unless someone was there to care for me. My only sister was now married and enjoying a career as a cellist while touring with a popular jazz band. Both my brothers were married and had large families of their own. Earsly solved the problem by calling her sister, Henrene Yuille, in Pittsburgh to ask if she would spend Christmas with me at my home in Detroit. With her husband's full blessing she agreed to come, along with her two young children, Sydney, Jr., and Marilyn. Thus I was assured of a lively and loving Christmas celebration.

Meanwhile, I continued to tour the hospital hallways and facilities in my wheelchair, spending hours that might have otherwise been filled with unrelieved boredom. One of my favorite places was the laboratory where blood analyses were performed. The young woman in charge, Marjorie A. Pryor, was generous with her time in showing me the equipment and allowing me to watch as she analyzed various blood samples. I was fascinated by the amount of information she obtained from a tiny drop of blood. Marjorie patiently explained the procedures and techniques used for the various types of blood tests. During our many conversations we found we shared a love of poetry, especially by American authors. One day she surprised me when I entered her lab by giving me one of her favorite books, *The Best Loved Poems of the American People.* On the flyleaf she wrote, "To Neal Loving, a swell fellow." This book provided me with much humor and inspiration during my long stay in the hospital, and to this day.

Another one of my favorite places to visit was Red's watch repair shop in the hospital basement. I was fascinated by the sounds and intricate movements of the chime clocks and the highly polished inner works of the many watches on display. The shelves were filled with all kinds of timepieces, including wristwatches, pocket watches, and mantel clocks. The simultaneous ticking of the watches and clocks, plus the chimes, provided background music for our hours of conversation. But I soon learned that Red was not a slave to his job. He loved to drive his battered old car to the woods of northern Michigan to hunt everything in season from deer and duck to rabbit. On other days when the fish were reported biting in nearby Lake St. Clair, he would hang his "Closed for the Day" sign on the door and head for his favorite fishing spot. This sign came as no surprise to those who knew Red and his love of the outdoors. To this day Red roams the country roads near his home like the free spirit he has always been.

Red and I referred to the man in the room next to mine as "the Melancholy Dane." He was a tall, blond, soft-spoken Scandinavian who always seemed to have an air of sadness about him. He would often stand in his doorway just to watch the visitors go by. Whenever I went by in my wheelchair with my leg clearly missing he would shake his head slowly as if in sorrow and express his sympathy for me. One day, after one of Red's visits to my room, we went wheeling down the hallway and saw the Dane standing in his doorway. Nodding his head to me he offered his usual mournful, sympathetic comments, which caused Red to stop and express his feelings. He told the Dane in no uncertain terms he was wasting his time feeling sorry for me. "Neal will soon be up walking around on his artificial leg," Red argued, "making it possible for him to drive, fly his airplane, and live a normal life. If you want to feel sorry for someone feel sorry for me," Red concluded; "though I still have my legs, I will be in a wheelchair for the rest of my life." We never again heard expressions of sympathy from the Dane on my behalf.

As Christmas approached, my high level of excitement reminded me of childhood days long ago. The thought of being home in familiar surroundings added joy to the usual anticipated pleasures of Christmas. Little Sydney and Marilyn wrote to me in their childish scrawl how happy they were going to be spending Christmas with me in Detroit. On the appointed day, four days before Christmas, Earsly arrived at the hospital to drive me home. The nurses gave me a rousing sendoff, saying they would miss me. Since they were like an adopted family to me, I felt the same way. Climbing into a car for the first time in five months, with Earsly at the wheel, I relished my freedom.

The Yuille family welcoming committee greeted me with enthusiasm as I arrived at the front door of my home. I was surprised and thrilled to sit in the homemade wheelchair my brother Bernard had made for me. The seat was bolted to a piece of plywood and mounted on four coaster wagon wheels. Although not as elaborate as a hospital wheelchair it had the advantage of being small enough to allow me to enter every room in the house, including the bathroom. Henrene had cleaned the house until it was spic and span and now the aroma of a home-cooked meal made me feel right at home. The children, Sydney and Marilyn, made sure there was never a dull moment.

One of the highlights of being home I had not even anticipated as I left the hospital. After five bedridden months I had forgotten the simple pleasure of sitting on a toilet. Since entering the hospital I had been restricted to bedpans and urinals, which were always cold and uncomfortable and often embarrassing. The indignity of sitting on a bedpan was referred to in hospital humor by the nurses as "sitting on the throne." But now with my crude but efficient wheelchair I could maneuver into the bathroom and make use of a modern convenience most people take for granted. I looked longingly at the bathtub and wished for a genuine, warm-water bath instead of the "bed baths" the nurses gave me every day. But with the cast still on my leg I had to forego that pleasure. One of the few pleasant aspects of having both legs amputated was that I could enjoy the luxury of bathing in a tub again.

Another advantage to being home was that my family of friends and relatives could visit me without the time-consuming 20-mile trip to Mt. Clemens. One of my special friends, whom I had known as a young teenager in our church, was tall, slender, always cheerful Wilhelmina ("Billie") Lewis, the medical officer of our CAP squadron. She worked in a doctor's office and therefore had a good understanding of my medical problems which, with her sense of humor, were kept in perspective. I always felt buoyed up after her visit both at the hospital and at home.

Other CAP members who visited me over the holidays, some who had witnessed my accident, were Erlaine Bishop and her father, Earl Conway, Telford Duncan, Clinton Walker, and many of the cadets. We enjoyed many hours of conversation unhampered by the confines of the two-hour visiting hour rule at the hospital. Sometimes, however, I would get very tired from these extended visits and, in spite of this extra activity, my appetite did not increase as predicted. Even with Henrene's good cooking I couldn't eat enough to put on the additional weight Dr. Thompson had hoped for. But surrounded by a loving and caring family of relatives and friends, my spirits were raised at a time when I needed a boost the most.

Since I had spent all the money I had saved for my college education on medical bills and had no source of income I was embarrassed that I could not buy Christmas presents for Earsly, Henrene, and little Sydney and Marilyn. But everyone was very understanding, including the kids, so I was able to fully appreciate the beauty and excitement of Christmas morning. We opened our gifts by the brightly decorated Christmas tree and then sang carols while tasting candies and fruits on the coffeetable. In the early afternoon, Henrene served a sumptuous Christmas dinner of roast turkey and all the trimmings. As the day ended my emotions were mixed. I was warmed by the love and joy the day had brought, bringing to mind words from the Bible, "My cup truly runneth over." But on the downside, I had to consider the risks of the coming operation and the distinct possibility of this being my last Christmas. Going to bed that night I remembered one of my favorite literary works from high school days, which helped restore my peace of mind before drifting off to sleep. This is the portion I recalled:

So live, that when thy summons comes to join the innumerable caravans which journey to the silent halls of death, go thou not like a galley slave scourged to his dungeon, but sustained and soothed by an unfaltering trust, as one who wraps the drapery of his couch about him and lies down to pleasant dreams.

Earsly drove me back to the hospital the day after Christmas to be welcomed by the nurses and staff like a long-lost relative. Club 328 was busier than ever as we exchanged holiday experiences. Some of them had also gone home for Christmas, so we had plenty of subject material.

During this post-Christmas reunion a patient was admitted to my room. Robert ("Bob") Colman was a brash, blond teenager, full of fun and mischief. Once again the racial barrier was broken. Bob had shot off part of his foot with a shotgun while climbing over a fence on a hunting trip. On New Year's Eve he coaxed one of his high school friends into bringing a bottle of wine to his room—against hospital rules. Bob managed to surreptitiously drink enough of the wine to become tipsy and uninhibited. Just before midnight he put on his call light and a very shy student nurse, Virginia Fisher, came to our room. Bob demanded she give him a kiss to celebrate the new year. She politely refused and turned to leave the room but as she neared the doorway Bob called to her, "Miss Fisher, if you don't give me a kiss I am going out into the hallway and yell 'Happy New Year' just as loud as I can!" Virginia stood there a moment, probably weighing her distaste for kissing a strange man versus having a patient disturb the peace of the hospital in the middle of the night. Sister Florian would surely take a dim view of the latter. After weighing the lesser of the two evils she leaned over Bob's bed and gave him a quick kiss, leaving the room before he could ask for another. With his New Year's Eve celebration over and the wine bottle empty, Bob was soon sound asleep.

After coming back to the hospital, I thought it very strange that Dr. Thompson did not come to see me as soon as I expected. When he finally made his visit we talked about my Christmas vacation but he made no mention of the operation. After the New Year celebrations were over I spoke to Mrs. Raemeyer and asked her to query him about setting the date. A few hours later she was back saying the amputation was scheduled for the morning of January 4. As I discovered later, Dr. Thompson was having problems dealing with his feelings about my surgery, and kept putting off setting the date of the operation. But I was glad the uncertainty was over so that I could begin to prepare myself mentally for whatever was to come.

The night before the operation was a sleepless one for I was not allowed any of my daily pain and sleep medication. There in the semi-darkness I tried to deal with my increasing fears and anxieties. At times I stared at my foot as though trying to fix its image in my mind for future recall. Looking at my toes and foot it was hard to control my emotions as I contemplated their loss. Fortunately these morbid thoughts were temporarily dispelled when a nurse came into my room seeking my assistance. A young woman down the hall was to have a cast put on her sprained ankle, a relatively simple and painless task. But according to the nurse, she was so frightened her body was visibly shaking the bed. The nurse asked if I would mind visiting the patient at this early hour of the morning to try to ease her mind. She felt if I mentioned the serious operation I was to have the same morning it might help to put the woman's fears in perspective. I did talk to the patient at length just to divert her mind from her fears, but I suspect she was as worried as ever when I left her room.

At about 5:30 A.M. I heard Gussie the cleaning woman start noisily down the hall with her buckets and brooms and cart. In spite of the noise I somehow fell sound asleep and had a dream that is as fresh in my mind today as it was that first morning. I dreamed I was sitting alone in the living room of my home reading a book when I heard a knock on the door. Rising to open the door I saw my mother standing in the entrance. Looking at her in surprise I asked, "Mother what are you doing here? I thought you were gone." Still dreaming, I heard her reply, "I have not left you, Neal, I am still here." Suddenly I was awake again as Gussie rattled into my room with her cart. Obviously I had been sleeping only a few minutes but it was long enough to provide a memory that comforted me as the nurses came in my room to "prep" me for the operation. To this day it is significant to me that from the day she died to that night before my crucial operation I had not dreamed of my mother. And for reasons beyond my understanding, I have never dreamed of her again. I sincerely believe she was with me on that one early morning I needed her the most.

Despite my many misgivings, the operation was a medical success. It was now necessary that I start preparing for my life as a double amputee. The first task was to build up my strength and energy as necessary to start the long and painful process of learning to walk again. In those days there were no physical therapy programs designed specifically for amputees. Under the guidance of Dr. Thompson and the nurses, I tried to get as much exercise as possible both in the wheelchair and by performing in-bed aerobics. This effort was also designed to increase my appetite and body weight. I weighed only 135 pounds when I entered the hospital and could only guess how much weight I had lost in the subsequent six months. But just the thought of returning home and resuming my life, even with artificial legs, was all the incentive I needed to start my plans for living at home alone. I discussed my plans with brother Bernard and although he wasn't enthusiastic about them he could not offer a reasonable alternative. Without a source of income I certainly could not afford to stay in the hospital. I had no idea how I was eventually going to make a living but was optimistic enough to think I could do so with sufficient amounts of luck and skill.

The first obstacle was obtaining Dr. Thompson's permission to leave the hospital. He agreed to give the necessary discharge orders as soon as my stumps had healed and no longer required medical treatment. On that happy note I asked Sister Florian to come see me so I could tell her of my plans. Just like at Christmastime, however, she absolutely refused to let me go home unless there was someone in the house to care for me. There was no one I could think of who could stay with me for such an extended period of time. I even told Sister I could not afford to accumulate hospital bills without a source of income. She told me not to worry about it and with a confident smile left the room. A few days later she was back with the news that at a special staff meeting it was decided that I would be offered free room and board at the adjacent St. Joseph Sanatorium for the rest of my life if I so chose. This offer was made despite the fact that I was a fallen-away Baptist, not a Catholic. I was deeply moved by the offer but still wanted to go home and become self-sufficient. Fortunately, my sister, Ardine, had become pregnant and had to give up traveling with her husband (who was business manager for the Earl "Fatha" Hines jazz band) until her baby was born. She was happy to come home and stay with me. My last obstacle was overcome.

With this stroke of good fortune I was in unusually high spirits. That same evening the night nurse came into my room with my daily ration of pain and sleeping pills. These medications (as were all the others) were always to be taken in the presence of the nurse. But with the student nurses visiting my room at odd hours of the night there were times I did not want to go to sleep immediately. As an act of faith, they would leave the medicine for me to take at my convenience.

That evening, trying to be humorous, I waited until a young student nurse came in to pretend I was in a state of despair. I told her I was considering suicide by taking in one dose all the medications saved over several weeks. The poor student nurse turned pale with shock and ran out of the room before I could stop her. Within minutes she was back with every nurse she could find and began to search every nook and cranny of my room for the supposedly hidden drugs. Realizing my joke had gotten out of hand I did my best to convince them it was all in fun. However, they kept up their search until they were satisfied I had not saved any medication. Realizing the depth of their concern, I apologized sincerely to those dedicated young nurses who were so concerned about my well-being and promised never again to joke about such a serious matter.

On Valentine's Day, February 14, 1945, I was discharged from St. Joe's amid numerous farewells and even a few tears, some my own. After my $6\frac{1}{2}$ -month stay, the doctors, nurses, and staff had become my extended family. With promises I would stay in touch and pay a visit when fitted with my new legs, I climbed into my Buick I had loaned brother Bernard and, at long last, was on my way home to stay.

Ardine had already been home for several days and had added her own special touch to decorating our home. My bedroom furniture was specially arranged so I could get in and out with my wheelchair without difficulty. Just being home again with my family was "seventh heaven." Ardine and I spent hours talking about the events in our lives, large and small, since her visit the day after I entered the hospital. Before going to bed I gave her the ample supply of pain pills and sleeping tablets given me before I left the hospital and told her to put them all in the garbage can. I was sure the nurses who worried about my faked suicidal tendencies would be happy to know I had absolutely no medication on hand.

As soon as I could arrange for transportation, I made my first visit to the Fidelity Orthopedic Company, where I met with the rotund salesman who had visited me in the hospital to discuss the purchase of my new prostheses. It was then I discovered one of the few advantages of being a double amputee. After a few preliminary questions the fitter casually asked me how tall I wanted to be and what size shoe I wanted to wear. Not many people get to make that decision. After considering the many possibilities I decided to retain my same height and shoe size so that, mainly for financial reasons, I could continue to use my existing wardrobe. With this important decision out of the way the fitter wrapped my stumps with wide elastic tape that I was to wear every day for a month. The purpose was to shrink the stumps to their natural size before fitting the prostheses. Then began the long and often very painful process of fitting my new legs, which required about three weeks to complete. After the final fitting I was ready to walk out to the Buick parked in front of the store. To my surprise the fitter brought my new artificial legs (with proper brown skin tones) into the fitting room wrapped in a large paper bag. I told him in no uncertain terms I intended to walk to the car with my legs and crutches, not riding in a wheelchair. In spite of the pain, I was proud and happy to be on my feet again! To commemorate the occasion the florist next door, who had been watching my progress during my fittings, gave me a small bouquet of flowers. Their bright colors seemed to reflect my feelings and hopes for an equally bright future.

Every day I walked around the house on my new legs from chair to chair, sometimes leaning on the wall for support or even falling when I lost my balance. Although the pain was very severe, especially when water blisters formed on my legs, I was determined to keep them on all day long. Gradually I gained strength and skill. Within a few weeks I was ready to attempt a walk, using crutches, from my house out to the front sidewalk. With neighbors peeking through their windows, I struggled along the walkway for what seemed an enormous distance until I reached the sidewalk and felt I had conquered Mount Everest! Watching the automobile and pedestrian traffic like a visiting tourist until the pain became unbearable, I started walking back to my house. The return trip was especially difficult because the walk was slightly uphill. Finally, sitting down in my living room chair, exhausted from my efforts, I felt my first baby steps had been completed and I was on my way to independence.

The news of my progress must have reached Detroit City Airport because Telford "Dunc" Duncan soon called, asking if I was interested in coming out to the airport for a visit. "Would an alcoholic like to have another martini?" I asked. That must have answered his question for he was knocking on my door just as I finished changing clothes.

Walking down the walkway with firm purpose, I reached his car parked on the street and climbed in. My home was not far from Detroit City Airport so the trip was short but, in my mood of high anticipation, it seemed to last forever.

Duncan's first stop was the airport restaurant where I was warmly greeted by the owner, George "Nick" Manteris, and the waitresses I knew so well. News of my presence spread quickly and I was soon surrounded by fellow pilots and mechanics as well as office employees and other airport regulars. It was a warm reception but I soon became impatient to get out on the flight line.

Duncan drove me around the huge hangar so I could see all the latest airplanes, and then out to the flight line where the sounds of engines and propellers were music to my ears. I was content to just sit there and drink in the atmosphere that had only been a memory for the last eight months.

The strain of walking on my new legs soon caused my newly healed stumps to swell, resulting in pain that even the joy of being at the airport could not alleviate. With reluctance, I asked Duncan to drive me home where, upon arriving, I immediately and uncharacteristically took my legs off to ease the pain. Sitting in my living room chair and thinking about my airport visit I realized my love of aviation was undiminished. But I still did not know if mental trauma from my accident might cause me to have an uncontrollable fear of flying. The answer could only be determined in the air. With mixed emotions I asked Duncan to take me flying as soon as possible.

On my next visit to the airport, Duncan drove directly to the flight line, where his Aeronca L-3, NC47426, was gassed up and ready to fly. It was painted in my favorite colors, yellow and blue (like the Waco and S-1), and was appropriately but unofficially named "Yellow Gal." Duncan had recently become the first black in the state of Michigan to earn his commercial pilot license and instructor rating. He was an outgoing, relaxed person with a natural ability to instill confidence in his passengers and students. We had a long talk about the mistakes I had made leading to my accident and the potential effects it might have on my skills and emotions as a pilot. We agreed I should start with simple maneuvers to test my initial reactions. If there were no negative signs we would continue on to more advanced maneuvers. If all went well we would fly out to Wings Airport, the scene of my accident, and to the degree possible perform the 180-degree turn and resultant spin just as it happened on July 30, 1944.

I climbed awkwardly into the front seat of Yellow Gal, fastened my safety belt, and then performed a cockpit check. After looking at the familiar dials on the instrument panel I was soon relaxed and impatient to be airborne. Duncan climbed in the back seat and closed the door. We went through the routine engine start procedures and called the familiar word "Contact" to the waiting mechanic. The 65-HP Continental engine came quickly to life, its vibrations shuddering through the fuselage. The tower called, "Aeronca 426 you are cleared for takeoff, runway 33." Pushing the throttle forward I felt the familiar surge of movement and excitement as we raced down the runway for takeoff. My eyes followed the airplane's dancing shadow moving along the ground, growing smaller as we continued our climb. The unbounded freedom of the sky I had been dreaming of for months was now a reality as we cruised in joyful flight above green farmlands.

Upon arriving in the practice area we went through basic turns and orientation maneuvers to test my coordination between hand pressure on the control stick and forces I needed to apply to the rudder pedals with my artificial legs and feet. After some initial awkwardness I was soon performing all the maneuvers with confidence and skill.

Encouraged by my performance we flew over Wings Airport for the crucial test. Starting at as low an altitude as feasible, I entered a 180-degree turn followed by a stall entry and spin, the same sequence of events that led to my accident. The ground rushed toward me, spinning in a familiar blur of green and brown. I recovered quickly and returned to level flight. Dunc leaned forward and patted me on the back. I smiled in return, happy in the realization that the fears or emotional scars that might destroy my love of flying had not materialized. During the short flight back to Detroit City Airport I tried to think of appropriate words to express my thanks to Telford Duncan for returning me to the realm of flight.

Whatever words I used, his eyes and ready smile told me he understood. The language of pilots, like love, is universal.

CHAPTER SEVEN

INDEPENDENCE

One contradiction in trying to become an independent double amputee was that my best friends and relatives were at times my worst enemies. Out of consideration for my safety and well-being, they were overly concerned about the risks I felt were necessary to meet my goal of becoming independent.

When I first started walking on crutches my sister understandably wanted me to stay inside our home, where she would always be available to help me whenever I had problems in maintaining my balance. She was sure I would fall and hurt myself if I went outside.

When I decided to give up my crutches and use only a cane the same overly protective advice was given. Similarly, whenever I discussed my plans for driving my car and even worse, flying an airplane, questions were raised about my mental stability. According to my loved ones, anyone who had spent $6\frac{1}{2}$ months in a hospital should be content to stay home and be safe and comfortable.

Earsly was an exception to this "safe at all costs" syndrome. After I had been on crutches for about a month Earsly came by my house with a problem. One of our CAP cadets, Sammy Harmon, had injured his ankle while performing routine exercises in preparation for his first parachute jump. His injury was so painful that he couldn't walk without crutches and the only ones available were mine. After a short discussion

Earsly and I decided that Sammy needed them more than I did so my transition to using canes started sooner than planned. Even Dr. Thompson had suggested using crutches for at least six months and many of my conservative friends agreed. To their dismay, I was delighted to get rid of the cumbersome crutches.

Such thoughts were not on my mind as I sat in the driver's seat of Duncan's battered old Mercury looking at the controls and trying to figure out how I could use them. I happened to be at Bay 12 in the main hangar at Detroit City Airport when Duncan called, asking that someone drive his car to the flight line. Seeing there were no drivers available at the time I decided to make my first attempt at driving a car. Cautiously moving my feet from the clutch to the brake pedals and then to the accelerator, I soon found a comfortable position and practiced the motions of driving. Gradually my confidence increased enough for me to start the car and begin to move it very slowly back and forth. I cautiously put the car in low gear and moved forward, making sure the road ahead was clear so that if I lost control there would be no crash. I had no problems. After parking the Merc on the flight line I moved out of the driver's seat so that no one would question me. The short trip was nothing special for any average driver but for me it was a breakthrough on my way to personal freedom.

The overprotective syndrome surfaced again when I called brother Bernard and asked him to return my two-tone green 1941 Buick I had loaned him during my stay in the hospital. He, too, expressed his concern for my safety and well-being. "After all," he said, "people with two good legs are getting killed every day on the road and you are taking an even greater risk as a double amputee." But his logic wasn't good enough for me. "If the Detroit Police Department Examiner says I am competent to drive a car and grants me a license then I will continue to drive my Buick. If I fail then you can have it back." Even though he wasn't convinced, Bernard drove the Buick to my home and wished me well.

I started my practice by driving back and forth in the back alleys of the neighborhood where I had no car traffic to worry about. Soon I was out on the streets driving with my old skills and confidence.

After taking my driver's test the examiner must have agreed, for he granted me a license with only the single stipulation that I had to have special devices. Unfortunately he did not identify on my license that the required special devices were my artificial legs. One day I was stopped by the police at a special road block for a routine vehicle safety inspection. Looking at my driver's license, the officer looked into my car in vain for special devices on the steering wheel or on the pedals. It took some convincing talk on my part, plus a look at my legs, before he agreed that my legs were my special devices.

Although I was doing quite well with my driving and was pleased with my flight in the Aeronca, I did not feel ready to start the serious dual instruction necessary for me to solo again. In the meantime, Earsly and Duncan were flying Waco 4711 whenever possible. Gasoline ration stamps for aircraft use were scarce so flights were few and far between.

One day Duncan was flying the Waco over the south side of Detroit when the Siemens-Halske engine quit. He skillfully landed in a hayfield with no damage other than to the hay. On examining the engine he found it was seriously damaged internally. This was a special problem for Earsly and me for the engine was built in Germany, and during the war no spare parts were available. We had a perfectly good airplane with a nonairworthy, nonrepairable engine. We dismantled the Waco and stored it, waiting for the day we could get parts, a day that never came. Our beloved Waco was grounded forever.

My first visit to St. Joe's was long overdue according to the correspondence coming from the student nurses. With the ink barely dry on my driver's license, I called the hospital to tell them I was on my way. I didn't tell them I would be driving alone, as it was to be a surprise. And a surprise it was! As I got out of the car at the hospital entrance they had their second surprise. They had never seen me standing erect during my 6 months in the hospital and to them I appeared to be 10 feet tall! They escorted me into the hospital to be greeted with obvious affection by doctors, nurses, hospital staff, and, of course, Sister Florian. After several hours of conversation I was invited to dinner. When it was over I started saying my goodbyes in preparation for the drive home. This idea was immediately vetoed by everyone present. The had rearranged the doctors' lounge, which was to be my bedroom for the night. My visit turned out to be an all-day, all-night party. It was a homecoming I can never forget.

Another trip I planned after discharge from the hospital was to Marine City where Mrs. Miller lived. She had retired as head librarian of the Marine City Library. Her late husband had been a Great Lakes iron ore freighter captain and had routinely guided his huge vessel by their house on the St. Clair River, about 30 miles northeast of Detroit. Mrs. Miller had entered St. Joseph Hospital early in January 1945 for a two-week stay. After the nurses had told her a few of their favorite "Neal Loving stories," Mrs. Miller sent word by the nurses inviting me to visit her in her room. I was too bashful to enter a strange white lady's bedroom, even in a hospital, so I stayed away. One day a nurse brought me a fresh bunch of Florida kumquats and a note from Mrs. Miller requesting I come to her room and say thanks for her gift like a gentleman should. Overcoming my initial reluctance, I went to her room and found her to be a lovely, gray-haired woman with a youthful sense of humor. It was the first of many such visits.

Before leaving the hospital she gave me a book written by Ernie Pyle, the famous newspaper reporter whose daily articles on the lowly foot soldiers of World War II made him world-famous. The book was a scarce collectors' item, but with her library connections she was able to obtain a copy for me. On the flyleaf she penned the following words above and below the book's title:

To one of the
BRAVE MEN
of St. Joseph Hospital

I never felt particularly brave but certainly appreciated the compliment.

Since Red had also met Mrs. Miller during her stay at the hospital, when she invited me to her home she also invited him. We arrived at our scheduled time and were encouraged to make ourselves comfortable in the lawn chairs she had placed on the patio which faced the blue gray waters of the St. Clair River. Her luxurious home gave evidence of her high social status. After reminiscing about our experiences at

St. Joe's she prepared afternoon tea and sandwiches served on elegant, expensive china. Red and I were too worried about breakage to fully enjoy Mrs. Miller's hospitality. But she was a gracious, thoughtful hostess and did her best to put us at ease. We enjoyed the visit but felt a lot better when we were able to leave without having embarrassed ourselves.

Another bright spot in the summer of 1945 was the Group 9 CAP Encampment held at Croswell Airport, about 75 miles northeast of Detroit. On Friday afternoon of the designated weekend, the cadets and officers of our squadron reported for duty at our training center near downtown Detroit to prepare for our first field trip. We loaded our cars with tents, food, and medical supplies, and after forming our convoy drove to Croswell Airport following carefully planned military procedures. Upon our arrival the encampment officer gave us our orders and a map identifying our assigned squadron area. With previously practiced skills we pitched our tents and set up our campsite. Everyone, including officers and cadets, slept on the ground on blankets and sleeping bags. I was the exception; with due consideration of my handicap I was assigned the one and only cot at the encampment, which was in the medical tent. Billie Lewis, our medical officer, later complained, in good humor, that her slender body felt every ridge and rut on the ground.

Each of the five squadrons was responsible for providing food for its own squadron members, plus inviting wing staff officers for a meal at least once during the encampment. For the other squadrons the standard fare was K-rations, a filling but otherwise unappetizing meal. But we had a young, talented cook in our squadron who prepared fresh, tasty, homemade meals for breakfast and supper. In the morning, the aroma of fried bacon and eggs wafted over the entire camp area. Our evening meals were equally inviting; I remember especially a delicious beef stew. Instead of rotating their meals with other squadrons according to schedule, the wing staff officers converged at our campsite for all their meals. For once the other squadrons were jealous of the all-black Parachute Squadron. The wing staff would later think kindly of us when it became necessary to ask for assistance at staff level.

Lee Rivard was a friend of Red Rapp who had bought a war-surplus Taylorcraft L-2 in the fall of 1944 but unfortunately had no aviation background. Of course Red suggested he come to see me at the hospital. A few days later Lee came into my room and it was friendship at first sight. I was favorably impressed by Lee's easy-going, jovial manner, his muscular build, and lean, tanned face typical of a true outdoorsman. His sense of humor was legendary among his friends, many of whom had been the subject of his practical jokes. Lee was a 49-year-old bachelor living with his French-Canadian father in Mt. Clemens not far from St. Joe's. He was a man of many skills, such as auto mechanic, painter, and house builder, and now he was gaining experience in aviation. We spent many hours together discussing the maintenance and flying characteristics of his Taylorcraft L-2. I also advised him on how to find a suitable airport and flight instructor. Lee had the natural coordination and judgment required of a pilot and qualified for his private pilot's license in minimum time.

After I had mastered the art of walking on artificial legs, Lee invited me to fly with him to Lewiston, Michigan (about 200 miles north of Detroit), where he had built a hunting cabin in a clearing surrounded by towering green trees, typical of the forests in upstate Michigan. He had already smoothed out a landing strip on his property within walking distance of the cabin. I had never been in the northern part of the state so it was an experience I looked forward to. On the appointed day in July 1945, the weather was warm and cloudless, ideal for flying. We loaded our few belongings into the luggage compartment and took off on a course to Bay City, where his cousin Emile was awaiting our arrival. Sitting in the cockpit behind Lee and watching the wooded countryside and emerald-green lakes reflecting the blue skies go by, I knew my friends and family were wrong. The joy of being airborne was well worth taking the risk they warned me to avoid. We made our planned stop at Bay City Airport where we had a short visit with Emile while the L-2 was being refueled. Soon we were airborne again on our way to Lewiston.

When Lee's landing strip came into view I could not believe my eyes. It was incredibly short with tall trees at one end and a dammed-up lake at the other. The strip was narrow and hemmed in with brush and trees on both sides. Since I was a native-born Detroiter accustomed to flying out of the lengthy concrete runways of Detroit City Airport, this type of bush flying required skills I did not possess. Lee skillfully flew his traffic pattern to final approach, closing the throttle just as we cleared the dam. Extending the wing spoilers, Lee landed the little Taylorcraft on the tiny runway with room to spare. Concealing my sigh of relief, I walked with Lee to his cabin. While he prepared our evening meal I walked outside to see and smell, for the first time, the wonders of a natural, primitive forest.

After a few days of tramping in the woods and observing wildlife I had never seen before, we flew home. It was a wonderful new experience for a city boy like me and Lee was generous enough to take me back many times. But I always had a feeling that a successful landing at Lee's airstrip required not only exceptional piloting skills but also a dash of good luck. Several years later Lee's luck ran out on final approach to the strip. Seeing he was too high coming over the dam, Lee extended the spoilers to lose altitude, not realizing his glide speed was too low. The L-2 fell to the ground with such force that the landing gear collapsed, resulting in so much damage to the airplane, propeller, and engine that it had to be scrapped. Lee never flew an airplane again.

I was with Lee when he played one of his practical jokes on six of his hunting buddies (and me) during the deer hunting season in the fall of 1945. We had all gathered at Lee's house in Mt. Clemens early one morning to gather up our needed equipment and load it into our respective cars before heading north to Lewiston. We made one stop at a general store on the main highway just outside Bay City where Lee bought all of the fresh provisions needed during our stay at his cabin. After putting his purchases in the car he said he had to go back and buy something he had forgotten. Minutes later he brought to the car a large object in a large paper bag which he did not identify at the time. Several hours later we were at the cabin unloading our personal and hunting gear. Lee, among his many talents, was an excellent cook and his supper was a fine example. The evening continued with many well-worn and oft-repeated hunting stories (more accurately known as lies) accompanied by a generous supply of beer. Before going to bed,

Lee opened up his large paper bag and showed us his last purchase. It was a new, but old-fashioned, metal chamber pot, more commonly referred to as a "thundermug." Its distinctive shape was covered with a gray enamel porcelain-like finish like old-fashioned cookware. He knew we would appreciate having this convenience which eliminated the need to go to the outhouse in the cold, autumn night. Lee took full credit for this latest luxury.

Early the next morning we awoke to the smell of fresh coffee and fried bacon being prepared by our chef, Lee Rivard. As we washed up, he picked up the well-used thundermug and walked by us to the outhouse where he noisily emptied it.

We eagerly sat down to a breakfast of fresh orange juice, pancakes and bacon, and steaming hot coffee. The first serving was eaten in record time and everyone called for second helpings. Lee came out of the kitchen smiling. He carried a thundermug containing the remaining pancake batter to show us the ample supply still available. As we looked in consternation, Lee carefully explained that he had washed it thoroughly before mixing the batter. Evidently no one was completely convinced for suddenly there were no more demands for second help-ings. Lee went back to the kitchen and returned with a big grin on his face, carrying the empty thundermug we had used during the night and a receipt that proved he had bought *two* thundermugs at the general store in Bay City! Even with this evidence that our pancake batter had been mixed in the new and unused thundermug, our appetite for pan-cakes had disappeared.

One day my sister Ardine showed me an article in the Sunday newspaper describing a federally funded tuition assistance program for handi-capped people, available without regard for financial need. The only criterion was that the applicant's educational goals enhance his or her potential for employment. It was administered by the Michigan Division of Vocational Rehabilitation. I wrote a letter to the state office asking for tuition assistance for the courses I planned to take at Wayne State University, beginning with the fall semester of 1945. My long-awaited start toward earning a degree in aeronautical engineering was finally

My parents, Dr. Hardin Clay Loving and Alma Loving, in the summer of 1937. My father died the next year.

George E. Tabraham, pilot, mechanic, educator, and principal of Aero Mechanics High School, Detroit. He was a mentor and supporter of my early efforts in aviation and inspired me to achieve when others said, "Don't try." (*Source:* B. O. Davis Aerospace Technical High School.)

My first "big" project, Ground Trainer, 1935. It was designed to provide a realistic airplane cockpit to sit in, as well as practice in fabricating a structure that was a step or two above model airplane construction. An "imagination machine" for young would be fliers.

Don Pearl Simmons, president of the all-black Ace Flying Club in Detroit. Don and his wife Kathleen would die when the club's plane crashed on takeoff in 1933. (*Source:* Cornelius R. Coffey.)

Sitting in the cockpit of my first glider, N15750, in 1936. This picture was taken at Rose Park near my home in Detroit, which provided enough space for the glider to be assembled.

Standing beside my first powered aircraft, a Waco Model 125, at Detroit City Airport in 1943.

Earsly Taylor, 1943, in my second glider, NX27775.

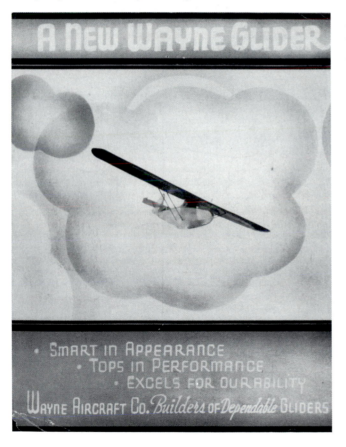

Cover of an advertisement brochure for Wayne Aircraft Company, Detroit. Earsly Taylor and I started the company in 1943.

Wayne Aircraft Company shop area and NX27775 (with the S-2 wing in background), 642 Hastings Street, Detroit, 1943. (*Source:* Wayne Aircraft Co.)

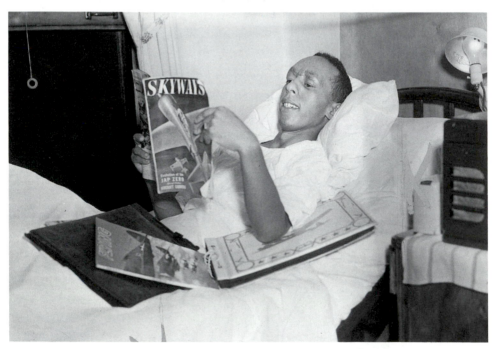

Recuperating at St. Joseph Hospital, Mt. Clemens, Michigan, in August 1944. (*Source: Negro News Review.*)

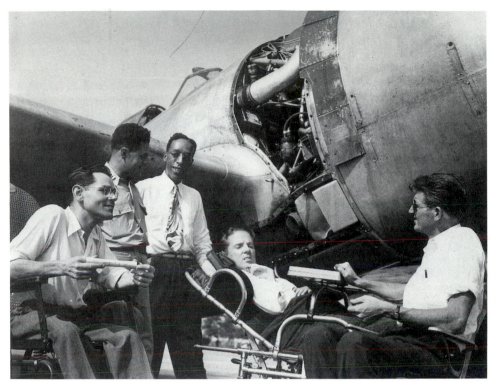

A courageous quartet of young men handicapped by paralysis and lost limbs were special guests of the AAF at Selfridge Field on August 5, 1945. *Left to right:* Norm Peltier, Chaplain George Khalel, Neal Loving, Van Wallace, and Elwyn "Red" Rapp. (*Source:* USAAF.)

King Walter Johnson and I flew to Decatur, Alabama, in 1946, to purchase an Army-surplus plane. This photograph was taken upon our return, in front my newly acquired Vultee BT-13, which still had its original military markings.

The all-wood wing structure of "Loving's Love," showing the inverted gull wing.

Neal and Earsly and Carl Barnett, Detroit City Airport, 1952.

Carl and Earsly just before flying the "Jamerican" VP-JAZ to Kingston from Detroit, July 1952.

"Loving's Love" disassembled for transport to Detroit City Airport, July 1950.

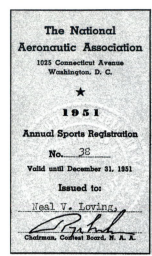
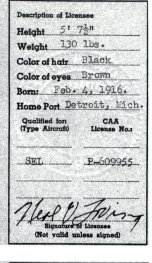

The National Aeronautic Association

1025 Connecticut Avenue
Washington, D. C.

★

1951

Annual Sports Registration

No. 38

Valid until December 31, 1951

Issued to:

Neal V. Loving,

Chairman, Contest Board, N. A. A.

Description of Licensee

Height 5' 7½"
Weight 130 lbs.
Color of hair Black
Color of eyes Brown
Born: Feb. 4, 1916.
Home Port Detroit, Mich.

Qualified for: (Type Aircraft)	CAA License No.:
SEL	P-609955

Signature of Licensee
(Not valid unless signed)

Fédération Aéronautique International (FAI) and National Aeronautic Association (NAA) pilot's annual sports registration.

The National Aeronautic Association

1025 Connecticut Avenue
Washington, D. C.

★

1951

Annual Sports Registration

No. 64

Valid until December 31, 1951

Issued to:

Neal V. Loving,

Chairman, Contest Board, N. A. A.

Description of Racing Aircraft

Make Loving Wayne WR-1
Registration No. 64
Type Low Wing Mono.In.Gu
CAA No. N 351 C
Make and Continental
Type of Motor C-85-12FJ
Bore 4.0625" Stroke 3.625"
Cubic Inch Displacement 188
Owner's Name N.V.Loving
Born (Date) Feb. 4, 1916.
Home Port Detroit, Mich.

Signature of Owner
(Not valid unless signed)

FAI and NAA racing plane owners annual sports registration.

FÉDÉRATION AÉRONAUTIQUE
INTERNATIONALE

NATIONAL AERONAUTIC
ASSOCIATION OF U. S. A.
INC.

Certificate No. 9307

The above named Association, recognized by the Fédération Aéronautique Internationale, as the governing authority for the United States of America, certifies that

Neal V. Loving

born 4th day of February, 1916 having fulfilled all the conditions required by the Fédération Aéronautique Internationale, for an Airplane Pilot is hereby brevetted as such.

Dated May 7, 1951.

CONTEST BOARD

Chairman

Secretary

[SEAL]

Signature of Licensee:

FAI pilot's license.

At Windsor Airport, Ontario, after a flight demonstration, August 1952.

"Loving's Love" in flight over Kingston Harbor, 1953. (*Source:* Amador Packer.)

Clare Therese Barnett and the Love at Palisadoes Airport, Kingston, May 1954.

Taxiing the Love at Palisadoes Airport, Kingston, 1954. (*Source:* Amador Packer.)

Rancho Boyeros Airport, Havana, on my return flight from Jamaica, May 1954. The Love always seemed to draw a crowd.

Torre Garde, Jamaica, where Clare and I spent our honeymoon. The short landing strip (*center*) gave Carl problems with the Piper J-3 Cub.

This was my entry, WR-2, in the EAA Design Competition for "roadable aircraft." Because of certain design characteristics to accommodate the roadable feature, it was not suitable, in terms of its handling or controllability, for amateur or less experienced pilots. I decided not to fly it and moved on to another design.

The WR-3, my successful design of a roadable aircraft, during a flight near my home in Yellow Springs, Ohio. (*Source:* Ed Embry.)

Lee Rivard working on the first roadable, N112Y, 1960.

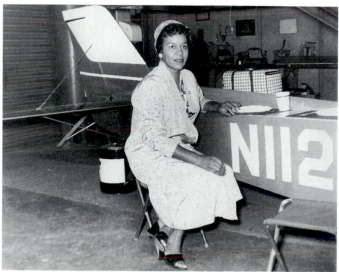

My sister, Ardine Loving Illidge, in 1960.

At work at the Flight Dynamics Laboratory, Wright-Patterson AFB, just before my retirement in January 1982. (*Source:* WPAFB PIO.)

Red and Helen Rapp, still dear friends after 50 years.

My family, after a talk I gave at the Annual Dinner Meeting of the Detroit chapter of Negro Airmen International, May 1990. *Left to right:* Bernard Loving and his wife, Bob Ella (deceased), Clare, Neal, Mae Loving (brother Robert's wife), Ardine Illidge (sister), and Robert Loving. (*Source:* Leavie Farro, Jr., and Associates.)

a reality. Mrs. Ailee Ervin of the Detroit office promptly answered my letter with the promise my tuition expenses would be paid by her agency. After my first visit to Wayne State to select my classes I went to her office to arrange for tuition payment. Mrs. Ervin was a warm, friendly person and a very able counselor. I told her of my handicap and my long-standing love of aviation. She gave me every encouragement but also reminded me of the many obstacles—after all, I had been away from academics for quite a while—that lay in my path before graduation. But the goal was worth the price and I started my studies with high hopes.

One of my new driving duties was driving Ardine to the clinic for her prenatal care. Her husband, Eric Illidge, was still on tour with the jazz band and could not be at home to take her. Occasionally I would have difficulty explaining to the nurses and staff at the clinic that I was her brother, not her husband. But her pregnancy went well and her son, Keith, was born in October 1945. I brought flowers to her at the hospital and otherwise was a stand-in for her husband. A few days later I drove her and the baby home, demonstrating that despite her fears it was a good idea that I had learned to drive again. Baby Keith was sometimes a hindrance to my college studies for his voice was loud and clear, especially in the middle of the night. It was embarrassing sometimes to complain to my fellow students about a baby keeping me awake nights when it was well known that I was a bachelor. The moral standards of that era frowned on unmarried fathers.

Another, more serious problem arose when an investigator from the Internal Revenue Service came to my home. In those days income tax payments were due on January 15 and mine was long overdue on the salary I earned in 1944. I told him about my accident and that I was going to college and would eventually earn a decent salary. But in the meantime I was unemployed and obviously unable to make the scheduled payments. Totally unmoved by my story he told me if I did not make full restitution within 30 days I could be fined up to $10,000 and/or sentenced to six months in jail. Rising from his chair he gave me the IRS payment form and left without a smile. After recovering from my initial panic, I began calling my family and friends to arrange a loan that would allow me to pay the IRS and stay out of jail. I was overwhelmed by the loving response of my family and friends and was able to make the overdue payment well before the 30 days were up. Relieved of my worries of going to jail, I went to bed so relaxed I managed to get a full night of sleep for the first time in weeks.

Early in December 1945, King Walter Johnson came to my home while I was working on homework assignments for my classes at Wayne State. I wasn't too happy about the interruption until he told me the purpose of his visit. He showed me a magazine advertisement by the War Assets Corporation, which was created after the war to dispose of all war-surplus assets. Among the items listed was a large number of surplus Vultee BT-13 basic trainers. Walter had flown BT-13s during his basic training at Tuskegee and was impressed by their strength and performance. The BT-13 was a two-place, all-metal, low-wing basic trainer powered by a 450-HP Pratt & Whitney nine-cylinder radial engine. It was equipped with a Hamilton Standard controllable pitch (two-position) propeller and fully instrumented, including radio, for day, night, and instrument flying.

Walter had written many letters to me at the hospital telling me of his experiences flying this high-performance airplane. He even sent me a picture of the instrument panel, which seemed to be so complex I told him it looked like a "plumber's nightmare!" It was obvious the acquisition price paid by the government for these airplanes was well beyond my financial means. I was amazed, however, when he showed me the ad where they were being sold for $975 with a 20 percent discount for veterans. Walter was still unemployed following recent discharge from the Army so he could not buy one himself. However, he agreed to buy a BT-13 for me in his name to obtain the serviceman's discount, reducing the price to a mere $780. With money available from a settlement with my medical insurance company, the purchase of a high-performance BT-13 was within reach.

With class assignments forgotten for the moment, Walter and I made plans for our trip to Decatur, Alabama, where the BT-13s were stored and available for purchase. The only time I could take off from my studies for this trip was during Christmas vacation. We planned our departure for the day after Christmas and our arrival back in Detroit in time for me to resume classes after New Year's Day. I purchased train tickets for our trip but in the meantime found it extremely difficult to concentrate on my studies while dreaming of owning and flying my own BT-13.

The excitement of Christmas in the presence of Ardine and her infant son Keith was overshadowed by my concerns associated with my first trip south of the Mason-Dixon Line to Alabama. The significance of the Mason-Dixon Line became readily apparent to Walter and me as our train crossed the Ohio River. On entering the border state of Kentucky we were forced to move from our unsegregated coach to the last coach on the train, the "Jim Crow" section. The quality of service and the conditions were significantly worse than those we had enjoyed on the trip from Detroit to Cincinnati. But such inconveniences were minor as we looked forward to selecting our BT-13 from the large supply in storage at the airport in Decatur, Alabama. On our arrival at the train station we went into the colored waiting room as required by Southern custom and hired a colored cabdriver to take us to the colored section of Decatur. We asked our cabdriver to recommend a place to stay since we knew we were not welcome at the white hotels. He took us to a small rooming house where we spent the night on lumpy straw mattresses in a dingy, miserably cold room. The next morning our landlady served us a breakfast of cold pork chops and grits. The sight of congealed fat in the chops and grits was more than either of us could stand. We settled for toast and coffee.

With breakfast finished, we took a cab to Decatur Airport where a large array of BT-13s were lined up on the flight line available for inspection. Walter walked up and down the line of parked aircraft, checking with a practiced eye the mechanical condition of each airplane and its aircraft and engine logbooks. After several hours of deliberation he selected one that had served as an instrument trainer at an Army training base in Greenville, Mississippi. Instrument training was less damaging to the aircraft structure than aerobatics.

After we showed the waiting mechanic a receipt indicating full payment for our designated BT-13, he began the lengthy process of removing it from storage and making it flight-ready for our trip home.

The entire cockpit canopy had been covered with an opaque preservative before storage which had to be removed before flight. However, only the front cockpit windshield and canopy area were cleaned. From my seat in the back I could only look straight forward. I scraped a little peep hole on either side so I could help Walter with his navigation. Before we left to return to our room in Decatur the mechanic started up the engine and I heard for the first time the distinctive sound of a Pratt & Whitney engine at full throttle. I couldn't believe it was mine.

The next morning the BT-13 was ready. After a quick preflight we took off for Huntsville, Alabama, for refueling for the first leg of our long journey home. Walter had not flown a BT-13 for several years but it did not take long for him to renew his piloting skills. After landing at Huntsville, we were beset by problems caused by a dead battery. By the time we had them resolved, bad weather set in. With this delay the probability of my arriving home in time for the start of classes at the end of the Christmas holiday became very remote. After several days of weather-watching we got a marginally acceptable forecast from the weather office and took off for Cincinnati. As we continued on a northerly heading it became painfully clear that neither of us was adequately dressed for the unusually cold weather now prevalent over large areas of the South. To compound our problem, the cockpit heaters were not working properly. Outside temperatures continued to drop as we approached another cold front coming south out of Canada. The weather conditions gradually deteriorated to below visual flight rules (VFR) minimums as we neared Bardstown, Kentucky, so Walter decided to make an emergency landing.

Carefully selecting a suitable farmer's field, Walter made a perfect short-field emergency landing on his first attempt. After a comfortable two-hour wait for the weather to improve, we took off again for Cincinnati. Soon the familiar outlines of Lunken Airport came into view followed by instructions from the tower advising us the wind was out of the north. We were cleared to land on runway 2.

For reasons he was never able to explain, Walter overshot this mile-long runway three times before making a successful landing in spite of having made a perfect short-field landing only hours before.

Hiding his embarrassment, Walter taxied to the hangar ramp, guided by a Queen City Air Service lineman.

We were both chilled to the bone as we climbed stiffly out of the cockpit to face the cold, snowy winds blowing across the ramp. Quickly removing our luggage from the BT-13 we rushed to the warmth of the airport waiting room. After making sure our BT-13 was properly tied down and refueled, we took a cab into Cincinnati where we had reserved a room at the Manse Hotel. As soon as we checked in, Walter and I each selected a steam radiator and sat for several hours before thawing out enough to go out to dinner. On arriving back at the hotel we quickly went to bed using all the available blankets, which were needed to get us warm and comfortable again.

The 220-mile flight to Detroit City Airport the next morning was accomplished without difficulty except for the continuing cold weather. Again, afraid of negative criticism from my well-meaning friends, I told no one except Earsly of my purchase. To avoid attention, Walter parked the airplane quickly in a remote section of the Detroit City Airport flight line and we left before anyone recognized us. But this was the first BT-13 to be parked for an extended stay at Detroit City Airport and it soon attracted the attention of the local aviation community.

As soon as I paid the tie-down fees at the airport office my identity as the owner could no longer be concealed. As usual, Duncan and all my well-meaning friends deplored my plans to fly it, citing the customary arguments of why a legless pilot shouldn't risk his life in such a high-performance airplane. It didn't help either that the BT-13 was frequently referred to during the war at basic training fields as the "cadet killer." Duncan even went so far as to predict I would kill myself before flying it 10 hours. But with Walter's steady assurance that I could safely learn to master the complexities of flying the BT-13 and his promise to give me the required dual instruction, I looked forward to this new challenge.

The first problem I faced on arriving home, though, was that I had failed to finish my classes at Wayne State, including the final exams. I was so ashamed of myself that I did not have the nerve to call Mrs. Ervin and tell her of my adventure to Alabama. I did not enroll for the spring semester but instead began studying the BT-13 flight manual in preparation for dual instruction prior to solo. My new flying activities were to keep me so busy that I did not re-enroll at WSU until the fall of 1954. The task of converting an ex-military BT-13 into its civilian version, NC63650, added to my already busy schedule. I had little time to dwell on my interrupted college career. So the year 1945 ended on both a positive and negative note.

CHAPTER EIGHT

THE FLYING SCHOOL

My New Year's Day celebration for 1946 did not include the traditional noisemaking and revelry. Rather, I went out to Detroit City Airport with King Walter Johnson and, with his assistance, taxied the BT-13 from the flight line down to Bay 12 in the main hangar. There, under the watchful eye of George Sentas, pilot, mechanic, and owner of Sentas Skyways, I started the long and arduous task of converting my former military trainer into a licensed civilian airplane. There were several Civil Aeronautics Administration (CAA) airworthiness directives to be complied with, plus innumerable smaller tasks to be completed before the conversion was accomplished. Some of the most time-consuming tasks were purely cosmetic. The natural aluminum finish of the BT-13 was dulled by years of exposure to the hot, southern sun. The job of cleaning and polishing an all-aluminum airplane the size of my BT-13 was immense. It had a wing span of 42 feet and was over 30 feet long. Fully loaded and ready for flight, it weighed over two tons (4,250 pounds).

By mid-March my grubby war veteran had became a shiny aluminum and blue civilian Vultee NC63650. George Sentas gave it a thorough inspection before issuing the required CAA airworthiness certificate. George was a very competent and likable man of Greek descent with a decided limp from a childhood accident. Since both of us were lame from our respective accidents we became like brothers. Our close relationship continued in both our personal and business lives until his untimely death in an airplane accident in the late 1950s.

Now that the Vultee was fully licensed by the CAA I was ready to embark on the long road to qualifying for my pilot's license. Once again, friends and relatives advised me to stay safely on the ground. As usual, I ignored them. Walter had loaned me his BT-13 flight training manual and I spent all my hours away from the airport studying everything from checkout procedures to advance flight training maneuvers.

In the midst of my intensive but enthusiastic flight manual studies came news of an upcoming joyous celebration. Red Rapp and Helen Starkweather called to announce their plans to be married on February 28, 1946, at a Methodist church near downtown Mt. Clemens. I was invited to attend, along with Hilda Hines (maid of honor) and her husband, Harold. Other than the minister, we were the only ones to attend the ceremony. The reception was held at Helen's parents' home and all of their many relatives and friends were there. I loaned the newlyweds my 1941 Buick for their honeymoon, which they said they would spend in Port Huron, only 20 miles away. The first postcard I received was from Atlantic City, New Jersey!

Before my first BT-13 flight lesson, Walter insisted I pass a "blindfold cockpit check." This required being able to touch every instrument, electrical switch, and flight control in the cockpit correctly on command while blindfolded. This was by far the most complex airplane I had ever attempted to fly and I was determined not to fail. I practiced the required cockpit procedures for hours.

On March 30, 1946, I climbed into the front cockpit of Vultee NC63650 for my first flight lesson as Walter got into the instructor's seat in the rear, giving me a reassuring smile. Even with the hours of preparation and familiarization I was still awed by the thought of flying this modern, high-speed, powerful airplane. The cockpit was large and roomy with a full instrument panel. I sat much higher from the ground than in anything I had flown before, including the Waco. Walter broke my reverie by calling me on the intercom system and gave orders to start the big 450-HP Pratt & Whitney engine. With a roar and a cloud of smoke it came to life. After finishing all preflight procedures I called the tower for takeoff instructions. Within minutes we were climbing rapidly, headed for the practice area. According to the brief entry in my logbook I "practiced gentle and medium turns" during our 30-minute flight. However, it would take volumes to describe my emotions as I purposefully guided the Vultee over St. Joseph Hospital. I soloed just two days later, after 2 hours and 50 minutes of dual instruction. I felt as if I had been born again.

One of the Michigan wing staff officers I met during our Croswell Airport CAP encampment was trim, white-haired Col. Louis Edwards, a true officer and gentleman. When he heard the story of my accident while on CAP duty, he returned to his office and searched the CAP regulations to see if I was entitled to federal insurance benefits. After several weeks of research he found I was covered by the War Survivors Insurance Program. Under this coverage, all my hospital expenses were paid by the U.S. government. This meant all the money I had paid to the hospital (as well as the money paid to the hospital by my insurance company) was to be returned to me.

In addition, I was entitled to $85 per month survivors' insurance, retroactive to the date of the accident. Since the accident occurred almost two years before, I was paid a lump sum for the accrued amount. Free of all debts, and with money in the bank, I was ready to plan my financial future.

In 1946, many returning war veterans were using their GI Bill benefits to learn to fly. Black veterans were, as always, excluded from white flight schools. Earsly and I met to discuss possibilities. We had closed Wayne Aircraft Company during my long stay in the hospital. We now decided to form the Wayne School of Aeronautics at Detroit City Airport. When we discussed our plans with airport management officials, they were quick to cite various reasons why we could not be given permission to open our flight school. None, in our view, were valid. We knew they did not want to offend the many white flying school operators who had lucrative businesses at the airport. Once again it was back to the NAACP, the Urban League, and other civil rights leaders for assistance. We then took our request directly to the Detroit Common Council for action. With pressure from the civil rights groups and a letter of recommendation from the Michigan Civil Air Patrol Wing Staff, the council tentatively granted our request, subject to approval by city airport management.

Earsly and I quickly found that airport management continued to throw obstacles in our path to discourage us from opening Wayne School of Aeronautics. They hastily drew up a new set of requirements specifically for our school. One required us to establish a code of conduct for our students, flight instructors, and office personnel, and submit it to the Detroit City Common Council for approval. No other flight school had to meet such a requirement. It took hours of paperwork, plus additional pressure from the CAP, NAACP, and the Urban League, before we obtained final, written approval from the council. The airport officials then told us there was no office space available for us on the flight line. Earsly and I promptly purchased a small trailer home and converted it to office space. Parked just west of the permanent flight line offices, we were ready for business as soon as we obtained state and federal approval.

With these roadblocks out of the way we now had to set up our flight school operation to conform to the standards of both the CAA and the Michigan State Department of Aeronautics. Personnel from these agencies were interested only in our ability to meet the technical requirements and exhibited none of the racial biases we had encountered before. They gave their full approval.

We selected Sentas Skyways as our aircraft maintenance agency and appointed Telford Duncan as our chief flight instructor (CFI). With Duncan's help we drew up the course curriculum for private and commercial pilot licenses and rules governing our proposed charter service. We then obtained with no difficulty a contract with the Veterans Administration to teach veterans how to fly under the GI Bill. By mid-summer 1946, we had our flight school certificate issued by the Michigan State Department of Aeronautics and were open for business. Earsly quit her long-time job as bookkeeper at a local gas station to take over the office duties as manager of our school. My principal function was to oversee the technical operations and teach all ground-school subjects, from aerodynamics to meteorology.

Our first airplane was the familiar Yellow Gal, NC47426, which we leased from Duncan. It was a two-place, war-surplus Aeronca L-3B converted to civilian standards. As soon as we officially opened our office and parked our bright yellow and blue Aeronca on the flight line, prospective students began signing up at a rapid rate. Although most of our students were black, we also had eager white students. One of our first was tall, red-headed Robert Sutherland. Bob was not a GI but his enthusiasm led him to build up his flying time faster than any of our other students. In fact, he became the first Wayne School of Aeronautics student to obtain a private pilot's license. So much for our image as an all-black flight school! Earsly and I were proud that Bob had selected our school over the thirty white schools operating at Detroit City Airport at that time.

Our flight school grew rapidly as prospective students, both black and white, came into our office in ever increasing numbers. In addition to Yellow Gal, we expanded our fleet to include a new Aeronca Champion 7AC, N1150E, Luscombe 8A's N45436 and N45744, and our flagship, Stinson 150, N8607K. This was a comfortable, four-place cabin plane we used for both flight training and charter service. The Vultee was maintained strictly for the personal use of Earsly and me and, of course, Walter Johnson. In that era of sexual as well as racial discrimination, Earsly was always the center of attraction when she flew our sleek silver and blue Vultee with the canopy open and her head scarf flying in the wind.

The airport management continued to keep a watchful eye on our operation through their contacts with control tower personnel, airport employees, and other flight school operators. The reports must have been satisfactory for we were finally offered office number 8 on the flight line. Wayne School of Aeronautics now had a permanent home and a reputation as a safe, well-managed operation.

One day a prospective student came in our office carrying a leather helmet and goggles. Earsly guided him through the paperwork and discussed the requirements of our training program. She also informed him that all of our training aircraft had enclosed cabins, making his helmet and goggles unnecessary.

Duncan started the new student on his flight training. After experiencing more than the usual difficulties, our young pilot made several satisfactory landings and was prepared for solo. Duncan climbed out and waved him off on his first solo flight.

The Aeronca taxied a short distance and then came to a stop. Worried that the student might have lost his nerve, Duncan walked toward the Aeronca. As he approached, the student taxied away but not before Duncan saw that the pilot had donned his helmet and goggles on this hot summer day in our closed-cabin airplane. His solo flight was successful but Duncan and Earsly banned further use of helmet and goggles. Our "Walter Mitty" was crushed.

On October 3, 1946, after a 70-minute dual instruction flight in Aeronca Champion N1150E, Duncan recommended me for my CAA flight test for a private pilot's license. My sleepless night was spent mentally rehearsing all the potential questions and flight maneuvers the CAA examiner might require during the test. Putting my anxieties behind me the next morning, I prepared myself, as well as Aeronca 1150E, for the flight to the CAA office at Wayne County Airport, 20 miles west, where my flight test was to take place. It was a short flight of only 35 minutes, but it seemed a lot longer.

The CAA examiner was polite but subdued in posing his questions prior to the flight test. I tried very hard to contain my excitement as I answered questions that I knew would weigh heavily in his assessment of my ability to fly.

After the oral examination we went out on the flight line where my Aeronca was waiting. After watching my preflight inspection he asked if I could manually prop the Aeronca, which had no electric starter. Having routinely propped our training airplanes on a daily basis for months I kicked my right leg in the air and vigorously pulled the prop through for a perfect start. We then climbed into the cockpit for my flight test, which lasted only 20 minutes.

The brevity of the flight test made me very happy for I had been told that if the test lasted much longer it meant you had failed. One of the maneuvers the flight examiner asked me to perform was a slip. Thinking carefully for a moment, I asked, "Do you want a sideslip or a forward slip?" When he specified a forward slip I further inquired,

"Do you want it to the left or to the right?" I performed a forward slip to the right as requested.

After one of my better landings we walked to his office where he gave me the good news. Not only had I passed the flight test but he was not going to follow the usual CAA procedure of restricting handicapped pilots with a private pilot rating to the model and make of airplane in which the flight test was taken. He accomplished this by making no reference to my physical handicap on my pilot's certificate. Only my medical certificate carries this information. This freed me of the requirement of obtaining additional ratings for every other make and model of aircraft I subsequently wanted to fly. Considering there were already four types of aircraft in the Wayne School of Aeronautics fleet, this would have been an expensive, time-consuming process. The examiner expressed confidence that I would use good judgment in choosing aircraft that were within my limitations to fly safely with my artificial legs.

Whenever I checked out in a new airplane in the years that followed, I always remembered the high level of responsibility expected of me by that very considerate CAA flight examiner.

There was a small coffee shop on the corner of French Road and Gratiot Avenue which Earsly and I passed every day on our way to work. Occasionally we would stop and pick up coffee and doughnuts for a quick breakfast at our office. One morning Earsly came in and ordered breakfast, stating clearly her intention to eat at the counter. She was surprised when the waitress brought the meal packaged for takeout service. When Earsly reminded her she wanted to eat at the counter, the waitress explained, "We don't serve colored people here." Undaunted, Earsly asked to see the manager and, probably to avoid what he thought might become a civil disturbance, he quickly came to the scene. Sitting down next to her he tactfully tried to justify his policy. He explained that sometimes colored laborers from the nearby Detroit Street Railway yards came into his shop; due to their offensive body odor, he refused to serve them. Earsly raised her left arm high and leaned toward the manager, making sure her armpit was within inches of his nose, and asked with quiet dignity, "Sir, do you smell me?" Obviously embarrassed, the manager ordered the waitress to bring Earsly her breakfast.

Without a word, Earsly rose to her full, statuesque height and with a final scornful look walked regally out of the coffee shop. Needless to say, neither of us ever went back.

One of our more unusual students was Mr. Smith (another "Smitty") from Cincinnati. There was no flight training available for blacks in Cincinnati so he would fly up to Detroit via American Airlines, take his flight lesson, and fly home. This was convenient since all major U.S. airlines used Detroit City Airport for their passenger services. The airline terminal was only yards from our office.

Smitty liked our Vultee so much he decided to buy one of his own and purchased a BT-13 based at Detroit City Airport. He asked me to ferry it to his home airport, Lunken Field, in Cincinnati. Because his airplane had a history of engine problems I decided to wear a parachute—just in case. Since this was a ferry flight I put my chute over my business suit so that I would look respectable coming home. The trip to Cincinnati was uneventful and Smitty met me on my arrival. After a brief discussion about the condition of his airplane he gave me my return ticket. I trudged over to the American Airlines departure gate with my parachute slung across my back and took a comfortable seat. When the boarding call came for American Airlines Douglas DC-4 service to Detroit I walked out to the airliner and up the boarding steps carrying my trusty parachute on my shoulder. It wasn't until I met the intense gaze of the stewardess on entering the cabin that I realized my position. How could I in a few words explain my motives for carrying a parachute on board a luxurious four-engine DC-4? My business suit, white shirt, and maroon tie gave no hint that I was a pilot. A suitable explanation was truly beyond my capability. To her credit, she did not inquire and I discreetly volunteered no information. But I still had to face the stares of seated passengers as I found my way to my assigned seat. No one said anything to me during the entire flight, for which I was grateful. To this day, I still have not been able to think of appropriate words I could have used to explain that situation to that knowledgeable and courteous stewardess.

Earsly kept our office and pilots' lounge comfortable and clean, with appropriate reading material on a coffeetable for our own use, as well as for visiting pilots. One day while at my desk I heard a visitor humming a popular tune and was impressed by the lilt and quality of his voice. I thought both his face and voice were familiar but could not place either one. He had a heavy-set build, gray-flecked hair, and a neatly trimmed beard. After glancing briefly at our magazines he stood up and thanked us with a pleasant smile on leaving. Later, I went to the nearby city gas office on the flight line to pay my daily gas bill and found the gas attendants talking excitedly about the famous personality who had just taken off, piloting his own personal airplane. Being curious, I asked who this famous person was. They looked at me as though I had been living on a deserted island. "Don't you recognize Burl Ives when you see him?" No wonder the voice I had heard was so melodic! Burl Ives was a famous folk singer who appeared regularly on radio shows and in Hollywood movies. Among his many popular recordings was my favorite, "The Blue Tail Fly."

One famous personality I did know fairly well was Jimmie Lunceford, leader of the famous Jimmie Lunceford Jazz Orchestra. Jimmie was a talented musician, a devoted family man, and a competent, multiengine-rated commercial pilot. He owned a war-surplus, twin-engine Cessna UC-78 converted to CAA standards which he routinely used for his own travel. Mechanical problems on one occasion required him to leave his airplane in Chicago, so he came to Detroit by commercial airline. After appearing with his band in Detroit he came out to City Airport for a visit. After the usual "hangar talk," Jimmie asked if I would fly him to Chicago to pick up his airplane. It was clear and cold at Detroit City Airport and Chicago's Midway with both reporting icy runways. But a band of snow showers west of Detroit extended all the way to the South Bend area, reducing both ceiling and visibility. Jimmie, an exceptionally proficient pilot with an instrument rating, assured me the flight would be no problem. Not having Jimmie's experience, I accepted his judgment. We rolled out the Vultee and fueled it in preparation for takeoff. After filing a VFR flight plan and upon receiving tower clearance, I took off with Jimmie smiling confidently in the back seat.

As predicted, the clear skies gave way to clouds and snow showers just west of Jackson, Michigan. To stay in visual contact with the ground as required by my VFR flight plan, I had to descend to 500 feet, an altitude at times below the height of some radio towers that lay in my flight path. The snowfall was heavy as we reached South Bend, Indiana. I was elated to see through the snow showers and get a glimpse of the golden tower of the cathedral at the Notre Dame campus off to my left, which was proof I was on course. As the south shore of Lake Michigan appeared the skies cleared and we landed at Chicago's Midway Airport without difficulty.

Knowing the hazards we had faced on our trip over I had second thoughts about flying through the snow alone to get home. I discussed the possibility of staying in Chicago for the night and leaving when the weather cleared. But Jimmie had more confidence in me than I had in myself. He predicted the snow showers would be blown south of my course by the strong northerly winds and I would have good weather for a safe flight home. With some misgivings, I gassed up the Vultee for the return trip to Detroit. Jimmie thanked me for flying him to Chicago and wished me a safe, pleasant flight home.

My hopes were as high as the bright blue sky that beckoned to me during takeoff. Less than an hour later my optimism was dashed as the cloud ceiling, due to the still-present snow showers, dropped to CAA VFR minimums and I could barely see the Notre Dame cathedral through the driving snow as I passed South Bend. Occasionally I had to drop below 500 feet to keep the ground in sight. On one occasion I was low enough to see the lighted windows and smoke from the chimney of a farmer's house. I imagined the occupants could well be saying, "Only an idiot would fly in this kind of weather." Although it didn't help my ego, I had to admit I had the same thoughts. But I persevered and the sky began to brighten as I approached the city of Jackson from the west.

As the vague outline of downtown Detroit came into view, the turbulence reached extreme levels. I called the Detroit City Airport tower for an airport advisory. They answered, "The visibility is unlimited; however, surface winds are 45 MPH gusting to 75. Braking action due to ice is poor to none. Be advised we will abandon the tower if the winds increase." I had never flown, much less landed, in winds of such force. But my dwindling gas supply dictated I could not delay much longer. If I had to abort the landing at Detroit City Airport it would be necessary to fly west again and land at Willow Run Airport where the winds were much lighter. As I approached familiar runway 33, turbulence bounced me against my safety belt as I tried to maintain an airspeed well above normal to compensate for the gusts. Fortunately, my skills were reinforced by a large measure of luck, sufficient to make a normal, smooth landing. Once I was stopped it was evident I could not turn the Vultee around on the icy runway due to the high winds. Realizing my difficulty, tower personnel called the airport restaurant and asked for volunteers to help push my airplane to the tie-down area. Once that was accomplished, everyone returned to the restaurant where I bought a round of hot coffee for everyone. In retrospect, I was glad the tower had not told me that an AT-6 army advanced trainer had groundlooped out of control several hours before my arrival.

With the arrival of summer weather, Jimmie Lunceford returned the favor. He dropped off his twin-engine Cessna UC-78 at Detroit City Airport and invited me to fly it to Chicago at my convenience. Duncan had just earned his multiengine rating (Earsly and I did not have one) so he had the privilege of being our flight captain.

Earsly and I rotated duties as copilot. Billie Lewis came along as passenger. On our arrival at Chicago's Midway Airport, Earsly and Duncan called their Chicago relatives to tell them we were on our way for an overnight visit. The four of us then walked to 63rd Street to wait for the next streetcar. I had been standing and walking extensively at the airport and with the long walk to the streetcar line my legs were extremely sore. I waited impatiently for the streetcar to come and the opportunity to sit down. When it did arrive there were no seats available so I had to stand in spite of the pain. After I had been on my feet for what seemed forever, a man sitting in front of Duncan left his seat. Like a true gentleman, Duncan generously offered the seat to a young woman standing next to him. When I gave him a pained look he became very apologetic and the next time a seat became vacant he made sure I was able to sit down.

In spite of my discomfort, I was flattered he did not consciously think of me as a handicapped person. Our flight home was uneventful but the blisters on my stumps were a constant reminder that artificial legs were never going to be as comfortable as my own.

Vera Brown wrote a daily column titled "Our Times" for the *Detroit Times*. Her first series of articles was on her experiences learning to fly in the late 1920s at an airport in the Detroit suburbs. She never lost her interest in aviation and often wrote articles about her airport friends. One such article was published during the winter of 1946.

High Heart

City Airport Manager Bud Burnett was pretty well shot up in a Hell-Diver over the Marshalls, leaving him with a bum leg. The other morning his leg was giving him what-for, so Bud dug up his walking stick his B. of C. pals had given him when he was in a south Pacific hospital. Leaning on the cane, Bud showed up at his office, and he stood looking out on the snow covered airport.

There he saw a young fellow painfully slogging his way through drifts and over ice. Bud watched his progress for a little while. Then the manager took his walking stick, stuffed it into the back of his wardrobe. He'll never carry it again. The young man? He lost both legs in a glider accident during the war. He's walking without a cane on two artificial legs and he does a sweet job of flying, fast stuff too. Bud says he has never been so ashamed of himself in his entire life.

The Michigan Department of Aeronautics sponsored a "Dawn Patrol" at a different airport each Sunday morning during the summer flying season where breakfast was available for all visiting pilots. We had never participated in one of these events so Earsly and I scheduled three of our airplanes, Aeronca N1150E, Luscombe N45744, and an addition to our fleet, Aeronca L-3 N47123, to attend the next one. Leonard Wiggins, our CFI at the time and former Tuskegee pilot, was in charge of the flight with five fully rated private pilots occupying the other seats in the three planes.

After the flight courses were carefully plotted and with a promise of good weather from the weather office, our fleet took off in the early morning for the popular Sunday morning Dawn Patrol at Grayling, Michigan. With nothing else to do Earsly and I strolled over to the airport restaurant where we took our time eating a rare full breakfast. This was quite a change from our customary quick snack of coffee and doughnuts. On returning to our office we placed two comfortable seats outside the door but near enough to hear the phone ring and relaxed. As we sat in the morning sun we congratulated ourselves on the joys of earning a living by operating a flight school.

Our peace was interrupted by a collect phone call from the operator at Edwards Corners, Michigan. We were mystified until we heard Leonard Wiggins on the line. He explained that Aeronca N47123 had experienced engine trouble but he had been able to make a safe landing in a swampy clearing in the woods. Wiggins and his student got out of the airplane quickly to warn the other airplanes that the marshy ground was too soft for takeoff or landing. In spite of the vigorous "waveoff" hand signals by Leonard Wiggins, the two remaining airplanes landed, one behind the other, and immediately bogged down in the mud. After an abortive attempt to take off in N47123, Wiggins decided it was time to call the office. Earsly and I took our two cars—needed to carry our six stranded pilots—and drove to Edwards Corners, 120 miles away. Our early morning joy was completely erased by this turn of events. Hours later we met a group of unusually subdued pilots standing in the swamp next to our forlorn but undamaged airplanes. Our return to Detroit marked the end of our only attempt to participate in a Sunday Dawn Patrol.

Several days later we borrowed a low-bed trailer from Lee Rivard and headed north to retrieve our airplanes since we were out of business until they were back at City Airport. Upon arrival at the clearing we started the lengthy process of loading the airplanes nose down, one by one, on the trailer and transporting them to the nearest airport. The roads were very narrow with trees on both sides. Occasionally telephone lines stretched across the road, which meant we had to lift them with makeshift poles to allow adequate clearance for the tail surfaces sticking high in the air. We were successful in getting the Luscombe and Aeronca N1150E to the airport without damage. But with N47123 we were in such a hurry we forgot to lift the first overhanging telephone line; it caught the tail surfaces and twisted them 90 degrees. In spite of this discouraging turn of events we knew at least our other two airplanes would keep us in business.

This good mood lasted until the airport manager stated that he would not allow us to fly our airplanes out until the proper CAA papers were in their proper place in the cockpit in each of them. We had removed these papers from the airplanes to prevent someone from stealing them while the planes were parked in the swamp and in our haste had left them in our office in Detroit. Frustrated, I lost my composure and told the airport manager, "You can keep the damn airplanes until hell freezes over!" Realizing my frustration he quickly relented and gave permission for my pilots to fly them to Detroit. This put us partially back in business but we still had the arduous task of dismantling N47123 and trailering it home.

Several days later we came back and dismantled the damaged airplane for return to City Airport. The twisted fuselage was eventually repaired and N47123 was airborne again, earning its keep. Although Edwards Corners, Michigan, is too small to be on the Michigan state map, it still looms large in my memory.

My first jet ride, like my first solo, was an exciting and unforgettable experience. Lieutenant Colonel Samuel ("Sammy") Massenberg was a former B-29 pilot who started his aviation career by attending one of my model airplane classes. Several years later he enrolled as a flight student at Wayne School of Aeronautics. Sammy had told Lt. Charles Phelps, a classmate during his U.S. Air Force (USAF) flight training, that he could pay off a personal debt by giving me a ride in a jet trainer. Lieutenant Phelps was a F-86 fighter pilot as well as an instructor pilot (IP) in the USAF's Lockheed T-33, a two-place jet trainer. He stopped by my office after arriving at Selfridge Field on a routine cross-country flight in a T-33. This young, professional-appearing black military pilot introduced himself and invited me to take a ride. Before he could change his mind I accepted and drove him back to Selfridge Field.

During the drive he expressed confidence in my flying skills, especially in a ex-military BT-13, to the extent that he offered to let me fly from the front cockpit, in direct violation of Air Force regulations. Only currently qualified USAF pilots were allowed to fly the T-33 from the front seat.

After suiting up in the pilots' ready room I walked to the T-33 for a preflight inspection. Approaching the sleek jet trainer, shining in the summer sun, I couldn't believe that I was actually going to pilot a high-speed, jet-powered military aircraft. Lieutenant Phelps showed me all the important technical features and then assisted me into the front seat. A sergeant standing by with the starting cart saluted me (at the moment I was pretending to be an Air Force officer) and went through the starting procedure. After Lieutenant Phelps familiarized me with the preflight cockpit procedures we started to taxi out for takeoff. I was surprised it took almost 60 percent power (over half throttle) just to get the airplane moving. Once on the runway I opened the throttle and after the slow initial acceleration typical of jets the T-33 gained speed rapidly and we were soon airborne, climbing like the proverbial "bat out of hell."

Lieutenant Phelps instructed me to level off below the solid gray overcast at 10,000 feet. But by the time I was in level flight I had punched through the clouds into clear blue sky above. Skimming just a few feet above the clouds at over 500 MPH was an exhilarating experience. The smoothness of the jet engine was unbelievable! With scarcely concealed joy I thrilled to the smooth, quick response of this high-performance jet. I had waited since 1927 to fly an Air Force fighter and, at the moment, was ecstatic. During our 1-hour and 45-minute flight we performed almost all the maneuvers within the T-33 performance envelope. After experiencing many high g-loads and head-wrenching rolls, my stomach began to rebel and for the first time in my long flying career I was anxious to terminate a flight. Once we landed my stomach returned to normal in time to conceal my problem from Lieutenant Phelps. I could not think of adequate words of thanks as we walked back to the pilots' ready room. There he made the following entry in my logbook: "T-33 #-9640, 1.5 hours. First jet orientation flight of all visual contact maneuvers: traffic patterns, landings, chandelles, lazy 8's, etc. Touch and goes, acrobatic maneuvers."

Leaving my IP at the officers quarters I drove home with my head still in the clouds. Without a doubt I had won championship bragging rights at Detroit City Airport after my never-to-be-forgotten (and clearly illegal) flight in a Lockheed T-33 advanced training jet.

CHAPTER NINE

BUILDING THE "LOVE"

By early 1947, Wayne School of Aeronautics was operating smoothly and all of the early growing pains were cured. With this new peace of mind and economic security, my thoughts focused once again on designing an airplane. The inspiration I was looking for came when pictures of several new midget racers appeared in the current aviation magazines.

Specifications for this new category of racer were established by the Professional Racing Pilots Association (PRPA) and the National Aeronautics Association (NAA). One of the objectives of this new class of racer was to make it affordable to average-income raceplane builders and pilots who could not obtain corporate sponsorship. The requirements reflected this philosophy by limiting the engine displacement to CAA-licensed 190-cubic-inch (85-HP) engines with no expensive modifications allowed. Also, relatively simple fixed landing gear and fixed pitch propeller were required. Strict standards for safety were established for aircraft structure, visibility, minimum wing area, and aircraft weight, making this class of racer comparatively safe and inexpensive.

Rigorous ground inspections and flight tests were required before approval for competition by the CAA/PRPA. The midget racers that evolved were, in effect, high-performance sportplanes. Although usually built primarily as racers, these little planes had good aerobatic and cross-country performance with speeds from 170 to over 200 MPH even though they were powered with only a standard 85-HP Continental four-cylinder engine. Races were sponsored by Goodyear Tire Company and Continental Motors Corporation. With this midget-class racer as inspiration, I started to design my newest airplane, the WR-1, better known in later years as "Loving's Love."

Remembering the negative comments I received when I bought the BT-13, I decided to keep this project a secret as long as possible. The ridicule and discouragement I expected from my peers was sufficient reason for my decision. Having no experience in designing a powered airplane and selecting a high-performance raceplane as my first project would surely cause my critics to question my sanity even more than before. Further, my plans to test-fly and race my own airplane would make them think I had suicidal tendencies. I told Earsly of my new project, of course, and she gave her support although I am sure she had mixed emotions when she thought of my glider accident. The danger was undeniable.

I set up my drafting board at home and since we closed our school every day at sunset, I had the benefit of going home early in the fall and winter months. After many hours of brainstorming and sketching, my thoughts crystallized into a basic design. The requirement for a fixed landing gear led to the unique feature of WR-1, an inverted gull wing mounted low on the fuselage. In this design the wing, instead of being straight from tip to tip, was shaped like a W when viewed from the front, with the landing gear attached to the lower points of the W. This design feature eliminated the drag of an external landing gear strut. In order to further reduce drag I made the frontal area as small as possible. To accomplish this I placed a large sheet of brown paper on the wall behind me and, sitting on the floor, traced my body outline in pencil. By form-fitting a curve to fit this outline, the front view of the fuselage was established. I am sure it decreased the drag as planned but it also restricted body movements so much that the cockpit was extremely uncomfortable if I sat in it for more than a few minutes.

With the basic design established it was now necessary to explore the unknowns of such elements as engine cooling requirements, power-on and power-off stability and control, stress analysis, and weight and balance, each requiring studies and tradeoff studies well beyond my training at Cass Tech. I bought college-level books on airplane design and stress analysis and corresponding mathematics texts to help in my design work. It was very discouraging at times, but as the racer grew on paper so did my enthusiasm. In the fall of 1947, the design of WR-1 was finalized and I submitted information and drawings to the PRPA for approval. Their letter in reply dated January 29, 1948, had these encouraging words, "The general design appears to be entirely sound and is approved subject to the final flight demonstrations."

Now began the tedious and difficult task of making up forty-two working drawings before starting construction. Initially, I had high hopes of starting the building phase in early 1948, and having the racer finished and ready to enter the Cleveland Air Races during Labor Day weekend. My plans changed when we had an unexpected surge of student enrollment in the spring of 1948, leaving little time to devote to my racing project. Reluctantly I covered up my drawing board and waited until the fall season to resume work. After a very successful 1948 summer season at Wayne School of Aeronautics I renewed my efforts to build and complete my midget racer in time for the 1949 Cleveland Races.

As with my gliders, I decided to construct my racer entirely of wood, principally aircraft-quality spruce. I found the price of aircraft-quality spruce in aircraft supply catalogs to be prohibitively expensive. I discussed my problem with Red Rapp, who was one of the few people other than Earsly who were aware of the WR-1. Red knew just about everyone in Mt. Clemens, including the owners of Hubarth and Schott, the largest lumber company in the area. In addition to the usual lumber company services, they specialized in making high-quality spruce ladders for fire departments all over the United States. After talking with lumber company personnel Red decided they had the quality of spruce and wood-milling skills to meet my specific needs.

With that good news, I drew up a long and exacting list of spruce strips, which called for hundreds of lineal feet in a variety of sizes ranging from $\frac{1}{4}$-inch-square strips for wing rib capstrips to 1-inch-square pieces for fuselage longerons. I wondered what kind of reception

Red would get when he presented this bill of materials that required aircraft-quality millwork for small wood sizes. We were certain they had never received such a request before. I was happily surprised when Red called and said Mr. Schott (supposedly retired) would personally take care of my order. The next step was to find a place to build my airplane and still retain the desired secrecy.

Earsly and I discussed my options and decided to use our former CAP meeting room, originally a library, in the basement of the Brewster Housing Project near downtown Detroit. Our CAP activities had essentially ceased with the end of the war. The lumber company delivered the spruce to my construction shop just a few days after Christmas of 1948. Mr. Hodo, chief of maintenance for the Brewster Project, looked at the odd-sized pieces of wood stacked near the wall and was mystified. Knowing what his reaction would be, I hesitated to tell him I was building an airplane. But not being adept at lying I told him the truth. He was too polite to say what he really thought, but his skepticism was painfully apparent. As I looked at that strange pile of wood and tried to visualize it becoming an airplane I began to develop my own skepticism. Nevertheless, I celebrated New Year's Day 1949 by starting construction of the WR-1.

When I conceived the idea of the inverted gull-wing design I wondered why other designers had not taken advantage of this obvious opportunity to reduce landing gear drag. Once faced with the realities of constructing this highly complex design I learned why. It took one entire month of intensive effort every night, six nights a week, just to build the main, W-shaped spar. My shopwork usually started after a late dinner at the airport restaurant. I usually worked until about 3 or 4 A.M., allowing me maybe four hours of sleep before returning to work. This was necessary to meet my goal of being ready for the 1949 races in Cleveland. One day in May, Mr. Hodo came and asked me to give a talk on my airplane building project to the National Technical Association (NTA), a professional organization of black engineers. Pressed for time, I was reluctant to miss even one evening of work, but given his friendly cooperation I felt obliged to accept his invitation.

Attending this meeting on the designated Saturday evening, like several other events in my life, was to significantly and permanently alter the course of my life. My talk on "The Design and Construction of a Midget Racer" was apparently well received by this technically oriented audience, which in itself was a source of encouragement. But, of course, they were unaware of the risks involved with racing aircraft. At the conclusion of the meeting a young man came up to me and introduced himself as Carl Barnett from Kingston, Jamaica. His West Indian accent clearly indicated he was not a black American. During our short conversation I learned Carl was in his senior year in the civil engineering department at the University of Detroit. His tall, slim but muscular figure was ideal for a member of the college track team. He spoke of his boyhood interest in model airplanes and aviation and said he came to the university to study aeronautical engineering. But when his advisor discovered Carl intended to return to Jamaica after graduation, he suggested switching to civil engineering. The merit of the advice was obvious: Jamaica had no aeronautical industry. He made the change.

Carl's interest in aviation had not diminished, however, and he applied for membership in the University of Detroit Flying Club. But just as in the secular world, racism was present at this Catholic university. Although Carl was a devout Catholic, his application was refused. During our short meeting I was so impressed by Carl's aviation background and enthusiasm that I asked him to come to my shop and see the midget racer under construction. He agreed, despite the lateness of the hour. His enthusiasm was evident as I showed him the wing, fuselage, and tail surfaces, which were complete but not covered. Carl quickly volunteered his assistance whenever his studies would permit.

Carl impressed me so much during our meeting that I invited him to learn to fly at Wayne School of Aeronautics regardless of his ability to pay. He had some money in the bank but admitted it was not sufficient to cover the cost of attaining a private pilot's license. He insisted, however, on applying all of his savings to his flight training. With the matter settled I drove him back to his dormitory, arriving long after the midnight curfew had passed. In view of the events that followed, it must have been fate that intervened to bring us together. As it turned out, neither of us wanted to attend the NTA meeting. Carl wanted to stay in his dormitory and study and I wanted to work on my racer, but forces beyond our control prevailed. Neither of us ever attended another NTA meeting.

Just a few hours later I met Earsly at the airport restaurant for Sunday morning breakfast and told her of my meeting with Carl and the offer I had made. Realizing I had made this offer without her knowledge and consent, I consoled her with the assurance that she would like him. This turned out to be quite an understatement.

Out of consideration for our usual busy weekend schedule at the school, I asked Carl to come out for his lessons on weekdays only. On the Monday morning following our initial meeting, Carl came out to the airport smiling with anticipation at his first meeting with Earsly Taylor. Walking out to the flight line, I put him in the pilot's seat of Luscombe N45436 for an introductory flight. It was a quiet, gray day with very little traffic to delay our takeoff. After reaching an altitude of 2,000 feet, I leveled off and demonstrated basic maneuvers and gentle turns before turning the controls over to Carl. Within a few minutes it was evident Carl had the natural skills and coordination of a born pilot. I directed him toward the college campus and he flew with such precision I found it difficult to believe this was his first experience at flying an airplane. After getting a bird's-eye view of the engineering building and his dormitory we headed back to Detroit City Airport. As we approached the airport he expressed the same concerns I remembered having on my first flight. The airport looked so small from the air. It seemed impossible a full-size airplane could land on such a postage stamp–sized space.

But the illusion disappeared as the airplane lined up for final approach and the runway appeared to rush up and touch the wheels. As Carl got out of the Luscombe his enthusiasm was the mirror of mine after my first lesson with Capt. Paul Hinds. We were truly brothers in our shared love of aviation. After Carl met with Earsly to arrange his next lesson, I drove him back to the campus.

The level of activity at Wayne School of Aeronautics increased with the onset of summer. I had to abandon my plans to race in 1949 and put off my work on the racer until later in the fall. Meanwhile, I ordered a fuel-injected C-85 Continental engine specially built (fully approved by the CAA) for midget racers directly from Continental

Motors. I felt like a kid at Christmastime when the engine arrived, gleaming like a jewel when I opened the packing crate. This was my first brand-new engine! The price was $625.

Other components I purchased included a McCauley Met-L-Prop and a new set of wheels, tires, brakes, and master cylinders from the Goodyear Company in Akron, Ohio. Although I enjoyed the summer flying season as always, I couldn't wait to resume work on my midget racer. During this period of waiting Earsly bought a stall-warning device for the racer to prevent a recurrence of my glider stall/spin accident. I appreciated her concerns.

Meanwhile, Jim Fitzhenry, our newest CFI, had been reading about midget racers in various magazines and was anxious to become a participant. Unaware of my racing project, but knowing my background in airplane construction, he asked me to do the design work for his own midget racer. Jim had already asked George Sentas to do the construction work. Only the problem of financing needed to be resolved. But he assured me he could raise the capital if I would agree to be the designer. I had guilt feelings when I told him I was too busy to get involved (this was true) in his racing project.

Carl came to the airport at every opportunity and was ready for solo well before logging the CAA-required eight hours of dual instruction. Jim Fitzhenry was able to solo Carl with minimum flight time. We knew he was very gifted as a pilot and we were not surprised that he flew like a veteran pilot with minimum required hours. Carl continued to demonstrate his natural flying skills in the advanced maneuvers required for a private pilot rating. Once again Jim was able to recommend him for his CAA flight test with the CAA minimum of 35 hours of total time. Carl passed the test with flying colors and became the newest pilot to earn his wings at our school. With the ink hardly dry on his certificate he asked if he could fly the Luscombe to Lansing, Michigan, on a solo cross-country flight to visit friends. I told him to check the weather the next morning and if it was suitable he had permission to fly.

The weather was terrible that morning with high winds, low clouds, and limited visibilities. Going into the airport restaurant I decided to take ample time and eat a full breakfast before going to my office. I was sure Carl had canceled his planned flight and was relaxing in his dormitory. While I was reading the newspaper over a hot cup of coffee, one of the tower controllers came in and asked why I had given permission for Carl to take off in such lousy weather. I was both shocked and scared and, leaving my breakfast unfinished, hurried to my office to wait for the dreaded phone call.

After several hours of agonized waiting, I decided to call the control tower in Lansing and check on his arrival. They told me Carl indeed arrived safely but had decided to remain overnight and return in the morning. I was immensely relieved but I was still surprised and angry that he would use such poor judgment.

Late the next morning Carl landed the Luscombe with his usual precision and taxied up to our office. Looking rather sheepish, he began his story before a tribunal consisting of Earsly and me. According to Carl, the weather didn't seem that bad, in spite of the tower operator's attempts to dissuade him from taking off. Due to poor visibility he relied on easily recognized landmarks, such as highways and railroad tracks, to stay on course. When Carl came to a fork in the double railroad track he had been following, he unfortunately took the wrong turn. He soon realized his mistake but, instead of panicking, tuned the airplane radio receiver to the Lansing low-frequency directional beam and followed it to a safe landing. The weather was below CAA minimums for visual flight when he arrived. The tower personnel reported his violation to the CAA office at Wayne Major Airport. He was ordered to stop by their office before returning to Detroit. The CAA punishment was a verbal chastisement and a warning not to repeat the offense. Earsly and I reviewed the series of events and gave Carl credit for exceptional use of his skills in making a safe landing at Lansing Airport. Then we berated him for taking off from Detroit City Airport in marginal weather. Earsly and I were so glad to see Carl alive and uninjured we forgave him but not before exacting a promise he would never be so foolish again.

When business at our school decreased in the fall season due to fewer daylight hours, I resumed my late evening/early morning, six-day work schedule at the shop. With the veil of secrecy still in place, only a few people were available for assistance. I relied heavily on Carl and Earsly for support. However, because of their other commitments I spent many lonely hours at the shop with only radio music for company. It was depressing at times but as WR-1 began to take shape during final assembly, my enthusiasm surged upward again.

Sometimes while sitting in the cockpit installing instruments, I visualized myself speeding around the racing pylons toward the finish line, leading the pack. Such flights of fancy did not last long for there was much work to be done if the WR-1 was to be ready for the National Air Races scheduled for Detroit, instead of Cleveland, over Labor Day weekend, 1950.

As the midget neared completion I went out to the CAA office at Wayne County Airport and applied for a registration number. On completing the application form, the CAA inspector presented me with a list of available numbers for my selection. Considering WR-1's tiny size, my prime objective was to pick out the smallest number, which turned out to be N351C. Satisfied, I went back to work with renewed energy. The next morning, while having breakfast with Ardine, I mentioned obtaining the registration number for my airplane. She was an ardent "numbers" enthusiast, always looking for "hot" new numbers to play. On hearing it was 351, she consulted the "dream book" she used to determine what number to play after a particular dream.

The answer visibly upset her, and she almost demanded that I change the number. The dream book said that if she dreamed blood, the number she was to play was 351! The obvious connotation was that my test flight in N351C would result in a bloody crash, a situation we both were familiar with. Fortunately, I did not believe in dream books and besides, I told her, "I would feel mighty foolish going back to the CAA and asking for a change of number because the dream book says it plays for blood." She was still very unhappy and made me promise I would not tell her the date of my first test flight. She didn't want to worry about it.

The next step was to write to the NAA in Washington, D.C., to obtain a racing number for N351C. The NAA was chartered by the Fédération Aéronautique Internationale (FAI), in Paris, to regulate all sanctioned races and supervise all attempts at setting official world records. I was happy to receive an NAA identification card assigning race number 64 to my racer. It was now necessary to obtain my FAI pilots' certificate required for competitive flying. This would have to wait until my flight test program was completed and I had flown around the racing pylons to the satisfaction of witnessing NAA and PRPA judges.

One late Saturday night in May 1950, I was in the basement shop alone working on the midget; my clothes were covered in accumulated dirt, paint, varnish, and dope. Not expecting visitors I was surprised to hear a loud knock on the hall door leading to the basement. Without changing clothes, I walked up the dark steps and opened the door. There stood Carl, dressed in a conservative blue serge suit, white shirt, and maroon tie, his Aunt Beryl and Aunt May from New York, and his younger brother Felix and sister Clare from Kingston, all immaculately dressed. They had come to Detroit to attend his June graduation from the University of Detroit.

If looks could kill, Carl would have been an instant corpse. Leading them downstairs in my dirty clothes, I was so embarrassed I wished I could climb into a hole and pull the dirt over me. But Carl was obviously proud as he introduced me to his family and showed them the nearly finished midget racer. It was soon evident they were more interested in the airplane than in my clothes but I remained uncomfortable until they left.

Going back to work I began to feel the positive effects of their visit. The Barnett family impressed me as a loving family with a distinctive West Indian background. I looked forward to meeting them again.

Carl brought his family out to the airport later in the week and showed them our flight school and the airplanes he had flown. He then asked me to take them for a ride in our four-place Stinson N8607K, which he had not yet been checked out to fly. It was almost dark when we took off, the horizon getting brighter as we gained altitude. The stars became increasingly visible in the darkening sky as we flew over downtown Detroit. The Barnetts were impressed at the thousands of surface lights twinkling in the dark. This was the first flight for all of them in a small airplane and their joy was evident in their smiles. Days later, Carl brought them out to the airport again for a final visit during which Clare, in a casual conversation, invited me to visit her family

home in Kingston. As exciting and pleasurable as it sounded, the
actuality of such a visit seemed as remote as flying to the moon! When
I tried to explain the improbability of my making such a visit she made
the mistake of thinking I wasn't interested. Knowing I was born and
raised in the big city of Detroit she assumed I wouldn't be interested
in coming to a small island like Jamaica. We parted on this note of
misunderstanding, but I made amends two years later when I visited
the Barnetts in Kingston.

Carl was a skilled painter, among his many talents, and volunteered
to spray sufficient coats of metallic maroon and cream lacquer on
N351C until it was as shiny as the proverbial new penny. When it was
finished, we stood back and admired the sleek appearance of the
WR-1, which had been, only 18 months before, a pile of spruce strips
on the basement floor. Our daydreaming over, we very carefully disassembled it in preparation for the trip to Detroit City Airport. During
this activity, Mr. Hodo came in with bad news. He had taken time to
measure the racer and check the interior dimensions of the hallway
that we had to pass through to get outside. After double-checking his
figures he came to the conclusion that the racer's 20-foot, one-piece
wing was too large to get through the hallway. The thought of cutting
my beautiful wing was too awful to contemplate. I said my prayers
hoping Mr. Hodo was wrong.

Several days later I assembled my crew for the long-awaited task
of taking the disassembled racer out of the basement and loading it
onto Lee Rivard's low-bed trailer. Carl and Lee were there, along with
student pilots Chuck Jenkins and Pancho Mobley. I held my breath as
we approached the hallway with the wing and was happily relieved it
went through with just enough clearance to keep the wing tips from
being scraped. It was a much closer fit than my own calculations had
predicted. The rest of the loading operation went quickly and we were
soon on our way, joining the light early morning traffic. The trip to
Detroit City Airport was uneventful.

Our arrival, however, was anything but uneventful. As we unloaded
the racer at Sentas Skyways in Bay 12, the crowd of onlookers was
so large we had trouble clearing the necessary hangar area. By the end
of the day, midget N351C was reassembled, looking even prettier than

I had dared imagine. However, the experts and critics soon gathered around offering unsolicited advice leading to one conclusion: I should not fly the airplane.

One engine expert, whose opinions I respected, said the unorthodox single intake for engine cooling and carburetor air located below the spinner was too small and he predicted the engine would overheat and fail soon after takeoff. The airport manager, a former Marine pilot, said he had read Japanese technical reports on a gull-wing fighter (a configuration similar to my racer) they had tried to develop during World War II, which had developed severe control and stability problems. He believed the WR-1 would have similar problems. My good friend Telford Duncan came by to tell me he had witnessed the near-disastrous first flight of a midget racer in Compton, California, in which the pilot was severely injured. He also pointed out I had no previous flight experience with racing airplanes and my pilot logbook showed only 800 hours of flying time. This, coupled with my artificial legs, led him and the other critics to the inescapable conclusion that I would crash on the first flight. Jim Fitzhenry generously offered to test-fly it for me but I quietly, but firmly, turned him down.

It took several days to hook up the flight and engine controls and to have all the bolts and nuts used in the assembly properly checked and safetied. These assembly procedures were completed on the evening of July 23 and we rolled N351C out into the fading sunlight for engine check and initial start and runup. Its distinctive inverted gull wing and shiny maroon and cream finish gave it the racy, streamlined look of a high-performance airplane. I took a moment to admire my creation before climbing into the tight-fitting cockpit, a procedure rehearsed many times before in the basement shop. A small army of observers were on hand for this momentous event. I tried to remain calm while completing my cockpit check as George Sentas pulled the propeller through to clear the cylinders. After actuating the engine primer and turning the ignition switch on, I called the customary "Contact!" George vigorously snapped the propeller around and without hesitation the Continental came to life with a staccato-like bark through the short, individual exhaust stacks. This was a sound not unlike the powerful Curtiss P-40 Hawk my fighter pilot friends from Tuskegee had told me about. Short plumes of orange and blue flames were visible in the semi-darkness. Glancing carefully at all the engine instruments, I was pleased that in spite of the gloomy predictions of the engine expert all were reading normal. During the engine warmup I took the opportunity to absorb the engine smells and vibrations that seemed to make my racer come alive for the first time. It was, I imagined, something like being present during the first breath of a newborn baby.

In spite of the doubts, my own and those of my friends, I was more determined than ever to be the first pilot to take N351C into the skies. The thoughts of possible disaster were ever present, but taking risks had always been a part of my life. As I sat there in the twilight, watching the bright orange and blue flames streaming from the four exhaust stacks, feelings of doubt and fear were overcome by the anticipated joy and excitement of my first flight in a high-performance racing airplane of my own design.

CHAPTER TEN

FLYING THE "LOVE"

With renewed enthusiasm resulting from the success of the first engine runup, my friends and I worked harder than ever to complete the remaining small jobs necessary to ensure that the midget was ready for flight. The first phase of the flight test program could not begin until every item on the checklist was completed. The brake cylinders needed to be filled with fluid and the braking action tested. The engine had to be checked for leaks, and the wheel alignment checked as well. Of particular importance, however, was determining the aircraft's actual empty center of gravity (c.g.), which can only be calculated when the airplane is fully assembled and weighed. George Sentas performed this important task and I was pleasantly surprised when he informed me that the actual empty c.g. was less than one-quarter of an inch from where I estimated it would be. A critical milestone had been passed, for an out-of-limits c.g. would most certainly cause severe control and stability problems during first flight.

One of our flight students, Glenn Forbes, a white, middle-aged professional sign painter, generously contributed his artistic skills to the midget racer project. His first effort was a large cardboard poster on which he lettered all of the pertinent technical information on the midget. Placing this sign in front of the airplane saved me a large amount of time for it answered most of the typical questions I had to respond to. His next task was to paint the racing number 64 on both sides of the fuselage, aft of the cockpit. Glenn painted the numbers with shiny black paint outlined by a silver-colored pinstripe border. Now the moment had arrived when a suitable name for N351C had to be selected and painted on both sides of the fuselage ahead of the cockpit. After much discussion among Earsly, Carl, and me, plus input from interested bystanders, it was named "Loving's Love," which it was. The gold leaf Glenn used to spell out the name in script lettering stood out beautifully against the metallic maroon and cream fuselage.

One other unfinished item was the interior. Jean Tygard, wife of fellow flight school operator Lank Tygard, had her own business specializing in aircraft interiors and was, fortunately for me, a good friend. Having heard about the racer, Jean came over to Bay 12 to see the newly christened Loving's Love. Looking into the bare cockpit she immediately offered to do the upholstering without cost. Within a few days she installed custom-made ivory-colored leatherette side panels with map pockets on each side plus matching seat cushions.

The flight testing program was now ready to begin. With the aid of eager volunteers I pushed Loving's Love out of Bay 12 and performed a thorough preflight check. With the racing number and name gracing both sides of her maroon and cream fuselage, the little gull-winged racer seemed eager to fly. I called the tower for taxi instructions and permission to use the active runway for high-speed taxi tests. With permission granted, I climbed into the cockpit and went through the now-familiar engine start procedures. The Continental started immediately and after a brief warmup a mechanic removed the wheel chocks. When I released the brakes, the midget moved past the many onlookers and parked airplanes on the way to the runway. I was immediately impressed by the sure response of my Love to every command. After clearance from the tower I turned onto runway 25 and began my first taxi run. The acceleration and control responses were beyond my fondest hopes. After several such runs at increasing speeds, incoming aircraft traffic made it necessary to clear the runway. As I taxied back and parked in front of our office on the flight line, my hopes and expectations reached a new high. All aspects of the preliminary tests were successful and I thought, "This dream of mine just might become a reality."

Earsly, Duncan, and a large portion of the airport population greeted me with smiles and congratulations as I climbed out of the cockpit. Questions flew fast and furious about midget 64's handling characteristics, engine cooling, control response, and braking action. It was as difficult for me as it was for them to believe how flawlessly the midget had performed. Maybe this was a sign of good things to come. Other than the rudder cables rubbing against the brake master cylinders (easily repaired), all subsequent tests were finished without a hitch.

On some tests, speeds of nearly 70 MPH were reached, which severely tempted me to become airborne. But Detroit City Airport was totally unsuitable for flight testing due to the short runways and congested housing developments completely surrounding the airport.

I decided to move N351C to Wayne Major Airport (now Detroit Metropolitan Airport) for initial flight testing. Ground tests were going so well that I let Carl climb into the midget and do enough taxi testing so I could get a second opinion. Later on, his big disappointment was that I would not let him fly it.

On Saturday evening, August 5, 1950, we loaded the fully assembled midget onto Lee Rivard's low-bed trailer for the 22-mile trip to Wayne County Airport. When loaded on the trailer, the midget constituted an extra-wide load requiring a continuous police escort. We called the county sheriff and state police, who had jurisdiction over the roads on our route, to get special permission for our wide load and the required escort service; both were cheerfully provided. We started our journey about 11 P.M., when highway traffic was at a minimum, as the patrol officers requested. In addition to the police escort we had several private vehicles driven by my friends in front and behind the trailer to keep overzealous motorists from trying to pass. One eager driver from Pennsylvania decided to try to pass and the police quickly put him behind our convoy and told him to stay there. About halfway on our journey we stopped at a coffeeshop for a break and to allow the traffic backed up behind us to move ahead.

Sitting next to a state trooper drinking coffee I sympathized with him for all the extra work my racer was creating for him. He just smiled and said how nice it was to work with law-abiding citizens instead of the criminal element he usually had to deal with. During this stop I discovered Glenn Forbes and his wife (she was with us) were celebrating their twenty-fifth wedding anniversary that day. I apologized for ruining what should have been a festive occasion. They both agreed this was the most exciting anniversary ever and certainly had no regrets. My gift to them was an anniversary wedding breakfast after our arrival at Wayne County Airport at about 5 A.M. It was the least I could do.

Since I was up all night, Earsly insisted I stay in bed this Sunday morning and get adequate rest. We agreed that extreme fatigue had been a prime factor in my accident. It was late afternoon when I came to the office and drew up a detailed flight test plan for the racer's first flight early the next morning, August 7, 1950.

Almost everyone at the airport wanted to know when I planned to test-fly the midget so they could witness the event. But as I had done during the construction of the racer, I kept my plans a secret to everyone but closest friends.

After a quick dinner at the airport restaurant I went home to get a full night's sleep before getting up at 5 A.M. and returning to the airport. Ardine had already asked me not to let her know when I planned my test flight so I went to bed without telling her of my plans for the morning. Unable to sleep, I rehearsed my flight test plan in my mind over and over again and tried to plan my reactions to possible emergencies. Worries crowded my mind as I remembered all of the dire warnings from my many friendly experts. They were almost unanimous in their opinion that my life span would be measured in mere seconds after takeoff. The question that came frequently to mind was "Where will I be tomorrow night, at home, in the hospital or morgue?" The answer was not far away.

When I arrived at our school office about 5:30 A.M., I found Carl there and asked him to help roll Stinson N8607K out of the hangar in preparation for the 20-minute flight to Wayne Major Airport. Flying with me, along with Carl, were Jim Fitzhenry and student pilot Jim

Frey. On taxiing up to the flight line at Wayne Major Airport, we were met by George Sentas who had already rolled the Love out of the hangar and performed his preflight inspection.

George was concerned about the gas tank cap; he didn't think it was vented, in which case a vacuum would form in the tank as fuel was consumed, shutting off the supply of gasoline to the engine and causing instant engine failure. George Barr, the Piper dealer at City Airport where I purchased the gas cap, had assured me it was vented. But George Sentas insisted on drilling two holes in the cap just to make sure. That one act probably saved my life. We learned later the cap was not vented.

After fueling up the racer I called the tower for taxi and takeoff instructions. Both a radio transmitter and receiver were installed in the plane but only the latter was working. The tower response was, "The wind is calm and there is no reported traffic. You are cleared for takeoff from the runway of your choice when ready."

It was about 6:30 A.M. when I climbed into the cockpit; I was wearing a parachute and, for the first time, a crash helmet. Glenn and Duncan, who had arrived with Sentas, stood by, quietly observing every detail, ready to alert me to potential problems. After fastening the canopy over my head I reviewed my test plan one final time. When the cockpit check was complete, I primed the engine and called "Contact." All engine readings were in the normal or "green" range after the Continental started so I called for the chocks to be removed and I was on my way.

The morning sun warmed the cockpit, adding to my enjoyment of this cool, sunny morning. But in the back of my mind unbidden fears came as I tried hard to remain calm. The voice of the tower came over my receiver, "Midget 64 do you read, over?" When I moved my ailerons in acknowledgment, he replied, "Roger, Midget 64 for your information, due to the nature of this flight, we have alerted the crash crew and fire truck just in case of an emergency." This, I am sure, was supposed to increase my confidence, but it only alerted me to the danger I was facing. When I finally reached runway 24, I performed a last-minute runup of the engine and magneto check. Sitting there, I wondered if I was about to commit suicide as my aviation friends had prophesied.

Taking a deep breath I slowly, but steadily, advanced the throttle until the Continental was developing full power at an RPM well above the customary red line. The Love leaped forward with a rate of acceleration never experienced before. Approaching takeoff speed I saw large red stains of aircraft gasoline flowing around my windshield, partially blocking my forward view. In a state of controlled panic, I immediately throttled the engine back to idle and after slowing down to taxi speed turned back to the hangar where Sentas and company were ready to offer advice and assistance. Meanwhile the tower, not knowing my intentions, called and cleared me for takeoff again. For a few moments I was in a dilemma. This new development added another potential element of risk to those I was already worrying about. Common sense dictated I should return to the hangar and have Sentas resolve the problem before another attempt at flight. But during the few seconds devoted to making a decision it became absolutely clear to me that if I went back to the hangar and climbed out of the cockpit, I would not have the courage to try again. It was obvious I did not fit the image of the typical fearless test pilot.

Still moving slowly along the taxiway I noticed the windshield was clean again with no additional fuel leakage. Remembering I had a full tank of 15 gallons of gasoline on board, I decided that even if the leak continued, this was enough fuel to keep me in the air long enough to complete an initial evaluation of the racer's flight characteristics. Satisfied with this rationale, I taxied back to runway 24 for my second attempt to test-fly my midget racer.

"Midget 64 you are cleared for takeoff." With renewed effort to control my fears I applied full power. Again, during the initial acceleration red gasoline stains appeared on the windshield. This time I deliberately ignored the situation, concentrating my attention on keeping the midget tracking straight down the runway. A slight touch on the stick and I was instantly airborne, climbing skyward at a spectacular rate as high as my heartbeat. As soon as my climb speed stabilized at 90 MPH the red stains disappeared, allowing me to breathe again.

A quick glance at the instrument panel indicated all the readings were normal but the noise level was incredibly high. Now that I was breathing again, I was able to calm down enough to look outside the cockpit to see what a beautiful morning this was for my first flight in the racer.

It was a special joy leap-frogging over the small puffs of early morning clouds forming under a clear blue sky. Leveling off in perfectly smooth air at 4,000 feet I throttled back to low cruise power and the airspeed settled on about 145 MPH indicated airspeed (IAS), or almost 160 MPH true airspeed (TAS). Then it was time to start my test plan: shallow turns, climbs, and glides. An especially important test was a series of stalls and slow flight to determine appropriate speeds for glide and landing. This series was followed by checks for longitudinal stability. I was pleasantly surprised that the Love was in almost perfect balance. The controls were quick and responsive in all axes, making it a delight to fly. Only a slight noseheaviness was detected, which was cured after postflight analysis. All of the engine temperatures were normal or even slightly below normal in spite of my engine expert's gloomy predictions.

After 30 minutes of flight testing I felt confident enough to return to the airport for my first landing. When I entered the traffic pattern the tower operator cleared me to land on runway 24. Starting my descent at a predetermined glide speed of 90 MPH, I lined up with the runway with a feeling of assurance I had not dreamed possible. Like the thoroughbred she was, Loving's Love smoothly approached the runway and touched down for a perfect landing. Checking my watch, I noted that I had been airborne for 35 minutes. Taxiing back to the hangar, I literally shouted for joy over the noisy Continental engine.

Duncan was the first to reach me. He had obtained permission from the tower to walk out near the runway to watch my landing. After I rolled to a stop he helped me remove the canopy and greeted me with words I shall never forget. With a smile as wide as his face he said, "Neal, it took off like an airplane, flew like an airplane, and by God, it landed like an airplane!" Smiling in agreement, I taxied to the hangar where Sentas and other onlookers were waiting to congratulate me. I shut the engine off and after wiping the perspiration off my face climbed out of the tight-fitting cockpit. Enjoying this moment to the fullest, I shook hands and hugged everybody in sight as part of my celebration of the unbelievably successful first flight of my newly fledged racer. As the excitement began to die down, I went over to my Love and patted her sleek fuselage in thanks for allowing me to safely complete the most dangerous and exciting flight of my career. Sentas came over to tell me he had given it a thorough postflight inspection and pronounced it ready to fly again. Putting the midget safely back in the hangar I made plans to make my second flight early the next morning. Climbing back into the Stinson with Carl, Jim Fitzhenry, and Jim Frey, I flew back to Detroit City Airport where I knew Earsly was anxiously waiting to hear the good news.

After Earsly's congratulatory hug, we sat and relaxed while I recounted the details of my first flight in Loving's Love. We then walked over to the airport restaurant where news of my successful test flight was already the principal subject of conversation. I found it difficult to eat while accepting congratulations and answering questions. I was very glad I did not have to hear the round of "I told you so's" that would have come if my flight had not been so completely successful. My pilot logbook entry for August 7 summed it all up in these brief words, "The thrill of a lifetime, first flight!"

Early the next morning I was back in N8607K heading for Wayne Major Airport, with Bailey Kailami and Pancho Mobley for company. Bailey, one of our flight students, was to be my chief mechanic when I entered the races the next year, 1951. With much more confidence than the day before, I rolled the Love out onto the ramp and completed my preflight inspection. I made a quick telephone call to the tower for takeoff instructions before climbing into the cockpit. Completing my cockpit check, I started up the engine and began to taxi to runway 24. The tower cleared me for takeoff and as I turned onto the runway the sense of panic of the day before returned with full force. Controlling my nervousness as best I could, I opened full throttle for takeoff and again the red gasoline stains appeared on the windshield. Now that I knew it only occurred during initial takeoff acceleration, I began my climb with confidence. Leveling off at 4,500 feet I continued my planned test schedule with more aggressive maneuvering at higher speeds and power settings than the day before. The Love continued to respond like a well-trained, high-spirited racehorse, raising my confidence to a new high.

Except for the cramped cockpit and the extremely high noise level I was beginning to relax enough so that I was able to enjoy being in the air with my homemade pride and joy. After 40 minutes of intensive testing I headed for runway 24 and started my approach. Lining up with the runway I began to overcontrol, causing the Love to oscillate above and below my desired glide path. During the landing flare I continued to overcontrol so badly the racer stalled about five feet above the runway. It dropped to the ground with such force that the quick release system I had designed to prevent being trapped in the cockpit in case of a crash landing inadvertently ejected the cockpit canopy. The canopy struck the runway while the midget was still traveling about 70 MPH, breaking the clear plexiglas canopy into tiny fragments and bending the supporting steel tube frame.

As I taxied back to the hangar my damaged ego was somewhat repaired by the knowledge that the Love seemed to be otherwise undamaged. However, my dreams of flying 10 hours in the midget as required by the PRPA prior to qualification were now over. It was impossible to install a new canopy and have 10 hours in my logbook in the two days remaining before the start of the races. My logbook entry for August 8 described my flight, "Flew fine, landed lousy."

Since I was still officially entered in the National Air Races scheduled to begin at Wayne Major Airport on August 10 I took the opportunity to join the racing pilots at their prerace meeting. Just to be in the company of such racing greats as Steve Wittman, John Paul Jones, Bill Brennan, president of the PRPA Bob Downey, and others fully compensated for all the trials and tribulations of building and test-flying N351C. Bob Downey invited me to join the PRPA, my membership card number 104 making me the first black pilot in the racing fraternity.

I also had the unenviable distinction of being the only legless racing pilot in the free world.

Now that I was ineligible to compete in the races, the race committee appointed me a pylon judge, where I was able to observe the races from a privileged vantage point. The 1950 races were marred by the fatal crash of the Anderson Racer resulting from structural failure. It carried race number 63, which made me wonder if I would be next with my race number 64. Despite the glory and excitement of air racing, the sobering thought of the inherent risks involved was firmly implanted in the back of my mind. I had always heard that racing pilots were courageous, fearless individuals but as I learned when I had the opportunity to know them better, their fears were not that different from my own.

September 2 was the date of my third flight, which lasted 1 hour and 45 minutes. The new canopy I had installed worked perfectly, instilling confidence as I rolled the Love around the sky both in fun and in the serious business of evaluating flight and structural characteristics. As the flight test program continued, it became increasingly evident that the performance of Loving's Love was exceeding my wildest dreams. Every aspect of my initial flight test program with the original McCauley Model 6156 propeller installed on N351C was completed without serious problems (the canopy failure was my fault).

Now it was my turn to say "I told you so" to my doomsday friends and critics. But I was too elated with the success of my initial flights in Loving's Love to need this type of satisfaction.

The following months were devoted to practicing specific maneuvers to increase my flight skills and occasionally flying the Love on cross-country flights to nearby cities, such as Toledo, Ohio, and Flint, Michigan. At every airport the Love became the instant center of attention. When I stepped out of the racer and the spectators learned that a black, legless designer/builder/pilot was at the controls, they were amazed. My presence inevitably attracted the local news media. I had come a long way since my lonely years in aviation.

In early October I bought a new Klip-Tip racing propeller sized especially for N351C by the McCauley Propeller Company of Dayton, Ohio. The first test propeller they provided had allowed the engine to turn only about 3,200 RPM in the air at full power. The new race propeller was predicted to allow the engine to reach about 4,000 RPM (well above the normal 2,575 rated RPM), with a corresponding increase in horsepower and speed.

On October 14 I completed the installation and was ready to test-fly the new propeller. When I opened the throttle for takeoff the additional power was immediately evident in the increased rate of acceleration. The rate of climb was also significantly improved and I reached 5,000 feet in record time. After clearing the area for aircraft traffic I started my speed runs, gradually increasing power and speed each time. Every run was normal and with speeds now approaching 200 MPH I had additional assurance I might someday be a serious competitor in the racing field. On my last test run I opened the throttle wide and watched the tachometer carefully as the RPM neared the 4,000 mark. Suddenly and without warning a loud explosion and a sharp tremor shook the fuselage. As I quickly throttled back, everything seemed to return to normal. Not taking any chances I flew back to Wayne Major Airport without further incident and made a normal landing. Once out of the cockpit I could see the nose of the racer was anything but normal. The 15-inch-diameter spinner around the propeller had broken off, the damaged back plate the sole evidence of its violent departure. But the propeller was undamaged and only a few small scratches were visible on the wing. It was clear Lady Luck had smiled on me once again. Undaunted, I ordered a new racing prop and was flying again on November 11.

On September 28, 1950, I received a letter from Herb Nipson, associate editor of *Ebony* magazine, expressing his intention to publish a story on my racer and Wayne School of Aeronautics. I was very flattered at the prospect of being featured in such a prestigious publication. My affirmative response was in the mail the next week. His second letter invited me to set a date for their reporter and photographer to fly to Detroit for the interview and photo session. I was also asked to arrange a plane rental so the photographer could take air-to-air shots of Loving's Love.

I set November 12 for our session, which fortunately turned out to be a beautiful day. Both the photographer, Bob Benyas, and the reporter, Mr. Sheifman, were very friendly and competent. The high point of their visit for me was the 35-minute in-flight photo session. I found it difficult to slow my high-performance racer down so I could keep pace with the relatively slow photo plane. It was also my second flight with my new prop and I was pleased with its performance.

After some post-interview correspondence with Herb Nipson, the multipage story appeared in the May 1951 issue of *Ebony*. In his last letter Mr. Nipson said, "If you should fly over to Chicago why don't you stop in and see us." I would accomplish that mission on September 17, 1951.

My photo flight for *Ebony* magazine was a new milestone for me as it was my first flight into Detroit City Airport in the racer. It was really like coming home! I based it there for the rest of the year in Sentas Skyway Services' hangar, enjoying the company and admiration of all my friends. During the year 1950 I flew the Love a total of 17 hours and 15 minutes. At times I could not believe it was true.

When I first rolled Loving's Love into public view in mid-July at Detroit City Airport it attracted much attention from the aviation and other media, including pictures and articles. One article appeared in *Skyways* magazine, a monthly national publication, which prompted Beverly Howard to write a letter to me, dated December 16, 1950. Bevo, as he was called by all his friends, was undisputed world aerobatic champion and owner/operator of the highly respected Hawthorne Flying Service in Charleston, South Carolina. Referring to my racer in his letter, he wrote, "I hope you will get it in condition whereby you will be able to enter it in some of the races around the country. I also hope I will have the pleasure of seeing you at some of these shows." Recalling some of my racial experiences in the ghettos of Detroit, this seemed unbelievable! Here was a world-renowned aviation figure and a true Southern gentleman actually looking forward to meeting me. It brought back memories of that dark morning when Dr. Thompson left my room after telling me of my mother's death. I remembered thinking, as I watched him disappear down the hallway, that my life would always be better from that day forward. This was living proof of that prophecy. I was to have the distinct honor of meeting Mr. Howard at the National Air Races in Detroit in August 1951.

With all the excitement of flying the racer I had not noticed the growing friendship between Earsly and Carl. In fact, when I found out about the relationship, they were already in love and making plans for their wedding in April 1951. This surprised many of my friends and relatives who thought Earsly and I would some day get married.

My first inkling of their romance was in December 1950 when Earsly invited me to her apartment for a pre-Christmas dinner. On entering her apartment I was surprised to see Carl already there. They used this occasion to tell me of their engagement and at that moment it was difficult to tell which of the three of us was the happiest! They made an ideal couple, sharing the same deep love of aviation that would become an integral part of their marriage. I felt privileged to be a part of this wonderful, new lifelong partnership.

During dinner Carl asked if I would be interested in driving to New York City over the holidays to visit his family. He was enrolled in a master's degree program at the University of Michigan Civil Engineering College but had arranged time off for the trip. Fortunately I had just bought a 1949 Buick Roadmaster two-door sedan and was looking for an opportunity to try it out on the highway. However, the winter of 1950/1951 turned out to be one of the worst on record and traveling conditions were not favorable. Undaunted, and with high hopes, we left Detroit on the first leg of our trip to the "Big Apple."

Bad weather made the roads barely driveable. We headed eastward for our planned visit with Earsly's sister Henrene Yuille and her family. They owned a small farm near the little town of Delmont, Pennsylvania, 30 miles east of Pittsburgh. Their farm was located off a small country road quite a distance from the main highway. Snow was piled so high along the sides of the country road we had difficulty picking out the correct driveway. All the driveways we passed looked alike, and if we drove up the wrong one we would be unable to turn around and return to the main road, which would have left us dangerously stranded. Luckily we chose the right one and soon we were able to see the snow-covered, rambling farm home of the Yuille family.

Making our way through the shoveled path to the door we were met by Henrene and her husband, Sydney. He had been waiting for us, ready with his tractor to pull us out of the snow if necessary. The ensuing hours were filled with family news and they were especially happy to learn that Carl was about to become their brother-in-law. We enjoyed our short visit with the Yuilles and for me it was a special opportunity to renew my friendship with little Sydney and Marilyn. I had not seen them since they had come to Detroit to help me celebrate my Christmas away from the hospital in 1944.

The weather gradually improved as we left Delmont, making the remainder of our trip to New York pleasantly uneventful. We stayed with Carl's Aunt Beryl, whom I had met at my shop when she came to Detroit for Carl's graduation in June 1950. Her husband, Uncle Flo (Hubert Floissac), was a very considerate and genial host. He enjoyed craftwork and had modified his bathroom to make it more accessible and convenient for me. As a typical first-time New York tourist, I toured the Empire State Building, Statue of Liberty, Hayden Planetarium, RCA Music Hall, and other familiar sights of New York City. The high point was my visit to the Metropolitan Opera where I heard Eleanor Steber sing the lead role of Violetta in Guiseppe Verdi's opera, *La Traviata*. It brought back pleasant memories of Dr. Thompson's gift membership to the Metropolitan Opera Guild while I was in the hospital. Carl was not an opera fan but both he and his 14-year-old cousin, Joan Floissac, Uncle Flo and Aunt Beryl's only child, insisted on accompanying me to the Met, much to my dismay. I was pleasantly surprised when they both apparently enjoyed the performance as much as I did.

Carl and I planned our return to Detroit so we could celebrate the coming of the new year 1951 with Earsly and other friends. On New Year's Eve I accompanied Carl and Earsly and Jack Walsh and his lovely new bride, Carol, to the beautiful Fisher Theater where special entertainment was scheduled to usher in the new year. As we sang "Auld Lang Syne" my heart was filled with joy as I looked forward to Carl and Earsly's marriage and the prospects of racing Loving's Love in the Detroit National Air Races of 1951.

The Barnetts were married in a quiet Roman Catholic ceremony a few days after Easter Sunday, 1951. I felt a special pride for if I had not given my talk on Loving's Love at the NTA meeting, this love affair would never have happened. The newlyweds were too busy for the typical honeymoon after the wedding. That would come later when, according to Carl's plan, they would return to his native Jamaica to establish their new home.

CHAPTER ELEVEN

THE AIR RACES

The dark, cold months of winter dropped flying activity at Wayne School of Aeronautics to its seasonal low, affording ample time to plan my racing schedule for 1951. Traditionally, the aircraft racing season started in May with the Air Pageant at Lovell Field, Chattanooga, Tennessee. My natural desire to enter the feature event, the Tennessee Products Cup Race for midget racers, was tempered by my knowledge of the racial prejudices common in the South. But I decided to submit my entry (with my picture so they would know I was black) just to see what response I would receive. If the answer was negative I would stay home. If my entry was accepted I planned to participate even though there were doubts about the type of treatment I would receive. On May 12, I received a telegram with the following message:

THANKS FOR YOUR ENTRY IN THE TENNESSEE PRODUCTS CUP RACE. WE WELCOME YOUR PARTICIPATION.

With some reservations still in the back of my mind, I confirmed my entry.

My first flight of 1951 in the Love was on February 18, a relatively warm day. I had received McCauley's latest racing design propeller and during the 1-hour and 45-minute flight I detected a vibratory response in a narrow band of RPMs I had not experienced before. On the next flight, February 25, the vibrations seemed to occur again, but I had no instrumentation on board to confirm or quantify my observations. I was to learn later that this was a quite common problem with midget racers and was due to the extremely high engine rotational speeds (well above normal design limits) required to be competitive in a race. The forces generated by the loss of a spinner and ensuing propeller damage could, in extreme cases, tear the engine from its mount with catastrophic, sometimes fatal, results.

I wrote to the McCauley Corporation in Dayton, Ohio, and received a prompt reply dated May 10 from the vice-president and general manager, S. M. Gamsu. In the opening paragraph he offered the following advice: "We have just started 10 racing props into process and will have one ready for your use on May 16. We suggest you fly down to Dayton on that day and check out the new AM6054 to see whether the vibration problem is encountered with the new prop."

This was a good news/bad news situation. The good news was that by flying to Dayton I would have propeller experts and proper instrumentation to resolve my vibration problems. The bad news was that because of the time involved, it was very unlikely I could arrive in Chattanooga in time to qualify for the races starting on May 18. Qualifying trials and speed runs for starting positions usually required the airplane and pilot at the race site at least three days before the first race. The *Chattanooga News–Free Press* reported my problem in part in an article they printed regarding my race entry:

> If Loving races here—he wrote that "bugs" in a specially designed propel-ler might ground him for the money run—it will be the first appearance of a Negro in a local air show. It is believed also that his flights will be the first by a man of his race in the South.

It was becoming increasingly clear that due to my flight to Dayton I would not be able to participate in the Chattanooga races. In addition to the mechanical problems, I had not made advance arrangements for transportation and motel reservations for my crew because I was still uncertain that I would even be allowed to participate in the races. Housing was, at that time, a major problem for blacks traveling in the South. Later I learned that race officials had arranged for me to enjoy the hospitality of a prominent black doctor whose home was near Lookout Mountain. I sent my regrets the morning of my departure for Dayton, May 17, 1951.

The weather forecaster at Detroit City Airport gave a favorable forecast except for east winds at 30 knots at my cruising altitude. This crosswind would reduce my ground speed for the 170-mile trip, my longest cross-country flight to date. This meant I would have to sit and squirm in my cramped cockpit, but such discomfort was a small price to pay for the never-ending excitement of flying Loving's Love.

The flight went according to plan and I arrived on schedule at Dayton Municipal Airport. Mr. Gamsu met me with a team of technicians and a new prop ready to install for comparison tests. First we conducted ground vibration checks on my old prop, with the engine running for a baseline. We then removed the old prop and installed the new AM6054 model. During a local 25-minute test flight I was overjoyed to find the vibration had disappeared.

After observing some additional ground tests, Mr. Gamsu gave his approval for the installation and wished me luck during the coming racing season. I was happily surprised when he also told me there was no charge for his services.

At the request of the tower I did a low-level, high-speed "buzz job" down the runway before starting the 1-hour and 15-minute flight back to Detroit City Airport. Several days later I received a copy of the *Dayton Daily News* containing a front-page headline,

Legless But Not Wingless
Double Amputee Flies Midget Racer

The accompanying article by staff reporter "Doc" Fisher included a picture of me in the cockpit.

Closed-course midget racing events are flown at speeds sometimes in excess of 200 MPH at a minimum altitude of only 50 feet. I had no low-level flight experience. Federal regulations prohibited flight below

1,000 feet except in sparsely populated areas. There were no such areas near Detroit due to continuously expanding suburban development. I called the CAA office at Wayne Major Airport and explained my problem. They were sympathetic but politely informed me they could not modify the regulations and therefore were unable to officially authorize any low-level practice flights.

Unofficially, their advice was, "Pick out a location near some large farms and other sparsely populated areas for your low-level flights. If someone complains we will merely ask you to move to a different practice area rather than file an official violation." With that assurance I selected an area near several large farms, adjacent to telephone lines and train tracks connecting Detroit and Toledo, and started my practice runs.

My first low flights were frightening experiences for they violated one of my cardinal safety rules: Always fly at a safe altitude. My instinctive reaction was to pull back on the stick and gain altitude. It was a long time before I became accustomed to seeing the ground rushing by only 50 feet below at speeds of over 250 feet per second.

As I told my friends later, with some exaggeration, "The telephone poles were going by so fast they looked like fence posts!" After a few attempts to practice low-level high-speed turns, I found it impossible to avoid passing over houses and farm animals. Remembering the CAA's advice about possible complaints, I flew across the Detroit River into Sarnia, Canada, where there were large unpopulated areas. After several hours of practice I felt about as comfortable as I was ever going to be at these dangerously low racing altitudes.

The 1951 National Air Races were scheduled to open on August 20 at Wayne Major Airport. I filed my entry in June and was accepted. There were two hurdles to overcome, in sequence, before I would be allowed to fly Loving's Love in a PRPA/NAA–sanctioned race. The first was to perform a set of predetermined maneuvers in full view of the race technical committee. If satisfied, the PRPA would issue a notarized qualification certificate good for the life of the airplane. The qualification maneuvers for the airplane were specified in entry requirements by the PRPA/NAA as follows:

Dive to 1.3 times max speed in level flight (266 MPH minimum)

Pullup to a minimum of 6.0 g's

Slow rolls left and right

Crosswind takeoffs without veering more than 30 feet

The max speed dive and the 6g pullup required more nerve than skill. The only time I planned to perform this test was for the race judges. However, I had no experience in slow rolls and needed skilled aerobatic instruction before performing that part of the test in my midget. For assistance I called on my good friend and fellow flight school operator at Detroit City Airport, Lank Tygard. He had been an aerobatic instructor during the war and was fully qualified to give me aerobatic instruction. He volunteered his services and then called Rose Ruby, one of the few flight service operators in the Detroit area who had a Stearman primary trainer, ideally suited for aerobatic training. Rose, a generous woman, on hearing of my need, refused to accept compensation for use of her airplane. Such unearned generosity always made me feel humble, searching for ways to return such favors.

On August 14 Lank and I flew over to Wayne Major Airport where Rose had Stearman N61988 waiting for us. After a careful review of the control-stick movements and engine power adjustments for slow rolls, we took off for a 50-minute flight. I had some difficulty keeping my feet on the cockpit floor when inverted (artificial legs are heavy) and keeping my sense of orientation while rotating 360 degrees around the horizon. After completing my lesson, we agreed I would need one more aerobatic session.

Two days later we were back in the Stearman for an additional hour of aerobatic instruction. I was now quite accustomed to being on my back for Lank insisted on practicing inverted flight until the Stearman's gravity-feed Continental radial engine quit for lack of fuel in the carburetor. The seven-cylinder radial would start again as soon as we resumed level flight. By now my aerobatic repertoire included snap rolls, slow rolls, accelerated stalls, and vertical reverses. The question now was, could I translate these new skills to the midget? The answer would come just two days later.

The second of the two PRPA/NAA hurdles was a qualification test required of all pilots without recent experience in closed-course racing. I was a true novice, never having seen, much less flown, a closed-course midget race. The stringent pilot qualification test included ten high-speed laps around the course, marked by a series of six 50-foot orange and black pylons, in full view of PRPA officials who would evaluate my competence. My hope was that the hours of practice-flying the midget down railroad tracks and over the flat lands of Canada had prepared me to pass the test.

On the Monday before the races were to begin, Wayne Major Airport was a beehive of activity as racing and aerobatic pilots in their showplanes, as well as commercial aircraft, began to arrive. Amid all this airport activity I took the midget up for a 35-minute practice flight. It was quite difficult to concentrate on my maneuvers while keeping constant surveillance for other traffic. After landing I taxied up to the hangar where my crew chief, Bailey Kailami, was waiting. Standing next to him was Mr. Champion, technical representative from Continental Motor Corporation (sponsors of the race), who had been listening to my engine during my flight.

After introducing himself, Mr. Champion gave me the bad news. My engine had a faulty fuel injector on one cylinder. He suggested it be replaced. After instructing Bailey to remove the engine cowl and defective fuel injector I flew back to Detroit City Airport in the Stinson to pick up a new fuel injector. We certainly had no time to lose. I came back in record time only to find my racer sitting on the ramp with the engine cowl fully in place. It was difficult to restrain my anger as I walked over with my new fuel injector ready for installation. Obviously this could not be accomplished until the cowl was removed, a delay I could ill afford. Bailey sensed my feelings and quickly explained what had happened.

After I had taken off in the Stinson, the news of my predicament reached the midget racing team from Los Angeles. Two of their mechanics came over with a spare injector and installed it in the Love. They ran the engine to make sure it was working properly and left, refusing payment for the injector or services. Bailey had re-installed the cowling prior to my arrival. I walked over to Bob Downey, head of the Los Angeles racing team and president of the PRPA, to express my appreciation. His words I can never forget, "Neal, we will give you all the help we can on the ground, but in the air we will fly like hell to beat you!" I was proud of this latest sign of my acceptance as a full-fledged member of the racing fraternity.

Bailey and I, along with the other ground crew members, went over every inch of the midget, giving it a super inspection to make sure it was ready for my qualifying trial the next day. During the inspection we found a small crack in the spinner. Not having the equipment for an on-site repair, I flew the racer back to Detroit City Airport for an all-night repair session.

George Sentas and his mechanics greeted me on my arrival and immediately began removing the spinner for repairs. George told me to go home and get some sleep, promising to have the Love ready to fly early in the morning. I was awake most of the night and listened to the sound of raindrops on the roof just before dawn.

On my arrival at the airport early in the morning the sun was out, shining and reflecting on the many shallow pools of water on the ground. Sentas pronounced the midget ready to race, so it was with full confidence I completed my preflight cockpit check. The air was smooth as silk as I took off into clear, blue skies and headed west toward Wayne Major Airport. My good friend in the tower, Bill Giddings, called as I was exiting the traffic pattern, "Good luck, Neal, at the races." His words were like a reassuring pat on the back.

That afternoon, August 18, I was scheduled to perform the required qualification maneuvers in full view of the racing technical committee. This flight qualification test was required of all new racing aircraft and Loving's Love was the only one that had not yet tested. During this qualification flight the airport would have to be closed completely to all traffic, local as well as departing and arriving aircraft. The airport traffic was extremely busy at this time and it took several hours before my clearance was issued. Climbing into the cockpit I noticed a solid layer of clouds had formed overhead. Mindful of the PRPA rule requiring all maneuvers to be completed at least 5,000 feet above the ground, I asked the technical committee chairman, Joe Hance, to check the height of the cloud deck. Glancing up with an experienced eye he assured me it was at least 10,000 feet. Satisfied, I closed the canopy and after engine start took off, climbing swiftly through the deserted skies. While mentally reviewing the maneuvers to be performed and the predetermined emergency procedures, I found myself suddenly enveloped in cloud. I dove out of the mist and glanced at the instrument panel, which indicated my altitude was only 4,000 feet above the ground. Now I had to make a very critical decision.

This was the last day of the aircraft qualifying trials and thus my only opportunity to became eligible to race. However, the element of risk was increased considerably if I elected to perform these potentially hazardous maneuvers below the 5,000-foot minimum. I would also be in violation of the PRPA rules regarding these tests. But I had come too far in my quest to become a racing pilot to quit now. I also thought briefly of my crew and friends on the ground who I knew were waiting expectantly for me to become the first black to successfully complete a midget racer qualifying trial.

Without further hesitation, I decided to go on with the qualification maneuvers. With Lank Tygard's instructions still fresh in my mind I performed the slow rolls left and right flawlessly while flying just below the base of the clouds. I now decided to change my test plan and perform both the high-speed dive and 6g pullup in one maneuver. Taking a quick look at the instrument panel and a deep breath at the same time, I pulled up into the dark clouds as far as I dared and then pushed over into a dive. My true airspeed was over 270 MPH as I plunged almost vertically out of the clouds. Having exceeded the 266 MPH minimum dive speed I rolled to the left about 45 degrees and pulled back on the stick until the accelerometer reached the 6g mark while simultaneously glancing at both wings for signs of possible wing failure. Doctors have told me that no one can see both left and right extremes of peripheral vision at the same time, but I am sure I was able to do so as I watched anxiously for signs of wing failure. At 6 g's, my little racer weighed almost 3 tons! Easing off on the back pressure on the stick, I leveled off dangerously below the 4,000-foot cloud layer. Confident I had passed the qualification test, my spirits were as high as the stratosphere as I descended rapidly toward the airport.

I taxied up to the ramp where the witnessing technical committee members were waiting. Joe Hance was the first to greet me as I removed my canopy. Peering into the cockpit and noting the registered 6.3 g's on the accelerometer, Joe assured me I had passed my qualification tests but was now required to confirm I had not violated the 5,000-foot altitude minimum. Trying my best to sound truthful I assured him I had stayed above the required height at all times. Grinning broadly he responded, "Officially I believe you and that is what the record will show; but unofficially you are a damn liar!" I smiled back, then taxied back to the hangar where my race crew was waiting.

After such rigorous flight testing, a thorough inspection was now required. As my race crew proceeded with the inspection I started mentally preparing for my pilot qualification test the next day. As a novice racing pilot I had to fly ten laps around the race course with technical committee members at each pylon to observe my performance. In spite of my low-level practice over farmlands I still was unfamiliar with a pylon-marked race course. I scheduled a ten-lap practice flight as soon as the inspection was complete.

It was late afternoon when the airport traffic finally died down sufficiently for the tower to approve my practice flight. Another race pilot, John Paul Jones, decided to do a tuneup flight as well, so we lined up, wing to wing, for takeoff. As we completed our engine runup I glanced over at John just 30 feet away and he looked so calm I was envious. In contrast, my heart was pounding and I was sweating profusely in the warm cockpit. Fortunately, as the starting flag dropped I became so occupied with my flying I didn't have time to think of being scared. My first problem, quite unexpected, was finding the orange and black race pylons that marked the course. They were highly visible at ground level, but in the air at only 50 feet they tended to disappear into the ground clutter. It was very embarrassing to find myself totally lost in the middle of an airport doing over 200 MPH at 50-foot altitude! After frantically scanning the horizon for what seemed forever I managed to orient myself. I learned to use prominent landmarks on the horizon for initial reference. When my ten practice laps were finished, I felt reasonably confident for my qualifying flight test the next day. I met John Paul Jones after our flight and asked how he could be so calm as he waited for takeoff. He broke out laughing, for he was about to ask me the same question! It was comforting to know that race pilots with far more experience than I had shared my prerace fears.

They all agreed, however, that such emotions quickly disappeared when the starting flag signaled the beginning of the race.

The next morning, August 19, I went directly to the pilots' ready room to get the latest weather and airport information. As I was leaving, Bevo Howard came over and introduced himself. He immediately impressed me with his friendly smile and modest, courtly manner. After a few pleasantries, Bevo asked if I would be kind enough to show him my airplane and discuss its unique design details. I could not imagine a man of his international stature asking a favor of me, an unknown black pilot with two wooden legs. Needless to say I was proud of the opportunity to meet him and thoroughly enjoyed my one and only visit with the famed Bevo Howard. He was killed a few years later while performing aerobatics at an air show.

Shortly after meeting Bevo, I met another long-time pilot, Walter "Walt" Carr, whom I had greatly admired over the years. Walt was chief inspector for the Michigan Department of Aeronautics and a greatly admired and respected figure in aviation. His flying career started during the Wright Brothers era and he was a true aviation pioneer. He had witnessed my practice flight the day before and said he wanted to discuss it with me. His face had a serious look as he told me he had bad news. Coming from him, this was bad news indeed! His words, conveyed in a sad tone of voice, were, "Neal, you are never going to win a race with 'Loving's Love.' " As I searched my mind for his reasons for such a statement, he broke out in a loud laugh. "I remember the old folks saying that exceptionally beautiful girls are probably too busy being pretty to amount to much. Your racer is just too pretty to win a race." I never did win a race, but I never agreed that was a valid excuse.

Joe Hance came over with the news that the airport would be closed within the hour to allow me to complete my ten-lap race pilot qualification trial. Carl Barnett and Bailey Kailami gave Loving's Love a detailed final inspection while I set up my lap counter in the cockpit. Then I checked the wind direction and velocity at the weather office so I would know what crosswinds I might expect. It was now 20 minutes before takeoff.

Finding a secluded corner I tried to relax as I planned my flight. Location of the pylons, prominent landmarks for course orientation, were committed to memory. The only mechanical problem I had to worry about was the spinner and I hoped the recent repairs would take care of it. All that was left to do now was to hope and pray. Before I climbed into the cockpit, Mike Murphy, the chief starter (also a famous aerobatic pilot) and one of the team of pilots who would be judging me, gave some advice. "You are the last pilot to qualify and will start in the last heat of the race, regardless of your speed. My advice is to take it easy for the first few laps, gradually increasing your speed until the last lap which you should fly at wide open throttle."

My excitement level reached almost unbearable proportions as my Continental came to life with smoke and its usual noisy bark. Closing the canopy I taxied out to the starting line and awaited Mike Murphy's signal to take off. I noted the strong tailwind coming from the left. Normally all takeoffs are made into the wind, but not so in a race. Racing airplanes line up usually six abreast on the starting line and always take off headed for the scatter pylon regardless of wind direction. This pylon is situated a distance far enough from the takeoff line to allow the faster and slower aircraft to separate, thus allowing them to negotiate the scatter pylon without being dangerously close to each other. However, the race did not officially start until the first airplane crossed the starting line. I kept the tail of the Love on the ground a little longer than usual, and my takeoff run was straight as an arrow as I headed for the scatter pylon.

Leveling off at the 50-foot racing altitude I turned steeply around the scatter pylon and headed for the starting line in front of the grandstands. Throttling back to about 160 MPH I managed to fly around each of the six colorfully marked pylons without getting lost. Sometimes the wind would drift me too close to the pylons but I soon learned how to compensate. I continued my race pattern at increasing speeds, raising my structural loads to the 4g level during my steep turns around the pylons. I even tried to spot the judges located at each pylon as they observed my flying skills and racing techniques. Starting my tenth and final lap I noticed I was well above the 50-foot altitude minimum.

Taking advantage of this chance to increase my speed, I dropped the nose slightly, opened the throttle wide, and headed for the starting line for the last lap. I had no time to look at my airspeed indicator but I could tell by the high-pitched sound coming from my engine that it was revving nearly 4,000 RPM which, along with the wind noise, was evidence I was traveling well over 200 MPH. This was faster than I had ever flown before in level flight and with it came a sense of exhilaration.

As the starting line flashed by, I made a slight correction for the crosswind and gently banked the Love as the first orange and black pylon approached. Suddenly I heard a tremendous explosion followed by violent shaking throughout the airplane. Over the nose I could see the engine cowl twisting and bouncing up and down so violently I was afraid the engine might tear itself away from the fuselage. Quickly turning off the ignition switch I eased the stick back to use my excess speed to gain altitude. The cockpit was deathly quiet as my airspeed diminished to a safe glide speed.

Gliding without power, I had only a few seconds before I would be back on the ground. I quickly scanned the area for a safe place to land. The active runways were too far away to reach from my low altitude. An emergency landing site had to be picked without delay. Looking around, I thought I could glide to one of the new runways under construction for the soon-to-be-opened Detroit Metropolitan Airport. The new runways were not approved for aircraft traffic and were being used to park cars of airshow attendees.

Aiming toward the nearest one and carefully noting the position of the parked cars, I touched down at nearly 70 MPH, passing startled bystanders as I maneuvered around the parked cars. With a fortunate combination of luck and skill, the landing was completed with no damage.

Almost before I came to a stop, emergency vehicles and fire trucks with flashing red lights surrounded my racer. Sitting there with my head bowed for a moment, I gave thanks to the gods that look after racing pilots in their time of need. When my "feet" were on solid ground again, my body shook in emotional response to this near disaster. Still not knowing what caused my problem, I walked around to the front of the airplane. The answer was clear. The spinner had ripped off but, unlike the last time, it came through the arc of rotation of the propeller and chopped about four inches off one blade. The resulting unbalance, aggravated by the engine turning nearly 4,000 RPM, almost ripped the engine from its mount.

As one astute observer commented, "'Loving's Love' was built hell for stout!" Other than a few surface scratches on the upper left wing, there were no external signs of damage. Concerned about my well-being, Carl and Bailey came racing up in a commandeered official car to offer whatever assistance I might need. Seeing I was physically and emotionally okay, they made plans to hook my airplane to a tow truck for the trip back to the hangar. The ignominy of having my crippled racer towed backward past the crowded grandstand was more than my pride would allow. I was determined to taxi my midget racer back to the hangar like good airplanes are supposed to do "come hell or high water." Now safely on the ground, I thought maybe the vibrations were not as bad as I remembered during those panicky moments in the air. Against the advice of my crew I climbed back into the cockpit and started the engine. Immediately the Love started to shake so badly that directional control was impossible. Bowing to the inevitable, my head hanging in shame, I allowed my damaged racer to be towed to the hangar for repairs. Not having a replacement prop or spinner, my opportunity to participate in the 1951 National Air Races was ended.

Once again the race officials appointed me as a pylon judge and I was forced to watch the likes of Bob Downey, Steve Wittman, and others speed by my lonely outpost. But I now had the deep satisfaction of knowing that I had not only successfully qualified my racer, but was now a certified racing pilot with license number 9307, issued by the Fédération Aéronautique Internationale.

The 1951 National Air Races marked the end of my brief and unsuccessful attempt at closed-course racing. This also marked the last year the aviation industry gave financial support to air racing events. Over the years, major racing events were sponsored by aviation companies such as Thompson Products, which awarded the annual prestigious Thompson Trophy to the winner of the unlimited closed-course racing class event. Bendix Corporation awarded the Bendix Trophy to the fastest airplane in a flight from Los Angeles to Cleveland. Each of these awards provided substantial cash prizes for the winners. But now the aviation industry wanted to rid itself of the daredevil image associated with aerobatic displays and air races and, without this support, air racing lay dormant for years.

Years later Bill Stead of Reno, Nevada, began reviving interest in major air racing. However, the prize money had to be raised strictly through the sale of tickets. For a long time it was difficult, if not impossible, to guarantee cash purses that would justify the financial investment required to produce and support a competitive racing airplane. Still, latent interest in air racing continued to grow. Today, the Reno Air Races have become a popular annual event with a secure financial future.

With competitive racing no longer a goal, I began to think of my Loving's Love as an inexpensive, high-speed sportplane, fulfilling in a sense my long-held desire for a high-performance airplane like the fighter planes of old. I added a small baggage compartment, additional instrumentation, and radios (unheard of in racing airplanes!) to make the Love more suitable for long cross-country flights. The Bendix PAR-3 radio receiver allowed me to hear control tower instructions, which I acknowledged by waggling my ailerons when taxiing or rocking my wings in the air. But the transmitter never worked, probably due to the short antenna length (limited by the small dimensions of the racer). This inability to transmit to the control tower caused many delays in taking off and landing. Many airports with busy airline traffic required all aircraft to have functioning two-way radio on board which prevented me from flying into airports such as Miami International or Idlewild Airport (now JFK) in New York.

Only two significant airplane modifications were needed. I installed a new spinner and mounting bracket and replaced the troublesome racing propeller with a slower turning cruise propeller. These changes made the Love more suitable for flying to faraway places, undreamed of before the momentous first flight on August 7, 1950.

CHAPTER TWELVE

TRAVELS

With my racing career apparently at an end, I began planning for the promised visit to the *Ebony* magazine office. To prepare Loving's Love for long-distance cross-country flying, I ordered a new spinner and cruise propeller (low RPM) and repaired the minor paint damage resulting from the spinner failure on the race course. I test-flew the new prop for 50 minutes on September 5, 1951, long enough to determine that Loving's Love was ready to provide safe, high-speed transportation. In a phone call to Herb Nipson in Chicago, we agreed on September 17 as the date for my visit.

My initial plan was for a nonstop, straight-line flight to Chicago. This would require flying over a substantial portion of Lake Michigan, a practice usually avoided by single-engine aircraft. To elude this potential danger, I decided to take the longer route, skirting the south shore of Lake Michigan as I had done when I flew Jimmie Lunceford to Chicago in the BT-13. My westerly heading would be against a headwind if the typical westerly winds were present. If they were unusually high, I planned a refueling stop to ensure adequate fuel reserves on entering the Chicago control zone.

The large volume of airline traffic at Midway Airport often meant delays in receiving a landing clearance so an ample fuel reserve was necessary. Another reason for making an intermediate stop was that extended flights in the cramped cockpit of the midget were sure to cause almost unbearable aches and pains.

The morning of September 17 was warm and beautiful with gusty winds out of the west. A visit to the weather office on my way to breakfast at the airport restaurant confirmed I would have stronger than average headwinds on my 270-mile flight to Chicago. During breakfast Earsly and I spread the sectional flight charts on the counter and discussed possible changes to my original flight plan. The strong headwinds would seriously increase the total flight time and hence the fuel required. A refueling stop at Bendix Field in South Bend, Indiana, was agreed upon to ensure legal fuel reserves. After returning to our office to pick up maps and flight gear we climbed aboard Luscombe N45744 for our 35-minute flight to Wayne Major Airport. Sitting on the right, I chatted with Earsly as she did the flying. It was one of the few opportunities we had to fly together. After a smooth landing, in spite of the strong gusty winds, Earsly taxied our silver and blue Luscombe up to the AC Sparkplug Division hangar where Loving's Love was ready and waiting on the windy, sunlit ramp.

After a few last-minute encouraging words from Earsly, I was ready for takeoff. The tower called as I taxied away from the hangar and gave taxi instructions and clearance for takeoff from runway 24. Strong winds blowing directly down the runway lifted Loving's Love into the air in record time. Runway 24's magnetic heading of 240 degrees put me almost directly on course to South Bend, so I continued to climb on a straight-out departure with occasional gentle turns to avoid the puffy white clouds that dotted my path.

Leveling off at cruise altitude I tried unsuccessfully to unfold my map but found my hands pressed against the sides of the cockpit before I could get it straightened out past the fold line. I finally had to tear away portions of the map, leaving only the portion showing my plotted course.

My little midget bounced around like a cork in rough seas, occasionally banging my crash helmet against the canopy with unexpected force. The extreme turbulence also made it difficult to maintain assigned altitude and planned course heading.

In spite of almost constant course corrections, the predetermined checkpoints came into view on schedule and after almost two hours of flying time the runways of Bendix Field appeared straight ahead. Putting my map away I entered the traffic pattern, fully alert for an audio or visual signal of recognition from the tower. Realizing the midget was a small target I circled the field several times below traffic altitude to give the tower personnel ample time to see me. They gave no signal so I scanned the area for traffic and decided there was no one else in the sky. Assuming I had clearance to land in absence of other traffic I started my final approach to the active runway.

As I passed over the airport boundary the tower operator finally spotted me and, assuming I had no radio contact, called the emergency crew, "We have an aircraft on final approach and making what appears to be a gear-up landing. Prepare for crash landing!" I heard every word of their transmission but could not respond since my transmitter was not working. Just as I touched down the tower operator called the emergency crew again, "Whatever landing gear the aircraft is equipped with appears be in the down position so the emergency is canceled." The wheels on the midget were attached directly to the lower apexes of the gull wing, hence no external landing strut was visible. His failure to see my landing gear was understandable.

After tending to the refueling of Loving's Love, I called the tower operator, who was both embarrassed and apologetic on learning I had heard all his transmissions. Had he been alert and used his binoculars he would have seen me as soon as I entered the traffic pattern. And if he assumed there was no radio on board, a flashing green light from the tower would have provided legal clearance to land. Our brief conversation concluded with his promise of prompt service on my departure.

My flight time to South Bend had been a long, bumpy 2 hours and 5 minutes, resulting in severe back and leg pain. For temporary relief, I decided to relax in a comfortable chair in the airport lounge before resuming my flight to Chicago. However, instead I found myself standing by the midget answering questions from interested onlookers. "How fast does it fly?" "Who designed and built it?" "How much does it weigh?" Answering these questions while standing on artificial legs caused such severe pains I decided the only way to get off my "feet" was to prepare for takeoff. As promised, the tower operator called as soon as I taxied away from the hangar and quickly gave me taxi and takeoff instructions. The wind direction had not changed so my takeoff was once again into the strong west wind.

The flight time to Chicago was only 40 minutes, so I had ample fuel reserves on board in case of traffic delays. Tuning my radio receiver to the tower frequency of Midway Airport, I listened to their transmissions to other aircraft in the traffic pattern and tried to spot them visually. A constant stream of aircraft flew in and out of Midway Airport, warranting its reputation at the time as the world's busiest. I was pleasantly surprised when an alert tower operator called as soon as I descended into the traffic pattern and gave me clearance to land. Turning off the runway as soon as possible, I taxied past numerous airliners, returning the stares of the pilots and passengers looking down at my tiny midget racer. On arriving at Butler Aviation my homebuilt Loving's Love was parked in a prominent place among the many expensive multiengine executive aircraft in the hangar. They even roped it off to keep curious onlookers from getting too close.

A phone call to Herb Nipson confirmed they were expecting me. I took a cab to the *Ebony* offices in downtown Chicago. This was my first visit to a large, all-black business organization and I was favorably impressed by the cordial receptionist in the luxurious visitors' lounge and the well-appointed private offices. My racial pride surged as I sat in the lounge waiting for my appointment and observed staff members going about their duties in a very business-like and professional manner.

Herb Nipson soon came and invited me into his office where he gave me a briefing on the history and current status of *Ebony*. At the appointed time I was ushered into the impressive wood-paneled office of John H. Johnson, owner, publisher, and chief executive officer of *Ebony*. He greeted me graciously and made me feel welcome during my visit. I thanked him for the coverage he had given me and told him how impressed I was with the resulting mail I received.

One of the more interesting letters was from a woman and her son living in British Guiana, South America. It was clear that *Ebony* readership extended well beyond the borders of the United States. Realizing Mr. Johnson had a busy schedule, I said goodbye and headed back to the airport. During the cab ride a strange thought came to mind.

I had spent the afternoon visiting the offices of an all-black publishing firm and suddenly remembered that the photographer and reporter who were assigned to do my story in Detroit were both white. Racial integration was, in this case, a two-way street.

While touring the facilities at Butler Aviation I noticed a special park bench reserved for the black baggage handlers and attendants. Several were there enjoying the warm sunlight. Inspired by fond memories of my meeting with "aeroportah" Smitty Smith from Cincinnati's Lunken Airport, I walked over and sat down with them. Their involvement in aviation was different from mine but I found their stories fascinating, especially when they talked of the personality traits of the many famous people they had met. On leaving, they paid me one of the most cherished compliments I have ever received. One of them spoke up and said, "Thanks for visiting with us. With all the attention you and your airplane have received we didn't think you would take the time to visit with working level people like us." It was a pleasure for me to tell them I enjoyed my visit more than they did.

Making sure my airplane was well taken care of, I went back to my hotel to await a call from Bob Sutherland, our first graduate of Wayne School of Aeronautics, now living in Chicago. He had promised years ago that he would treat me to my first steak whenever I visited him. Shortly after I unpacked Bob called, offering to pick me up for that promised steak dinner. After a happy reunion in the hotel lobby we drove to a restaurant where we swapped flying stories while feasting on juicy steaks.

When our meal was over Bob suggested we visit Nick Rezich, owner of the Pylon Bar, famous for its polished wooden bar with miniature racing pylons at each end. Other aviation memorabilia decorated the walls. Nick was a well-known aviation personality in Chicago who often flew his antique Travelaire biplane to nearby air shows. He also performed as announcer and commentator at local air shows and fly-ins.

As Bob drove to the predominantly Polish neighborhood where the Pylon Bar was located, I began to have misgivings. In the past, I had found racial prejudices to be at their strongest in singularly ethnic areas. Bob brushed aside my concerns as we entered the Pylon Bar and asked the bartender to let Nick know we were there. We were told he was away at the moment but would return soon. While we sat at the bar sipping our drinks, I noticed a patron surreptitiously signaling to Bob that he wanted to talk. Realizing my presence was causing a problem I suggested we leave. In his innocence, Bob's only comment was, "Be patient, Nick will be here soon and will be glad to see you." The bar patron, now aware he was being ignored, finally came over, tapped Bob on the shoulder, and in a whisper asked for a private conversation. Bob excused himself and walked out of earshot. As I watched their animated conversation, I could tell Bob was getting very upset. It was clear that the patron was unhappy at having a black man seated at an all-white bar. Bob, a well-built six-footer, looked down on the skinny, gray-haired senior citizen and vented his anger, loud enough for everyone to hear, "If you speak one more word about my friend leaving this bar I will wipe up the floor with your scrawny body." Sitting down next to me again, a very irate Bob Sutherland insisted we stay long enough to prove we were not intimidated (I was). But Nick never returned and I was glad when we left, even without the pleasure of visiting with him.

The next morning I arrived at Midway Airport to prepare for my return to Detroit. During my preflight inspection the owner of Anderson Propeller Company came over for a look at my racer. He introduced himself as Mr. Anderson, the designer and builder of the Anderson Special, NAA Racing Number 63, which I had seen involved in a fatal crash at the Detroit National Air Races in 1950. Although he was not a pilot, we talked about the unique handling characteristics of our respective airplanes. He described how his pilot had complained about the difficulty he had keeping his racer straight on takeoffs and landings, especially in a cross wind. Mine, I contended, was always directionally stable, even with adverse winds. Anderson was very skeptical of my claims and bet five dollars I could not take off on Midway's northwest runway with the existing crosswind without applying brakes to keep it straight.

Having full confidence in N351C, I took Anderson up on the bet. He could observe my flight from his office located at the approach end of the northeast runway. If I applied brakes, the sound of skidding tires would be audible. During a brief lull in airport traffic the tower cleared me for a crosswind takeoff. I held the tail down a little longer than usual, and the midget was off the ground without the slightest touch of braking action. Mr. Anderson did not realize that the limited motion of my artificial legs prevented me from ever using brakes for directional control. It was the easiest five dollars I had made in years.

After collecting the bet I took off for a nonstop flight to Detroit. With the prevailing westerly winds now providing a tailwind, my nonstop flight home required only two hours flight time.

Carl Barnett received his master's degree in civil engineering from the University of Michigan in June 1951, shortly after his marriage to Earsly. Now that the 1952 New Year's Day celebrations were over he was planning his return flight to Jamaica with his new bride. Carl was determined to open a flight school in Kingston to provide Jamaicans with the opportunity to learn to fly, an opportunity he had not had until coming to the Wayne School of Aeronautics. Earsly and I had decided to turn over one of our Piper J-3 Cubs, N42026, as their first Jamaican trainer. It was completely dismantled in June 1951 and then completely rebuilt and refinished. Instead of the customary Cub yellow, Carl painted it a beautiful Diana Cream with medium-green trim. Earsly, with the skilled help of Jean Tygard, upholstered the interior in cream-colored leatherette with matching seat cushions similar to those in Loving's Love.

Carl applied to the Civil Aviation Department (CAD) in Kingston for Jamaican registration of his newly finished Cub. The CAD, in accordance with British regulations, issued the all-letter registration marking of VP-JAZ. But Earsly's inventive mind came up with the unique name "Jamerican." Carl made the first test flight on July 3 and I made the second the same day. The purpose of these flights was to test the extra five-gallon fuel tank we had installed to provide extra range for the overwater flights on their way to Jamaica. The Cub's normal cruising speed was only 70 MPH, so the maximum range with the standard 10-gallon fuel tank was only 210 miles, or less in case of a headwind. The extra five gallons proved to be a necessity. Carl made the final check flight on July 9 and VP-JAZ passed with flying colors.

Wayne School of Aeronautics was full of activity the morning of July 9. In addition to our usual student flight activity, Carl and Earsly Barnett were busy preparing to start their arduous and potentially hazardous 2,600-mile flight to Kingston, Jamaica. It took considerable time and ingenuity to store a 10-day supply of baggage and equipment for two people in the tiny luggage compartment of the Cub. The ramp was soon crowded with well-wishers who came to see them off. Of course, there were doubters on hand who questioned the wisdom of the undertaking.

I gave them my own special hug and wished them godspeed. They boarded VP-JAZ as I climbed into blue-nosed Cub N6822H. After engine starts, we taxied in formation to runway 33. Taking off together we circled the field before heading southeast toward Cleveland. Passing over the Detroit River into Canada I flew close enough so we could trade hand signals and wave final goodbyes. After 20 minutes of formation flying I slowly turned away and headed back to City Airport. My eyes blurred with tears as the cream and green Cub "Jamerican" disappeared in the smog-covered horizon.

Returning to my office I sat by the phone like an expectant father waiting for a call from the hospital. They promised to call from Pittsburgh, where they would spend the night with Earsly's sister Henrene and her family. After what seemed an eternity, the Barnetts called me to say they had a nice flight to Pittsburgh and would be leaving the next morning for New York. With that anxiety off my mind I was finally able to relax and enjoy my first good meal of the day.

For the next two weeks I received a virtual travelogue of picture postcards from the flying Barnetts.

New York, July 11: My loving buddy; This is your Thursdays card. We felt like Arthur Godfrey landing at Teterboro. We ignored the turnpike and came directly over the mountains.

Brooklyn, N.Y.: All the Floissacs send their best. We will head for Baltimore Friday about noon to stop with U/Alan. The "Jamerican" is performing swell.

Baltimore, Md.: We are lost in the airport lobby looking for U/Alan but no can find. Arrived Baltimore at 1900, Friday.

Richmond, Va., July 12: Today we left Baltimore and my U/Alan. The weather is holding out and so is OUR Plane. Thundershowers a day away in Savannah. 4.6 gal/hour, speed about 70 MPH.

Jacksonville, Fla., July 13: Hello Elder Pilot; Our luck's holding out so well I'm fearing we will run out. Weather bad everywhere but where we are. Saw plane's shadow in rainbow for first time.

Miami, July 14: Hello Flash; At the speed that we have been traveling we are now in Miami. Tomorrow we see the Cuban Consul for clearance to land and proceed through Cuba before going to Key West.

Key West, Fla., July 15: Had to stay overnight in Key West—strong winds—Customs and immigration couldn't be hurried. Carl and Earse

Havana, Cuba, July 16: Hello buddy. We had a good crossing to Havana from 0845 to 1047. The Continental sounded like a Pratt & Whitney! But office to give us permission to continue through Cuba closed at 11:30 AM so we have to stay till 8:30 AM tomorrow in Havana.

Camaguey, Cuba, July 18, telegram: ARRIVED CAMAGUEY OK. ETA KINGSTON FRIDAY NOON.

Carl and Earsly's first landing in Jamaica was at Vernam Field, an abandoned U.S. Army Air Force base about 20 miles west of Kingston. They had run low on fuel and decided to land before the engine quit. The Barnett family and friends were assembled in the terminal at Palisadoes Airport in Kingston waiting anxiously for news as the scheduled arrival time of VP-JAZ passed without word of their whereabouts.

After a safe landing Carl walked down the country road until he found a telephone and called the tower at Palisadoes Airport. News of their arrival was relayed to the waiting Barnetts. An airplane was dispatched with extra fuel so that Carl and Earsly could continue their homeward flight. The return of Carl and his bride to Jamaica was a joyous occasion and duly celebrated in true Jamaican tradition. I received a phone call at my office from Carl and Earsly with the news of their successful flight and a question, "When are you coming to Jamaica?"

Before Earsly left Detroit I told her not to send me a pretty postcard from Jamaica with the usual words, "Having a wonderful time, wish you were here." I asked her to wait a few days and then send me a letter with a realistic description of Jamaica and its people. I received a nine-page letter from Earsly dated July 24 in which she described the daily life of the Barnett family in their home in Kingston. She also wrote about the limited flight activity of the few privately owned airplanes based at Palisadoes Airport. Both she and Carl had met with the local CAD regarding their plans to open a flight school with VP-JAZ. Earsly's letter also described the beauty of the lush tropical island and its people so well I knew I had to visit Jamaica as soon as possible.

Carl and Earsly's departure left an aching void in my life that I could not fill. With the advent of fall and the decreasing flight activity at Wayne School of Aeronautics I found myself flying the midget racer more often. It was one of the few ways I had of forgetting my loneliness. During one of these flights I decided to land at the airport in Windsor, Ontario, just across the river from Detroit.

While there I was invited to put on an impromptu air demonstration for Cec Raven, president of the Windsor Flying Club, and officials of the Department of Transportation. They were so impressed that they asked me to give a similar flight demonstration at the annual Windsor Air Show the next day. After I agreed they invited me to leave Loving's Love in their main hangar and promised transportation back to my home in Detroit. The next day I became quite a celebrity. My show in front of an enthusiastic Canadian audience was well received, especially since this was the first time a midget racer had been flown in their area. The fact I was a black, double-amputee pilot probably added to my audience appeal.

The air show was followed the same evening by an annual ball held in the main hangar. Talking to club officials after my flight demonstration at the air show I was surprised to be invited to attend as a guest of honor. With little time to lose, I drove home for a quick bath and change of clothes. Ardine came in just in time for me to tell her I was on my way to Windsor to attend the ball.

On entering the brightly lighted and decorated lobby I was greeted by Cec Raven, various club officers, and other guests. Within minutes a formally dressed waiter came over and asked my preference for a drink. As a dedicated pilot, I had avoided alcoholic drinks all my life, so I politely turned the waiter away. My Canadian hosts seemed to be offended and asked in hurt tones, "Are you one of those Americans who thinks he is too good to drink with his lowly Canadian cousins?" With the honor of the United States at stake, I relented. Being ignorant of liquor menu items, I asked the waiter to make a selection for me. His choice was a whiskey sour. From then on every time my glass was even slightly empty, he was there with a refill. One of the principal sponsors of the ball was the Hiram Walker Distilling Company and they were more than generous in supplying the liquor.

Seeking respite from my drinking companions I went into the main hangar where the lights were low and the dance band was playing soft, romantic music for the many guests, members, and friends of the Windsor Flying Club. My plan was to find a secluded corner where I could sit in peace and quiet. While my eyes were trying to adjust to the relative darkness I felt a heavy hand on my shoulder. One of the flight instructors whom I had met at the air show insisted I sit with him and his party. Trying to make the best of the situation I started talking airplanes and especially about Loving's Love, hoping to divert attention from the fact I was not drinking. My nearly empty glass caught their attention and I was invited to join them for the next round. When I tried to refuse they responded in hurt tones, "You were having drinks with the officers and guests out in the lobby. Does that mean you are too good to drink with us ordinary members?"

Once again my reputation was at stake. Once again I was back drinking whiskey sours. After waiting a decent interval, I reminded them I had a long drive home. I thanked my hosts and exited the back door of the hangar to avoid more invitations to drink.

With an unsteady gait, I stepped into the cool night air. It was obvious I was considerably less than sober for the first time in my life. The thought of being arrested for drunken driving, especially in a foreign country, was enough to scare me into some measure of sobriety. In spite of my apprehensions, the trip across the Ambassador Bridge and past the customs and immigration personnel was uneventful. The next morning Ardine insisted she heard me bounce against every wall in the house before I finally staggered into bed.

There was a steady flow of letters between the Barnett family and me. As Christmas approached they invited me to spend the holidays in Jamaica. Carl and Earsly knew how little flying activity there was at that time of year in Detroit and suggested it would be a wonderful opportunity to visit this largest and most beautiful of the Caribbean islands. Their logic was so persuasive I wasted no time in notifying all my students that the school would be closed from December 1 until my return from Jamaica. After arranging for the coverage of remaining school business during my absence I began to plan my Christmas vacation in paradise.

Having experienced the warm friendliness of Canada, I decided to fly to Jamaica via Trans-Canada Airlines. The first leg of my trip was a Douglas DC-3 flight from Windsor to Toronto on December 6, 1952. I was greeted at the airport by my friends Allen and Gail Martin, whom I had met after a flight demonstration with Loving's Love at Toronto Island Airport during the summer of 1952. Allen was a Trans-Canada employee and an expert freelance aerial photographer. When my flight demonstration was over, Allen arranged a flight in a Piper Tri-Pacer to take air-to-air shots of Loving's Love. Several weeks later I received a beautiful 16" × 20" black-and-white photo, framed and ready for hanging. This was one of the fringe benefits of flying a midget racer—the opportunity to make new and rewarding friendships. I enjoyed the Martins' hospitality until the early morning hours of my overnight visit. Although I was very tired from a long and busy day, I still had difficulty going to sleep. The prospect of being in Jamaica in less than 24 hours was so exciting I found it almost impossible to relax.

The weather was bitterly cold and ice crystals glistened on top of the red and white fuselage of the Trans-Canada Douglas DC-4M. As I walked cautiously up the boarding steps, a nattily uniformed stewardess greeted me and offered to take my heavy winter coat. Smiling, she explained, "I'll take your coat since you won't be needing it for a long time." Once again, it was difficult for me to realize that in a few hours I would be on the warm and sunny island of Jamaica.

The prevailing favorable exchange rate enabled me to travel first-class on Trans-Canada for the same price as coach class in the United States. Sitting in the luxury of the first-class section enjoying all the amenities I felt like pinching myself. Was this the same person who as a little boy had dreamed of riding in a Ford Trimotor? The distinctive sound of four 1,400-HP, 12-cylinder Rolls-Royce engines coming to life snapped me out of my reverie.

This was the only model of the Douglas DC-4 series using these engines, similar to those installed in the famed Spitfire and Hurricane fighter aircraft of World War II. Minutes after our on-time 11 A.M. takeoff, we were climbing through the cloud-laden skies heading south toward our first stop at Nassau in the Bahamas. During the five-hour flight the stewardesses offered all of the luxuries of first-class service: appetizers, predinner cocktails, wine with the three-course dinner, plus after-dinner liqueur. I tried to eat as much solid food as possible to counter the aftereffects of my second experience with alcohol. I rationalized my new behavior pattern with the knowledge I would not have to drive home.

Sitting in my window seat I watched the snow-covered plains and mountains give way to green fields as we reached the warmer climate of the Southern states. Our course took us east of the Atlantic shoreline, where the waters changed to the distinctive bluish-green color of the tropics. Out of this seemingly endless expanse of ocean a tiny speck of land appeared, followed by the pilot's voice advising of our approach to Nassau. As we taxied up to the terminal I couldn't believe my eyes as I saw people walking about in summer clothes. This was supposed to be wintertime! The warm tropical air and bright sun that greeted me as I stepped out of the cabin was unbelievable. Just five hours before I was in the frozen winter of Canada. Walking down the sidewalk to the terminal building I saw my first palm tree waving in the warm breeze. This, I said to myself, must be paradise. On entering the terminal I was offered a rum punch, courtesy of the local rum distilleries. While sipping my punch during the 30-minute visit in the airport lounge I realized that Nassau was only a sample of the wonderful things to come.

Airborne once again, we headed south on a course that took us over Cuba, then across the Caribbean to the north coast of Jamaica where we would start our letdown for Palisadoes Airport in Kingston.

By now the skies were dark except for the occasional twinkling lights of cities passing below. Only the stars lightened the skies. Soon the safety belt sign came on and the captain announced our arrival in

Kingston in 10 minutes. The lights of Kingston became visible on my left as the captain called our attention to the newly reopened and brightly lit Carib Theater. Ahead I could see the runway lights of Palisadoes Airport extending into the sheltered waters of Kingston Harbour. Out of the right window a small cluster of lights was identified as Port Royal, which had almost been destroyed by an earthquake some 200 years before. My excitement was almost unbearable as I thought of seeing Carl and Earsly for the first time in five months. Meeting the other members of the Barnett family, especially Clare and Felix whom I had met before in Detroit, was also sure to be a happy reunion.

The airliner turned suddenly quiet as we stopped at the gate and the engines were shut down. The passenger door opened to the warm tropical night and Trans-Canada station agent Dennis Campbell quickly boarded and walked directly to my seat, the first person to welcome me to Jamaica. He was a good friend of the Barnetts and offered to help me through the time-consuming process of clearing customs and immigration. With his assistance my tourist visa was soon issued and I was free to join my adopted Jamaican family. The guard waved me through the gate where I was immediately engulfed by the loving welcome of the Barnett family. Carl and Earsly gave me an enthusiastic embrace followed by an introduction to his father, known to everyone as Uncle Les. His full name was Leslie Arthur Barnett; his wife, Jeanne Alexandria Hannah Barnett, was Aunt Jeanne to all her family and friends. This was followed by my reunion with old friends Clare and Felix.

Carl rescued my luggage from the baggage claim area and loaded it into his new Ford Zephyr Six before we headed for home. As we drove down the narrow Palisadoes Road I began to worry when Carl stayed on the left side of the road. I panicked at the sight of approaching traffic, for I was sure we were about to have a head-on collision. But the cars went racing by unnoticed by anyone but me. I kept my fears to myself until I realized that driving on the left side of the road was a legacy of British Colonial rule.

The house was dark as we turned into the driveway of the Barnett home on Oakdene Avenue. Aunt Jeanne offered me an evening meal but due to the lateness of the hour and still sated from Trans-Canada's luxurious food service, I politely declined. But when she showed me her homemade Jamaican fruit salad I could not turn her down. It was far more flavorful than the bland canned fruit sold at home.

The next day was Monday, a working day for the Barnetts, and due to the lateness of the hour we agreed to go to bed and continue our celebration in the morning. I was shown to the guest bedroom where I quickly undressed and climbed into bed. My mind and body were so tired that even the excitement of being in Jamaica could not keep me awake for very long.

As the foggy remains of sleep left my body the next morning I began to have a sense of unreality. This was wintertime, how could I be hearing birds chirping outside my bedroom window? Raising myself up and looking out the open window I saw flowering bougainvillea, their red flowers brightened by the warm tropical sun. A beautiful bouquet of bright, colorful flowers was on the bedroom table. I thought of pinching myself to make sure I wasn't dreaming. Earsly's voice in the hallway calling me to breakfast assured me this was better than a dream. It was a wonderful reality.

CHAPTER THIRTEEN

IDLE MONTHS IN PARADISE

Getting out of bed, I was startled by the unfamiliar sounds and smells of my new surroundings. Warm sunlight streamed through the open windows and I could hear passersby talking as they walked in front of the house. Fragrance from the flowers in my bedroom joined with that of the colorful bougainvillea and poinsettias that almost touched my window. Putting my bathrobe on over my pajamas, I joined the Barnetts at the breakfast table.

Earsly had described the breakfast scene in the Barnett household in the second paragraph of her first and very informative letter to me:

> You will really enjoy meal times in this home. Breakfast is the only (slightly) disorderly meal. Clare and Fil leave home about 8:15–8:30 AM, Daddy leaves a little earlier when he is in town. Momma usually goes to Mass every morning before breakfast. This means that everyone is up early and taking turns in the bathroom, then eating in shifts. The maid and the cook are quite busy feeding the family as we come out, one by one, for breakfast (Carl and Earsly last, of course). There is not much time spent at breakfast as everyone must be about their daily work.

This was exactly the scene when I arrived in the dining room. All of the family was at the table except Carl, always a late sleeper. Aunt

Jeanne was sitting at her customary place at the head of the table where she served a plate for each family member. Uncle Les sat at her right, with Clare and Felix on the left side of the long, dark mahogany table. I was greeted warmly with a round of "Good mornings" from everyone and then introduced to Violet the cook, Irene the laundress, and Edgar the gardener. The first breakfast item was a plate of sliced paw-paw, which had the color and texture of cantaloupe but a totally different taste. I was glad Earsly was there to tell me about the new fruits and vegetables that I would experience at the dinner table. I was never quite sure what to do with them once they were on my plate. Should I sprinkle salt, or pepper, or sugar? Whatever they were, I looked forward to tasting exotic, tropical treats such as mango, calaloo, ackee, cho-cho, and more. But when Violet brought a plate of eggs and bacon to complete my breakfast, I felt like I was back home in Detroit.

Uncle Les and Aunt Jeanne welcomed me into their family like an adopted son. Uncle Les was not quite as tall as Carl, thicker around the waist, with a mustache and, appropriate for his age, a receding hairline. His voice was deep and authoritative, befitting his responsibility as superintendent of two Jamaica Public Service (JPS) hydroelectric stations on the north coast of Jamaica. He and Aunt Jeanne lived in a company-owned home near the little town of Lodge, not far from one of the hydroelectric stations located on the White River.

Every other Saturday they would drive into Kingston for the weekend, leaving again on Monday morning. Our visit this morning was cut short by their departure for Lodge but with the promise that I would be invited to accompany them on a future trip, which would provide me with the opportunity to sample life in the rural areas of Jamaica. Aunt Jeanne was a slender, attractive woman with a warm but regal air about her which prompted some of her family to call her "Lady J." Beneath that air of dignity was a sense of humor few could match. She could tease with such a serious look through her narrow-rimmed glasses, it was difficult for her victims to realize they were being harpooned until it was too late. I hugged her as I would my own mother before she left for the drive to Lodge, with the bright promise of seeing her again in two weeks.

Carl designed the Barnett home on Oakdene Avenue in Eden Gardens, Kingston, while he was still a civil engineering student in Detroit, and the house was completed in the summer of 1952. I had looked over his shoulder as he drew up the floor plan and was impressed by its unique features, especially the bathroom that was divided into separate compartments so that several people could use the facility at the same time and retain their privacy. After breakfast I took a bath, dressed in my latest style summer clothes, and came out of the bedroom ready to explore the house and its surroundings. By this time Carl had finished breakfast so I had a guided tour by the designer himself. We walked out to the front yard where the morning sun was drying the dew from the brilliantly colored flowers and shrubs. The "wet" season in Jamaica typically ends in late fall, adding to the lushness of the foliage in time for the Christmas season. This certainly wasn't like Christmas in Detroit. But there was obviously no sense of loss for Earsly; she said, "The only ice I want to see from now on is in my rum and Coke!"

The house was built with typical Jamaican construction materials, ivory-colored, stucco-like exterior walls and dark-red wooden shingles. There was a long verandah on the front of the house with three wide double doors entering the living room. Flowering shrubs lining the front of the verandah attracted various species of hummingbirds, including the famous "Doctor Bird," a national symbol of Jamaica. The male has a long black tail resembling the formal swallow-tail black dress jacket Jamaican medical doctors wore in years gone by.

When the family was away at work I would sit in a comfortable chair on the verandah for hours watching the birds, goats nibbling at weeds along the road, horse-drawn breadwagons, and pedestrians. In the evening the Barnetts would gather on the verandah to discuss the day's activities while watching the moon rise over Long Mountain directly ahead of us. During a full moon the sky was so bright we could even read a newspaper by "moonshine." One thing Earsly had commented on in her letter was the total lack of window or door screens. There were surprisingly few insects but almost every room had its resident lizards. They were small and harmless but it took me awhile to become accustomed to them for they were not known in Detroit.

Occasionally a "norther" would come streaming into Jamaica, lowering the temperatures to below the normal, midday 86° Fahrenheit reading. This happened early in December. The local newspaper, the *Gleaner,* headlined the event across the front page, "Cold Wave Strikes Jamaica. Temperature Drops to 76 at Midday!" I promptly cut this headline out of the paper and sent it to my family and aviation friends at Detroit City Airport. Nick Manteris posted it in his restaurant. As dramatic as it sounded, I don't think anyone suffering through Detroit's winter weather had any real sympathy for me.

One of the first social functions I attended in Kingston was a Christmas party given by the "Old Boys" (alumni) of St. George's College where Carl had completed his high school education. I met some of his childhood friends and enjoyed the humor and wit with which almost every Jamaican seems to be endowed. However, there were times I missed parts of conversations due to the fast-paced Jamaican accent. As an invited guest I tried to describe my difficulty as delicately as possible. "Jamaicans have a beautiful accent," I explained, "but I cannot always understand the words." One of the "Old Boys" smiled as he replied, "You are the one with the accent, not us. We are having trouble understanding you!" This put my American ego back in its proper place and from then on I tried to help them understand *my* accent.

Keeping up with the dialogue was often difficult at the Barnett dinner table as well, especially when Clare and her mother engaged in spirited conversation. On one occasion my puzzled look caused Uncle Les to lean toward me and whisper, "Don't feel ashamed, Neal. When those two start talking even I don't try to understand what is going on!" Aunt Jeanne was from Sierra Leone, West Africa, and had a combination Jamaican-African accent that was unique.

During the Christmas season I was introduced to two traditional Jamaican meals: curried goat and rice, and saltfish (salted cod) and ackee. Goat meat is standard fare—a spicy dish well seasoned with curry and hot Jamaican peppers served on a bed of white rice. I found a glass of rum and dry ginger ale helped cool off my tastebuds. Only tourists drank rum and Coke. Ackee is the fruit of the ackee tree and when cooked has a bland taste and strongly resembles scrambled eggs in appearance and texture. Saltfish and Jamaican peppers are added to the ackee and the result is what the Jamaicans refer to as "sawfish and ackee." Although ackee is found in the other Caribbean islands, only in Jamaica is it used as a food source. Sampling these native dishes was a continuing source of pleasure for me.

The one thing Jamaicans generally lacked was a decent-sized, healthy Christmas tree. The one at the Barnett house was so scrawny by American standards I didn't think a tree seller could give it away. But Clare, Earsly, and Aunt Jeanne did a wonderful job of decorating the tree with tinsel, green garlands, and tree ornaments. With all the Christmas gifts under the tree, and the glow of multicolored lights, the Barnetts (and I) were caught up in the joyous spirit of the season.

We attended midnight mass at Holy Trinity Cathedral near downtown Kingston and then went home for refreshments before going to bed. After breakfast we opened our gifts amid cries of excitement and words of thanks. The traditional Jamaican Christmas dinner was served shortly after midday, featuring ham and turkey plus the Jamaican fruits and vegetables I was now becoming accustomed to. For me, the highlight of the dinner was dessert, Aunt Jeanne's Christmas rum fruitcake. The aroma of white rum and port wine used in making the cake tempted my tastebuds even before the first bite. Each piece of cake was covered with a warm port wine and butter sauce. I left the dinner table basking in the warm glow of the Barnetts' Christmas hospitality, enhanced considerably by the rum in Aunt Jeanne's fruitcake.

My birthday on February 4 was celebrated with Jamaican-style birthday cake and gifts from each member of the family. Accompanying each gift was a short poem composed for the occasion. I don't remember the gift Earsly gave me but the poem she wrote was unforgettable and signed "By Earsly 'Joyce Kilmer' Barnett."

> To think that I should live to see
> A cho-cho growing in a lignum vitae tree.
> A tree in unfamiliar garb did dress

Against God's will to manifest
That poems are made by fools like thee
But only this fool would attempt a tree!

The inspiration for this "poem" came from an experience I had one day while outside admiring the garden. On seeing numerous cho-cho on the limbs of the lignum vitae tree I made the mistake of assuming that the tree produced cho-cho as a fruit. The second mistake was telling Earsly about it. She explained the lignum vitae is a hardwood tree and produces no fruit whatsoever. The cho-cho is related to the squash family and is a climbing vine. That story is now a permanent part of the Barnett family storytelling tradition.

Carl and Earsly formed Wings Jamaica, Ltd. (now the largest in the Caribbean), shortly after their arrival and began their operations out of Kingston's Palisadoes Airport. There were no office facilities available on the airport so they built their own one-room office and flight lounge. VP-JAZ was their only trainer and was kept quite busy taking young Jamaican men and women into the air for flight training. Carl wasted no time in getting me back into the cockpit for a local flight over Kingston and suburbs. The city of Kingston was built on Ligaunea Plain, which is as level as the plains of Kansas until it ends abruptly at the base of a mountain range. The ground suddenly rises to form numerous mountains including Blue Mountain Peak towering 7,500 feet above the sea shore only 20 miles away. I was awed by the height and shapes of the lush, green mountain ranges with their narrow winding roads passing through tiny villages.

As I gently banked VP-JAZ into a 180-degree turn we headed back toward the quiet, blue-green waters of Kingston Harbour and Palisadoes Airport runway jutting into the harbor like an aircraft carrier. As we circled for our landing, the white-capped ocean waves of the Caribbean appeared to stretch out to the crystal-clear horizon. The thought came, "This must be Shangri-La!"

With my check flight completed, I was now ready to demonstrate my flying skills to Clare. She had a new pair of yellow slacks, which were appropriate when entering the awkwardly placed front seat of a Piper Cub. With clearance from the tower I taxied out to the runway full of confidence that this would be a perfect flight and enhance my reputation as a skilled "elder pilot." The wind was light and the temperature and visibility typical of a beautiful day in Jamaica. We flew over sights she was familiar with, especially her home on Oakdene Avenue. Clare was able to point out some of the landmarks in Kingston that were unfamiliar to me.

After about 40 minutes of flying I headed back to the airport promising myself to make a smooth, airliner-style landing with the hope of making a favorable impression on my passenger. The tower flashed a green light, giving me clearance to land. There was no other traffic to distract me as I flew my best traffic pattern and lined up on final approach to the runway. As I slowed the Cub to proper glide speed, my ego assured me this would be a perfect landing. Passing over the airport boundary I slowly pulled back the stick until the attitude was correct for a three-point landing. My complacence was shattered abruptly when the Cub struck the ground and careened disgracefully high. Frantically coordinating stick and throttle movements I tried landing a second time, resulting in an even higher bounce. By now Clare was laughing at my efforts and started counting my series of landings loud enough for me to hear. "That's one," she counted, ". . . that's two . . . that's three." I finally gave up and let the Cub bounce on its own until it ran out of energy. This proved the old adage "Pride goeth before a fall."

Shortly after New Year's Day 1953, Uncle Les called to invite me to his home on the north coast near the town of Lodge. Since no public transportation was available, Carl agreed to take time off from his job at Jamaica Public Service for the drive. It didn't take me long to pack my luggage and load it into Carl's Ford so we could be on our way. Heading westward on Spanish Town Road we dodged donkey carts and goats grazing off and on the narrow highway. We passed by sugarcane fields and roadside stands selling everything from tropical fruit and vegetables to hot and spicy jerk pork. The road to Spanish

Town was the only level stretch of road on our way to the north coast. After passing through Spanish Town (the capital of Jamaica under Spanish rule) we drove over the ancient Flat Bridge spanning the Rio Cobre River.

Following the curves of the river we passed the abandoned JPS hydroelectric station at Bog Walk where Uncle Les worked many years ago, prior to the construction of the new station at Lodge. Driving through the town of Moneague we left the river and started our long and tortuous climbs and descents over the several mountain ranges that lay between Kingston and the north coast. The straight-line distance to Lodge is only 35 miles; by road it is 64 miles, a long and sometimes spectacular $3\frac{1}{2}$-hour drive. As we followed the twisting, narrow roads I became concerned that the road wasn't wide enough for two cars to safely pass, much less the trucks and buses that honked incessantly to warn of their approach. To relieve my worries, Carl stopped the car and measured the road width with his civil engineer's tape measure. Technically he was correct but it still bothered me when we had to pass on the outside edge of the road which usually dropped precipitously to the valley below. I was to learn that portions of the road were aptly known as "Devil's Race Course"!

The village of Lodge (not far from a town named Hand-to-Mouth) consisted of five unpainted, ramshackle buildings housing all the local businesses at a single road intersection. The stores had large, barn-like doors that were open during business hours and closed up at night. There were few, if any, windows in these buildings. A few minutes later we drove up a steep hill leading to the Barnett home. Aunt Jeanne prepared lunch for us followed by a tour of the hydroelectric plant by Uncle Les who was respectfully known to his employees and the villagers as "Mistah B."

Returning to the house, we sat on the front verandah sipping rum and coconut water while admiring the bright green of the valley below and the coconut and banana trees growing on the slopes of mountains across the valley. There were few signs of civilization to spoil the natural beauty. On moonless nights, the black void of earth brought out countless, brilliant stars, forming galaxies that filled the sky. This was unspoiled tropical beauty at its best.

On the Saturdays when they were at Lodge, the Barnetts drove through the nearby town of Ocho Rios, past the rust-colored aluminum ore loading docks, to St. Anne's Bay, a fairly large north-coast town. Uncle Les would take care of his payroll account at the local bank while Aunt Jeanne shopped for groceries, fruits, and vegetables. The local open-air markets were filled with local farmers selling fresh produce. No fresh meat was sold due to lack of refrigeration. I especially enjoyed listening to the country Jamaican dialect (different from Kingston) although it was almost totally incomprehensible to me. The pungent aroma of Jamaican spices mingling with those of ripe oranges, bananas, and mangoes was a treat to the senses. I was usually ravenously hungry by the time we arrived home for lunch.

My Christmas vacation in Jamaica was now continuing into the spring months; I was reluctant to leave my tropical paradise. But I could not ignore the realities of earning a living since Wayne School of Aeronautics remained closed until my return.

It was with mixed emotions that I went to the Trans-Canada ticket office and made reservations to return home on April 25. My remaining vacation time in Jamaica was filled with trips to Mandeville, Montego Bay, and St. Thomas, to experience as much of Jamaica's mountainous beauty as possible before returning to Detroit where the highest things to be seen were downtown office buildings.

The Barnett family accompanied me to the airport where my farewells were tinged with sadness, quite different from the joys of my arrival. It was with sincerity that I used the German expression "Auf Wiedersehen" ('til we meet again) in my farewell. On the plane, I watched the familiar sights of Kingston disappear as Trans-Canada's DC-4M climbed through the ever-present clouds over the mountains and headed north to Nassau and Toronto.

Reopening Wayne School of Aeronautics for business kept me so busy I had little time to miss my Jamaican family. Notifications had to be sent out to all students, unpaid bills taken care of, and airplanes inspected and made ready for flight. It was May 16 before I test-flew Piper Cub N6822H and turned it over to a waiting student pilot. Luscombe N45436 and Stinson N8607K were also placed on the flight line and Wayne School of Aeronautics was again ready for business.

With the pent-up rush of flying activity it was June 4 before I was able to return to Wayne Major Airport and take to the air in Loving's Love. This was one of the few things I truly missed during my long stay in Jamaica.

Shortly after my return to Detroit, I received a very formal-looking letter from Jamaica with Aunt Jeanne's return address on the envelope. In it was a business-style statement that read:

> To: Mr. Neal Loving
> Wayne School of Aeronautics
> Detroit, Michigan
> DR. TO Mrs. L. A. Barnett 25 June 1953
> Lodge P.O. Jamaica, B.W.I.
> For: Board and Lodgings, Car Drives, Tea Served in Bed, Storage of Rubbish, Personal Secretarial Services, Destroyed Mail Left Behind, Pains Endured During Your Stay Caused By Having You Around, Wear and Tear on the Bed, Food, Fruits, and Water Consumed, Total $1000.00.

I sent her a check for 15 cents to cover postage and asked for a more detailed, itemized account. Aunt Jeanne's sense of humor was equal to the occasion: I never received another bill. I still treasure this document as an example of her never-ending sense of humor.

During the summer of 1951 Paul Poberezny and a group of his friends met in the basement of Paul's Milwaukee home to finalize the organizational rules of the newly formed Experimental Aircraft Association (EAA). The purpose of the EAA was to unify all amateur aircraft builders into a single organization with sufficient power to influence the CAA into creating regulations that would legitimize and broaden their activities. Experimental aircraft such as my midget racer were subject to restrictions that limited their use for general flying. As a result of EAA efforts, the CAA created the Amateur-Built Aircraft category, making it possible for homebuilt aircraft to fly with the same freedom as factory-built aircraft, except for commercial operation. N351C was one of the first to be licensed in this new category. However, in the summer of 1953, I was still unaware of the EAA and was surprised to discover many years later that I had influenced some of the rules instituted by the EAA in 1951. In his book *This Is EAA,* Duane Cole, a member of the famous Cole Brothers aerobatic team, recounts a portion of one of those early meetings:

> They solidified and voted into the bylaws many of the policies we had formulated in the original group. For instance, from the very first, we had agreed that no one could be excluded because of race, color, or religion. The issue had come up in our first meeting in 1951, while we were discussing other sportsman pilots and homebuilders to whom we would extend an invitation to join if we ever began an expansion program. I was beating the drums for Neal Loving, a friend of Marion's and mine from Detroit. Neal ran a flight school at the Detroit City Airport where in off hours he designed and built a nifty little gull wing racer. The workmanship on "Loving's Love," as it was called, was superb. But I guess the main reason for wanting him in the club besides his ability to design and build was that he was a heck of a nice guy.
>
> At first, when someone said they had heard that he was black, then asked if it were true, I got a little hot. However, when I realized that the question had not been asked derogatorily, I was glad it came up. It gave us the opportunity to establish from the very beginning a unanimous belief that no man is better than another because of the color of his skin or the church he attends.

I was to meet Paul Poberezny in November 1953.

Ever since my return to Detroit, the thought of going back to Jamaica was never far from my mind. After sorting through several possibilities, I decided to emulate Carl and Earsly's pioneering flight in 1952 by flying Loving's Love from Detroit to Jamaica. When I told my friends of my intentions the reactions were the same as when I planned my first test flight in August 1950. All the sensible reasons why I shouldn't try my Jamaican flight were emphasized. N351C was a racer, not a cross-country airplane; it had no shock absorbers and landing speeds were near 70 MPH. The round-trip flight would require almost 800 miles of overwater flying where a forced landing was almost sure to be fatal.

Loving's Love now had over 100 hours of flying time and, except for spinner problems at racing speeds, had no problems whatsoever. The 2,200-mile flight to Kingston should take no more than 17 flying hours and there was no reason to believe my trusty Continental engine would quit just because I was over water.

Full of confidence, I contacted the Foreign Flight Planning Office of the Aircraft Owners and Pilots Association (AOPA), asking their assistance in obtaining clearances to fly over Cuba and into Jamaica. In response to my request, Lillian B. Wall, AOPA Flight Service, in her letter dated November 10, 1953, provided the requested flight information, and recommended a company that would rent flotation gear (such as a "Mae West" jacket), shark repellent, and other emergency equipment for an overwater flight. It was already my intention to wear a parachute. The grim prospects of ditching in the ocean were firmly impressed on my mind as I went ahead with my plans for a scheduled departure on December 1, 1953.

In mid-November 1953, a gentleman came into my office and introduced himself as Paul Poberezny. He was a big, genial, easily likable man, obviously filled with enthusiasm when he spoke of the aims and objectives of the Experimental Aircraft Association. I had not heard of the EAA before and was happy to know that other people were as interested in building airplanes as I was. Before he left my office I promised to join his organization without delay. Fulfilling my promise I became EAA member #522. He described our meeting in his monthly column, "Homebuilders Corner," in the December 1953 issue of the EAA magazine *Experimenter.*

I'm here again with more news and gossip about who is doing what. I took a short week-end trip over to Windsor-Ontario, Canada and talked to PAUL OLESIK at the Windsor Airport. He is of the opinion that you fellows over in the United States are very fortunate in being allowed to build aircraft, as they are not allowed to over in Canada. He had hopes of building a Loving Special designed by NEAL LOVING of Detroit.

On my return from Windsor, I stopped at City Airport in Detroit and had a fine talk with NEAL LOVING, designer and builder of the Loving Special which many of you have seen at the air races in Detroit and in aviation magazines. It is a low wing inverted gull wing, all wood construction, combination race-sport plane. In fact, NEAL is leaving for Jamaica with it, a distance of 2200 miles from Detroit, the first week in December. NEAL feels that the organization will be a great success as long as it is kept from being absorbed by a strictly professional group, it will be the backbone of general aviation, and I might add that when an organization gets too big for its britches it is on its way out—so let's make sure it doesn't happen to the EAA.

Continuing preparations for my Jamaica flight, I purchased a full set of sectional and world aeronautical charts (WAC) as recommended by the AOPA Flight Planning Service for my entire route from Detroit to Kingston. Remembering my difficulties in unfolding my maps on my flight to Chicago, I laid out segments of my course to Kingston and trimmed the border to 10 miles each side of my intended track. After fastening the various map sections together with transparent tape I rolled my completely mapped course (almost 10 feet long) over a cardboard tube; when completed it resembled a roll of toilet paper. Even in the cramped confines of Loving's Love I could locate my position on the map at any time. If I were to stray more than 10 miles off course I had a supply of WAC charts to cover the additional area. With this problem solved I had only one major remaining concern. My pilot rating was restricted to visual flight rules (VFR), which required that I remain in constant visual reference to the horizon or ground. However, it was possible during flights over large expanses of water out of sight of land that the horizon could disappear in light fog or haze. Without proper training and equipment, a VFR pilot, without a doubt, would suffer complete loss of control within seconds. With this in mind I installed a venturi-operated turn and bank indicator to provide an in-cockpit visual reference. On November 23, I went up in the midget to practice straight and level flight and procedure turns, using only the turn and bank indicator, airspeed, and altimeter for reference. This I hoped was sufficient preparation in case I ran into haze or clouds while flying over the Caribbean. After a 45-minute practice flight I was sure I could make a 180-degree turn and return to my point of departure if such conditions blocked my flight path. With newly acquired confidence I looked forward to my flight to Jamaica but remained keenly aware that unforeseen hazards could arise to compromise my personal safety.

One logistics problem that remained to be solved was how to get my long-term luggage to Jamaica. I had added a small baggage compartment behind the pilot's seat, which was the same size as the box the laundry used to pack my dress shirts. This box became my only on-board luggage, which I reinforced with tape and string to hold essential items needed during the long flight to Jamaica. My cousin Bernadine Garner volunteered to send my larger pieces of luggage to Kingston by air freight. With all preparations complete, I notified all my flight students that Wayne School of Aeronautics would be closed on December 1 and prayed the weather would be favorable for my departure. But Detroit weather is unpredictable during the winter months and my carefully laid plans were almost thwarted.

CHAPTER FOURTEEN

RETURNING TO JAMAICA

The normal weather pattern for the Detroit area during the late fall season is characterized by a number of cold fronts sweeping south out of Canada. These fronts are usually accompanied by clear visibilities and northerly winds, ideal conditions for my flight to the Caribbean. My plan called for an early morning start from Detroit with stops at Lexington, Kentucky, and Chattanooga, Tennessee, before reaching Atlanta, Georgia, for an overnight stop.

Waking up the morning of my planned departure, December 1, and looking out my bedroom window, I could see the weather was just the opposite of what I had hoped for. A light misty rain was falling, with low ceilings and limited visibilities. A warm front had passed through the Detroit area, bringing warm, moist air and southerly winds out of the Gulf of Mexico. Flying in such conditions in a high-performance racing airplane like Loving's Love would not only be illegal but possibly suicidal as well.

Giving up hope of keeping to my early morning schedule I drove to my cousin Bernadine's house with my considerable luggage needed for an extended stay in Kingston. After deciding on the date of shipment, we sat in the living room and talked of the joys and hazards of my solo flight to Jamaica. She, along with many others, was concerned about my safety. I tried to allay her fears evident by the tears in her eyes.

After doing my best to cheer her up I said goodbye to my sad cousin and walked out into the light drizzle to my car. I had a leisurely breakfast at the airport restaurant before visiting the weather office for their latest forecast. They predicted the weather would improve by early afternoon so I made preparations to leave as soon as possible, hoping to reach Lexington before sunset. My original goal of reaching Atlanta was clearly out of the question.

My good friend and current CFI at Wayne School of Aeronautics, Carl McKay, borrowed a Commonwealth Sky Ranger two-seater and flew me over to Wayne Major Airport where my little racer was gassed up and ready to go. As the sun peeked through the clouds, I called the weather office again. Their report indicated I would encounter improving but not particularly good weather farther south. Cincinnati was reporting a 1,200-foot ceiling and three miles visibility, while Lexington had a 1,500-foot ceiling with four miles visibility in smoke and haze. The conditions were above minimums for visual flight rules (VFR) so I crammed my shirtbox luggage into the small compartment behind the seat and climbed aboard. Settling into the cockpit with a parachute, Mae West vest, shark repellent, marker dye, and other emergency equipment was even more difficult than usual. After handing me my maps, camera, and sundry items, Carl was finally able to tuck me in and put the canopy over my head. It was 2 P.M. when the Continental snapped to life. After a final wave to Carl, I taxied out for the beginning of my 4,800-mile round trip to Jamaica.

LOGBOOK ENTRY: December 1, 1953
Detroit—Cincinnati, 220 miles, flight time, 1.92 hours.

I taxied down runway 24 to runway 15 where the tower gave me the welcome words, "Midget 64, you are cleared for takeoff and a right turn to the south as requested." Eagerly pushing the throttle forward I watched the runway markers racing by and, easing the stick back, climbed toward the base of the low-hanging clouds. Leveling off at 2,500 feet, I made a gentle turn to the right and headed toward haze-veiled Toledo. I was still squirming and tugging, trying to get all the loose and sundry items stowed in their proper places. Toledo slid by quickly but the horizon ahead was obscured by haze and cloud bases now down to 1,300 feet. This was certainly not the good ceiling or visibility I had hoped for.

Vandalia Airport, Dayton, came into view on my right, its runways bathed in a brilliant patch of sunlight. Circling gracefully overhead was a USAF C-119 cargo transport, its broad aluminum wings reflecting the sun's rays like a gigantic mirror. A slight correction to the right put me on course for Cincinnati, which appeared shortly like a blob of black smoke on an otherwise gray and featureless horizon.

The time was now 4:15 P.M. with 83 miles to go. Sunset was about 5:00 P.M. and I was still fighting the headwind coming out of the south, which reduced my groundspeed and narrowed the margin for error.

As I crossed the Ohio River, the valleys of Kentucky's famed bluegrass country began to disappear in patches of fog. If Lexington turned out to be below minimums on my arrival I would not have enough time to get back to Cincinnati before dark. Unaware of making a conscious decision, I made a gentle 180-degree turn back toward Lunken Airport in Cincinnati. The tower promptly called and gave me clearance to land. I taxied up to Queen City Air Service where a helpful mechanic assisted in removing my canopy. Reaching for the buckle to release my safety belt/shoulder harness I discovered to my embarrassment that in my hurry to leave Detroit I had not fastened it. This, I said to myself, is not a good way to start a 4,800-mile flight.

LOGBOOK ENTRY: December 2, 1953
Cincinnati—Lexington, 103 miles, flight time, 0.93 hours.

After an overnight visit with friends, I returned to Lunken Airport where Loving's Love was the center of attention. After answering as many questions as I could while gassing up, I climbed into the cockpit with the usual battle of trying to put everything in its place. The mechanic then helped me with the canopy and I was ready to go. After I started the engine I began looking for my map to Lexington. Feeling foolish not being able to find it, I shut off the engine, removed the canopy, and climbed out. I could not think of an intelligent excuse to offer on finding I had been sitting on it. That was the second dumb thing I had done, and I was still only 220 miles from home!

Getting started again, I confidently aimed the nose of Loving's Love across the bluegrass hills of Kentucky toward my first stop at Chattanooga. My aura of well-being lasted until I noticed none of my preestablished checkpoints were coming into view. After another 180-degree turn back to Lunken Airport, I checked my magnetic compass heading with the runway headings and found my compass was off about 15 degrees. I decided that maybe my habit of hanging my earphones over the stick in close proximity to the compass was causing compass error. Taking no further chances I followed the railroad and highway from Covington, Kentucky, to Lexington.

Having wasted so much time at Lunken Airport in Cincinnati I decided to stop in Lexington and stay overnight with Ernest "Cheeko" Bush of Bluegrass Airmotive. Cheeko was a pioneering black commercial pilot in the South whom I had not yet met. After our initial meeting he invited me to dinner where we discussed our mutual problems and interests as black pilots in the all-white world of aviation. We had many things in common.

The next day we were at the airport to solve my compass problem. Placing the midget on the compass rose located behind the hangar we were able to make the proper corrections. By the time we finished this time-consuming task the weather was so bad I had to postpone my departure.

On December 5 the weather was good enough for a local 20-minute test flight and a "buzz job" as requested by the Bluegrass Airport tower. The continued bad weather prompted me to send a telegram to the Barnetts in Kingston, "DELAYED BY BAD WEATHER AND GOOD FRIENDS. ETA NOW FRIDAY 10 DECEMBER. WILL CABLE."

LOGBOOK ENTRY: December 7, 1953
Lexington—Knoxville, 163 miles, flight time, 1.83 hours.

The terrain around Detroit was generally flat and marked with neat, orderly north-south and east-west section lines. Flying a correct heading using these patterns as a reference was comparatively easy. But I soon found that mountain flying required a new set of skills. I had planned to head for Chattanooga and then Atlanta, but the narrow roads winding through the Cumberland Mountains were of no help to my "flat land" navigational skills. I still did not have full confidence in my compass and winds aloft were unpredictable. Trying unsuccessfully to hold a steady heading in the bumpy air, I became lost over rugged mountain terrain. After several agonizing minutes I identified the strange city ahead as Knoxville. With a sense of relief I decided to land and refuel. I also wanted to get rid of my bulky winter flying jacket that was causing me to perspire profusely. Altering my course, I began my descent toward the comforting sight of the runways at Knoxville Airport. With confidence renewed, I entered the traffic pattern and was soon taxiing up to the terminal.

My shame at getting lost was somewhat alleviated when I heard many compliments paid to the sleek, racy lines of my Love. Not wanting to carry my winter flying jacket all the way to Jamaica, I asked a mechanic who was admiring my racer to put my jacket in a suitable box and send it to Bernadine in Detroit. After giving him five dollars for his troubles, I gassed up and took off for Chattanooga.

LOGBOOK ENTRY: December 7, 1953
Knoxville—Chattanooga, 90 miles, flight time, 0.75 hours.

The Appalachian Mountains run generally in a southwesterly-northeasterly direction that was almost parallel to my new course. By keeping this mountain range on my right and following the Cumberland River, I made it to Chattanooga's Lovell Field quickly and easily. Lovell Field was the site of the Tennessee Cup Race in 1951, which I was unable to attend. It was surprising the number of people who recognized me and the Love from the pictures and publicity that had appeared in the Chattanooga newspapers. It was a pleasant experience meeting these aviation enthusiasts with whom I could share my interest in air racing. We talked about past races and speculated on what my fortunes might have been had I been able to compete. Contrary to my initial misgivings, I found I was accepted as a member of the racing fraternity without regard for my color, even in the South. I spent so much time in Chattanooga I abandoned plans to reach Macon, Georgia, that night. Instead, I took off for Atlanta into the typical southerly headwinds.

LOGBOOK ENTRY: December 7, 1953
Chattanooga—Atlanta, 120 miles, flight time, 0.83 hours.

I was now gaining confidence in my compass accuracy and comfortable enough flying over mountainous terrain to relax and enjoy the scenery. Atlanta Airport appeared straight ahead on schedule so there was ample time to plan my approach. Entering the traffic pattern on downwind leg, I looked in vain for a sign of recognition from the tower. Midget racers were rarely seen outside of airshow events so I must have taken them by surprise. After circling several times I decided to land on runway 21, following a departing twin-engine Beechcraft.

On reaching the hangar for transient aircraft I called the tower by phone to apologize for my unauthorized landing. Instead, they greeted me with profuse apologies for their own lack of vigilance. With a sense of relief I went back to my racer to find it had been moved to a prominent spot in the hangar surrounded by plush executive aircraft. The office call board requested special protection be given N351C to prevent damage by a constant crowd of spectators. Feeling it was in good hands, I took a cab into town where I spent the night at the newly opened Waluhaje Apartments. It was somewhat embarrassing when the smartly uniformed bellboy offered to carry my grubby tape- and twine-covered shirtbox luggage to my room.

LOGBOOK ENTRY: December 8, 1953
Atlanta—Macon, 98 miles, flight time, 0.75 hours.

I had an early morning breakfast to allow a full day for my flight to Miami, with a stop in Jacksonville. When I checked out of my apartment, the desk clerk called a black cab company and I was soon on my way to the airport. As we neared the airport the driver turned onto the road leading to the airline terminal; I asked him to take the one leading to the general aviation side of the field. Obviously surprised, he asked, "Do you fly one of those little airplanes?" When I said yes, he continued, "What kind of airplane are you flying, one of those Piper Cubs?" "No" I replied, "I built it myself." His skepticism was evident as he went on, "Where did you get the blueprints?" When I informed him I was also the designer and builder he looked at me in complete disbelief.

Arriving at the parking lot in the back of the hangar I invited him to come see my airplane. We walked around the corner of the hangar, where I was surprised to find my racer was not where it had been parked the night before. Seeing my puzzled look, the cabbie asked sarcastically, "What's the matter, boss, can't you find your airplane?"

A crowd of people had formed a large circle out on the ramp. I suggested to the cabbie, "Maybe my airplane is behind those people." "You mean to tell me your airplane is hiding behind those people?" he asked in obvious, total disbelief. Without answering I walked toward the crowd. As I drew near, the mechanic who had parked my airplane the night before recognized me and announced to the waiting crowd, "This is Mr. Loving who designed and built this beautiful racer." As he spoke, the people stepped back and there was Loving's Love (only four feet high) glistening in the morning sun. The bewildered cabdriver left, still shaking his head in disbelief. As he disappeared around the corner of the hangar I wondered what his reaction might have been if he knew I was a double amputee on my way to Jamaica!

When I went to the office to pay my hangar bill, the secretary was unable to find a standard hangar fee for my airplane on her rate chart and called the owner/manager to set the price. In a typical Southern drawl, he told me how proud he was to have my airplane in his hangar and no payment would be accepted now or if I returned anytime. I was pleasantly surprised by this act of hospitality, which went a long way in changing my own racist image of the South.

I called the tower for takeoff clearance, which was promptly granted. Despite the busy airline traffic the tower asked for a buzz job down the active runway. In the air once more I headed for Jacksonville. This area of the South was a veritable paradise for pilots as there were dozens of abandoned military fields available for forced landings.

Once I reached cruise altitude my legs began to hurt so much from extended periods of standing I decided to attempt to take my artificial limbs off to relieve the pain. Much to my relief I managed to remove them and place my stumps on top of my artificial legs. Pushing my artificial legs by hand provided adequate rudder control. The disquieting thought of bailing out in my parachute came to mind but my high comfort level made me willing to take that risk. In fact, I made a practice of taking them off on almost every flight thereafter. What would the CAA say if they knew? The little racer, however, did perform some very erratic maneuvers whenever I inadvertently touched the stick while awkwardly putting them on again.

Now relatively free of pain, I turned my attention to the clouds beginning to form ahead of me. Soon the lowering cloud bases forced me to descend to an altitude of only 1,300 feet. Although I was now over reasonably flat terrain, I decided to land at Macon, Georgia, to check with the weather office. The forecaster promised the clouds would dissipate by early afternoon. This was good news indeed!

LOGBOOK ENTRY: December 8, 1953
Macon—Jacksonville, 190 miles, flight time, 1.75 hours.

Navigating to Jacksonville was quite easy by following the main highway winding its way through the beautiful but ominous Okefenokee Swamps. The thought of a forced landing in these lush wetlands was as disturbing as it was over the mountains. Continuing on, I landed in Jacksonville in CAVU (ceiling and visibility unlimited) weather after fighting brisk headwinds all the way. As I taxied up to the terminal people came out in such large numbers I thought there must be a fire. As the crowd formed around me, one of the onlookers said tower personnel had alerted the flight operators to the impending arrival of my gull-winged racer. Again the barrage of questions from a growing audience delayed my plans for a quick takeoff. This extended period of standing made my legs hurt more than ever.

LOGBOOK ENTRY: December 8, 1953
Jacksonville—Ft. Lauderdale, 330 miles, flight time, 2.5 hrs.

Miami was 330 miles distant and sunset only three hours away. If the headwinds continued during this last leg of the day, it would be near dark before I arrived. N351C was not equipped for night flying. After a snack at the airport restaurant I headed for the Love, brushing off the customary questions as courteously as I could. Fueling had already been completed. I was airborne in minutes on the longest single flight of my journey so far. My only diversions were skirting scattered rain showers and squirming in the cramped cockpit to relieve a nagging backache. After a flight of over 2 hours, the runways of Broward International Airport appeared dead ahead as a beautiful rainbow arced across my left wing and a shaft of brilliant sunlight broke through the broken clouds, creating a perfect ending to a perfect day. Taxiing up to the Sunny South Air Service hangar amid the usual curious crowd I felt I knew why a person like me would build a racing airplane. There was no rational, practical justification for the time, expense, and risk involved. But the unique satisfaction derived from creating and flying one's own airplane cannot be obtained on lesser, more mundane terms.

LOGBOOK ENTRY: December 10, 1953
Ft. Lauderdale—Havana, 265 miles, flight time, 1.83 hours.

It took two days in Miami to iron out all the red tape associated with international flight. As a member of the Aircraft Owners and Pilots Association (AOPA) #99852, I made use of their Flight Planning Service, which provided a list of suggested contacts in Miami with special emphasis on the U.S. Custom and Immigration Service (CIS). My concern was due to the lack of a transmitter in my midget racer, which prohibited me from arriving or departing from Miami International Airport where all government services were available 24 hours a day. Broward Airport lacked these facilities. After several phone calls I discovered the local CIS was located at nearby Hollywood, Florida, where they served the boat traffic in that area. F. W. Raggett, Sr. (CIS), informed me that there was no problem with my taking off from Broward but I was given strict procedures to follow on my return. He suggested that when filing my flight plan in Havana I request them to advise Miami Approach Control of my intended arrival at Broward International Airport (instead of Miami) and notify customs and immigration authorities there.

Loving's Love did not have sufficient fuel to fly to Havana and return to Miami nonstop. This was a serious concern, in the event that I couldn't land in Havana and had to return to Miami. The AOPA had warned me of potentially poor runway conditions at both Havana and Camaguey, Cuba, which might damage the midget on landing. Logic dictated I locate an alternate airport. I called the U.S. Naval Station at Key West to ask if I could make an emergency landing there. The naval officer I spoke with was very understanding and said although he could not authorize my landing in advance I would be welcome if an emergency arose. However, he warned, the runways were made of sharp coral and were comparatively short. I decided landing at that alternate airport where help was available was infinitely better than ditching in shark-infested waters.

Red tape now out of the way, I checked the weather along my route to Havana. The forecast was for good weather except scattered showers. After giving N351C an extra-thorough preflight inspection I took off, climbing rapidly into the sunny Florida skies. I accommodated the tower's request for a buzz job and headed for Havana in accordance with my VFR flight plan. I proceeded on a south-southwesterly course, keeping the Florida Keys in sight, which curved in front of me like an inviting finger.

Flying over the naval station at Key West I checked my compass with the runway heading and proceeded out over the open water. I was surprised that I did not experience the worries the experts told me to expect when flying out of sight of land in a single-engine airplane for the first time. Flying over open waters, engines were always supposed to develop imaginary sounds of trouble called "automatic rough." Instead I was fascinated by the varying patterns and shades of water which produced a mosaic of color and shadow.

Worries did arise as the forecasted showers blocked my path to Havana. It was necessary to drop well below the 10,000-foot cruising altitude I had promised everyone I would maintain over open water. From that high altitude, they told me, on a clear day I should be able to see Havana from Miami. I managed to maintain my course in spite of dodging rainstorms along the way. Halfway across the open water I spotted a Douglas DC-3 high above me headed in the opposite direction. If it was Miami-bound I was on course. True enough, after several false impressions of landfall caused by cloud shadows on the water, Havana came into view, slightly to the left of the long nose of the Love. Staying to the east of Havana to avoid prohibited areas, I circled Rancho Boyeros Airport looking for rough spots on the runway. After deciding to land beyond the normal touchdown area, I made a smooth landing and taxied up to the terminal building. A mass of excited Cubans came out to greet me in a torrent of completely unfamiliar Cuban Spanish.

Climbing out of the cockpit, perspiring freely, I heard the sound of a familiar American "Hello" with a Cuban accent. It was Mr. De la Cal, a broker who specialized in filling out the myriad Cuban immigration and customs forms required of arriving American pilots. Approvals for nine separate clearances from as many Cuban agencies were needed. I considered it a bargain when Mr. De la Cal charged only five dollars for completing an incredibly intimidating array of Cuban forms.

LOGBOOK ENTRY: December 10, 1953
Havana—Camaguey, 330 miles, flight time, 2.33 hours.

It was now 1:30 P.M. and Camaguey was 330 miles away. I was still fighting the southerly headwinds and once again faced the possibility of not being able to return to my point of departure in Havana should the weather or runway conditions prohibit a landing in Camaguey. The only available alternate airport was Cienfuegos, where the runways were too rough and short for a safe landing in the midget.

But risks were an inherent part of this venture so after filing a VFR flight plan I took off into the prevailing southeasterly headwinds shortly after 2 P.M. Climbing to 3,000 feet I could see the mountain-studded south coast of Cuba paralleling my course. Below, the flat, green farmlands stretched eastward while to the south were deep-green swamps reminiscent of Florida. Each little red-tile-roofed Cuban town stood out distinctly in clear sunshine untainted by urban smog. Passing over the town of Cienfeugos, I could see a range of green, lush mountains to the south.

The steady, even beat from the short exhaust stacks on my faithful Continental engine was very reassuring against the contrasting thoughts of being forced to bail out over such strange and desolate country. Looking behind toward the setting sun, I eased the throttle forward to compensate for the increasing headwinds. Soon the mountains dwindled into flat sugarcane fields and a quick navigational check indicated I had only 15 minutes flying time before arriving in Camaguey.

I had checked the sunset hour with the Havana forecaster and knew there was an ample 20 minutes of daylight remaining. Just as I was about to relax, ominous rainclouds appeared on the horizon with my destination still 12 miles away. New worries now cropped up in quick succession: How extensive was the shower activity? Would I have time to circle long enough for the showers to dissipate and still land before sunset? A return flight to Cienfuegos was impossible due to lack of fuel and time. Bailing out in my parachute would surely break both my legs on landing. The thought of being in a foreign-speaking hospital away from family and friends was unpleasant. Detouring slightly to the south I followed the railroad tracks which, according to my map, would lead me to the airport. Skirting the edge of a shower as I neared Camaguey, I could see another at the far boundary of Agromonte Airport. The runway was clearly visible between the showers. It seemed a miracle, like the parting of the Red Sea.

Abandoning my usual circle of the field, I angled just enough to one side to fly a base leg, hoping the tower would see me in time to issue a landing clearance. Minutes after my landing the rainclouds brought an end to the remaining daylight. Thankful to be safely on the ground, I taxied up to the terminal building where an admiring and cooperative group of Cuban officials and Pan Am employees took care of my flight plan and other official paperwork. Reporters and other news media representatives came out to write a story for the Camaguey newspaper which carried the following headline the next morning:

PILOTO NORTAMERICANO LLEGO A CAMAGUEY EN AVION DE UN SOLO MOTOR RUMBO A KINGSTON, JAMAICA.

The airline employees reserved a room for me at the Pan Am Club across the street from the airport. A gray-haired Spanish-American War veteran with a drooping mustache insisted on carrying my shirtbox luggage, presumably out of sympathy for my handicap. Arriving at my room, I offered to pay him for his services but he insisted, "No dinero, no dinero." Since neither of us understood the other's language we searched for a way to communicate. We solved the problem by pointing to various objects in the room and calling their names in our respective language. There was a lamp table by the bed and pointing to it I said "table" to which he responded "mesa." We spent several minutes laughing as we continued our "conversation." Later I went down to the dining room for a Cuban dinner. I was soon joined by several Cuban pilots who were determined to prove that their rum was better than their rival Jamaican variety. After downing enough samples to prove their point I was treated to several cups of strong Cuban coffee which fortunately had a sobering effect. I returned to my room with enough dignity to preserve my reputation as a sophisticated, experienced, international pilot. Before going to bed I placed a telegram by phone to the waiting Barnetts in Kingston:

ARRIVED CAMAGUEY O.K. WILL LAND PALISADOES TOMORROW AT 12 NOON, EST.

LOGBOOK ENTRY: December 11, 1953
Camaguey—Kingston, 250 miles, flight time, 2.08 hours.

Walking across the street to the airport lobby, I saw the ramp outside filled with curious Cubans waiting to see the legless American pilot whom they had read about in the local newspaper. In this large crowd of people was a delegation of Cuban doctors and nurses interested in talking to me about my prostheses. Several of them spoke English so we were able to discuss my medical problems and adjustment to wearing artificial legs.

During the conversation I noticed about a half-dozen teenage boys staring at me with more than casual interest. Leaving the group, one of them approached with a shoeshine box. Gesturing with his hands he indicated he wanted to shine my shoes. Nodding my head in agreement I placed my foot on the box and soon heard the sound of his shoeshine rag popping away. I then noticed the popping sound had stopped and, glancing down, I saw the teenager was surreptitiously feeling my leg to see if it was truly made of wood. Turning and with a confirming smile to his cohorts he continued his task on the other leg. Pleased with his new knowledge, his response to my offer to pay for the shoeshine was "No dinero, no dinero."

It was too early to leave Camaguey for my scheduled noon landing in Kingston. I went out in front of the terminal building with my camera to take pictures of Loving's Love with the Camaguey tower in the background. Fidel Castro's revolution was imminent and there was a large contingent of heavily armed Cuban soldiers standing guard.

Not wanting to be accused of being a camera spy, I went back into the terminal without taking a single picture. The Pan Am desk clerk laughed heartily on hearing my fears and waving toward the smiling Cubans admiring my racer said, "Take all the pictures you want. Next to Kid Gavilan [famous pugilist born in Camaguey] you are the most popular man in Camaguey!" With that assurance I took my pictures and prepared for takeoff.

Filing my flight plan an hour before scheduled departure I had time to complete my preflight in unaccustomed leisure. Airborne at 9:56 A.M. and after complying with yet another tower request for a low-level pass, I turned on course for the last leg of my flight to Kingston. The air was quite turbulent below the broken cumulus clouds but beyond the strip of land forming the Golfo de Guacanayabo the sky cleared enough to allow me to safely climb above the broken cloud layer. Here the air was silky smooth and milky white clouds stretched to the horizon.

Climbing to a comfortable 6,000 feet for the first time since leaving Detroit, I finally had time to admire the blue Caribbean below, flecked with dark shadows from the clouds above. Navigation was simple as I leap-frogged towering cumulus clouds dotting my course like giant highway markers. Other than an occasional glance at my instruments and compass I was free to enjoy the extraordinary beauty of this fliers' world. Occasionally, cloud shadows gave the false impression of land ahead, which I learned to ignore. Finally the shapes and colors of the north coast of Jamaica appeared ahead in haze and mist. I started my letdown toward the Rio Cobre Pass which would lead me to Kingston.

Minutes later the familiar rust-colored aluminum ore loading docks near Ocho Rios came into view. Passing near Lodge, with mountains on both sides rising into the clouds above, I could see the road Carl and Uncle Les almost always used when driving there from Kingston. Staying below the cloud deck, I followed the swift, twisting valley of the Rio Cobre River to the dazzlingly white-stuccoed but aging buildings in the plaza of Spanish Town.

With startling suddenness the mountains dropped sharply away to the flat expanse of Liguanea Plain where the colorful buildings of downtown Kingston were etched against the clear blue sky. Circling Palisadoes Airport with casual familiarity I started my approach over the harbor waters to runway 15. As I kept a watchful eye on the tower, a green flare soon arced across the sky inviting me to land.

Touching down at 12:07 P.M., just seven minutes behind my estimated time of arrival, I taxied up to the terminal filled with the joy of my arrival and the anticipation of a happy reunion with the Barnetts. I took a moment to look at the tiny wings that had brought me safely to Jamaican soil. Then glancing at the placid waters of Kingston Harbor and the mountains beyond I said a prayer of thanksgiving for yet another impossible dream come true.

CHAPTER FIFTEEN

A NEW LOVE

An airport attendant waved me off the taxiway onto the ramp reserved for foreign aircraft arrivals and gave the signal for engine shut-off. One of the airport employees watching my arrival must have been a Royal Air Force (RAF) veteran. On hearing the fighter-like sound of my engine as I taxied up, he exclaimed, "Migawd, a Rolls-Royce!" The sleek lines of the midget had some resemblance to the famous Spitfire fighters of the RAF during World War II.

The resemblance was purely superficial: my 85-HP, 200-MPH racer was a far cry from the 1,400-HP, 400-MPH Rolls-Royce–powered Spitfire. My laughter at his remark was dimmed when a very officious, uniformed government employee peered into the cockpit and asked in heavily British-accented Jamaican words, "Did you spray your aircraft 30 minutes out sir?" It was routine procedure to spray the cabin of inbound airliners to prevent unwanted insects from entering the country. If I had done so in the close confines of Loving's Love the fumes would probably have asphyxiated me. To avoid the problems associated with breaking a government regulation in a foreign country, I lied in answer to his clearly stupid question. "Yes sir, I sprayed my aircraft 30 minutes out as required." Noting this information on the government form he directed me to follow him to the customs and immigration office along with my shirtbox luggage. The inspection of the shirtbox, fortunately, went quickly but I thought it was going to take forever to fill out all the necessary forms and obtain corresponding approvals. Finally receiving my tourist card I was free to enter the visitors' lounge where I was sure the Barnetts were waiting.

Flashing my tourist card at the uniformed guard I passed through the gate into a large crowd of milling people in the terminal. To my utter surprise and disappointment there wasn't a single familiar face in the crowd. Was it possible the Barnetts had not received my cablegram? I thought of calling them on a pay phone until I realized I didn't know their phone number nor did I have Jamaican coins. It seemed like forever before Carl and Earsly rushed through the airport entrance waving their arms wildly to attract my attention. After affectionate hugs and kisses we drove home to wait for Clare and Felix to come home from work so they could join in the reunion. The senior Barnetts were still at home in Lodge but planned to be in Kingston the next day (Saturday) for their weekend visit.

Leaving the passenger area we walked out into the hot midday sun and boarded Carl's car for the ride home. Driving down the narrow Palisadoes Road we passed several hulks of wrecked freighters rusting away in the salt-laden water, silent testimony to the power of past tropical hurricanes. Turning left onto Windward Road we drove past the old and now unused Pan American Airways terminal located on the shore of Kingston Harbour. During the late 1930s and early 1940s, giant four-engine flying boats stopped here on their way from Miami to South America. Known as Clipper Ships, they pioneered passenger-carrying flights all over the world.

Passing the wooden open-front stores and colorful sidewalk vendors typical of Kingston we turned onto Mountain View Road which follows the edge of Ligaunea Plain adjacent to Long Mountain. A left turn at Deanery Road brought us to Oakdene Avenue and home. Edgar the gardener opened the iron-grilled gates and we drove into the flower-bordered driveway leading to the shaded verandah fronting the house.

While waiting for dinner we sat in comfortable porch chairs sipping refreshing tropical drinks and catching up on our pent-up reservoir of conversation. Carl and Earsly took great joy in pointing out an embarrassing "hare and tortoise" comparison of our respective flights from Detroit to Jamaica. They had taken 10 days to complete their 2,600-mile flight via New York City, flying a 70-MPH Piper Cub. My route was more direct, only 2,200 miles, in a high-speed racing airplane and I took 11 days! Whatever inflated ego I might have developed from the success of my flight was quickly dissipated.

Dinner was a happy reunion with Clare and Felix as well as Violet's wonderful Jamaican cooking which I had sorely missed back in Detroit. After our meal we returned to the red and white tiled verandah and greeted additional family friends and relatives as they came to welcome me back to my second home in Kingston. Amid all the joyous conversation with my Jamaican family, I was plagued by continual back and leg pains due to the long hours of cramped sitting in my otherwise wonderful Loving's Love. Earsly very thoughtfully brought extra back cushions which, with the aid of a few rum and gingers, did much to relieve my symptoms. It took months of relaxed living in Jamaica for my leg pains to subside to normal everyday levels. Truly, the exhilaration and pleasure of being "home" in Jamaica helped me forget my discomfort.

The next morning Uncle Les and Aunt Jeanne arrived from Lodge for their weekend visit and I rushed out to open the car door for them. Their warm greeting made me feel like the "prodigal son." During lunch we enjoyed our "labrish," a Jamaican colloquial expression for conversation. I was still having difficulty understanding Aunt Jeanne's special brand of labrish but understood her perfectly when she said her Christmas fruitcakes were already baked. The holidays were sure to be a season of great happiness for me.

One late afternoon in December Carl drove me out to Palisadoes Airport for my first local flight in Loving's Love. Rolling it out of the mammoth British West Indies Airways (BWIA) hangar into the evening sun I found it hard to believe my homemade airplane could carry me so far from home. My pains were still very much with me so I limited my flight to only 35 minutes. The air was smooth and clear as I took off near sunset for a short flight over Kingston and the nearby mountains. Circling the harbor on my return I marveled at God's handiwork evident in the brilliant red and orange colors of the sun's dying rays as they were reflected by the dancing waves of the Caribbean. It was an ideal subject for a Jamaican picture postcard. At Carl's request I dove over the water and leveled off for a 200-MPH low-level pass over the runway. Pulling up sharply in exuberance, I took one last look at the lights of Kingston brightening in the dusk of evening before entering my final approach and landing. It felt wonderfully strange to be taxiing up to the BWIA hangar instead of Bay 12 at Detroit City Airport.

The Christmas holiday season was celebrated with parties and small family get-togethers followed by attendance at midnight mass at Holy Trinity Cathedral. On Christmas Day all the Barnetts converged on the family home on Oakdene Avenue for the traditional Christmas dinner. Turkey, ham, rice and peas, cho-cho, and tossed salad were among the items on the main course, followed by Aunt Jeanne's fruit-cake served with warm port-wine sauce. After dinner we retreated to the verandah and while relaxing in our comfortable porch chairs watched the bright full tropical moon rise over Long Mountain directly in front of us. In a moment of reflection I recalled a poem written by Theresa Caver, a gifted young black Detroit woman afflicted with polio. Miss Caver had her own radio program on Windsor station CKLW (across the river from Detroit) which she devoted to reading her own poetry and the literary works of other authors. She began every program with these words accompanied by the soft musical sounds of violin and organ in the background, "When beauty's weight would break this heart in two, But for the ease of sharing it, whatever would I do!"

I celebrated New Year's Eve 1954 by accompanying the Barnetts to church services followed by attending traditional parties where revelers gathered in bright party dress to make merry under the mistletoe. It was just like being in Detroit except we were sitting outside in the moonlight instead of inside a heated house. Generous quantities of Jamaican fruit punch added to the gaiety of the occasion. At midnight we joined in the loud choruses of "Happy New Year" amid the sounds of whistles and firecrackers resounding throughout the neighborhood. I joined Carl, Earsly, Clare, and Felix and others in the merriment until we all ran out of energy in the early morning hours. It was a relief to go to bed for my legs were aching from the day's activities but it was a small price to pay for the exciting memories of my second New Year's celebration in Jamaica.

My winter vacation extended into a spring filled with trips to Lodge, visits with Maria and George Feurtado in Mandeville, flights in VP-JAZ to Boscobel and Port Antonio (where Carl, Felix, and Clare were born), tours of the local rum distilleries, and more. A bus stop was only one block from the Barnett home where the fare was only a thruppence (three cents) for a ride to downtown Kingston. During the day when everyone was at work I frequently rode the bus downtown to the end of the line at South Parade and King streets. Large department stores such as Issa's and Nathan's were located on King Street, Kingston's main downtown thoroughfare. Also in the area were numerous small shops and street vendors as well as large government treasury and court buildings. Clare worked in the treasury building and I occasionally stopped in for a quick visit. On the sidewalks colorfully dressed vendors enticed pedestrians into buying everything from souvenir items to fresh coconuts and mangoes. The sounds and smells here were typical of almost every Jamaican town and village.

As spring approached I found myself looking forward to spending more of my time with Clare. Prior to this, Carl and Earsly were my almost-constant companions as we shared our common interest in aviation. Clare was very quiet and reserved (the opposite of Carl) and rarely intruded in these conversations. But as I came to know her better I found she had a lively sense of humor, like her mother, and that we had many shared interests. Our sense of values, love of music, conservative ideals, and love of family were much the same.

One day she took the day off from work so we could have lunch together at Kingston's beautiful Hope Botanical Gardens, a setting of colorful and exotic tropical flowers. After that experience I awaited her return home from work every day so we could spend as much time as possible together during the last few weeks of my visit. Sitting on the verandah we talked and played records from her collection, including such mutual favorites as Carl Maria von Weber's "Invitation to the Dance" and Richard Strauss's waltzes from his opera, *Der RosenKavalier.* One day we talked Carl into taking a day off from his busy schedule and driving us up to Lodge for a visit with the senior Barnetts.

As we were driving up the narrow mountain road leading to Lodge, Carl questioned the two of us sitting at his side, "Wouldn't it be nice if you two were to get married?" Before either of us could reply he gave his own skeptical answer, "No, it will never happen, you two are both too old and set in your ways." We smiled at Carl's comment and continued to enjoy our conversation until we arrived at Lodge. Driving up the steep driveway to the house we were greeted by Uncle Les and Aunt Jeanne who were waiting for us. Carl had dinner with us before driving back to Kingston, leaving Clare and me to share a few days with her parents before their semi-monthly return drive to Kingston.

Clare's mother was an expert seamstress and her clientele kept her busy making custom quality clothing. Her other great interest was flowers. Her garden contained many species growing profusely in carefully tended plots. They provided an incredibly colorful view from the verandah, the lavish array of brilliant tropical colors of her flowers contrasting beautifully against the lush, green mountain background of coconut and banana trees. Clare and I spent many happy hours in this lovely environment sharing our thoughts and ideas.

"Mistah B" had his own hobby, keeping a few cows on the large property surrounding his house. During my stay at Lodge, one of his cows gave birth to a calf. This was a new experience for a city boy like me, whose knowledge of beef was limited to what I saw in the meat market. Our few days in this idyllic retreat ended when we joined her parents for the long drive to Kingston on Uncle Les's favorite road, the "Devil's Race Course."

It was now mid-May and my return to Detroit could not be put off any longer. After informing my office manager at Wayne School of Aeronautics, Dick Paridee, of my intentions I set my departure date for May 19, 1954. This was followed by a flurry of last-minute visits around Kingston. The evening before my departure was spent on the verandah visiting one last time with the Barnett family. But unlike my departure the year before I made a special effort to spend most of my time with Clare. Clearly our bond of friendship had taken on a new and deeper meaning.

LOGBOOK ENTRY: May 19, 1954
Kingston—Camaguey, 250 miles, flight time, 2.00 hours.

As I taxied away from the BWIA hangar, Carl in VP-JAZ with Clare in the front seat followed me out to the runway where the tower signaled our clearance for takeoff by shooting off a bright green flare. My brief logbook entry reads, "Farewell to Clare in JAZ. Cruise altitude 7000 feet." We flew formation for a few minutes as Carl took some 8mm movies and Clare waved her last goodbye. Waggling my wings in farewell, I headed for the Rio Cobre Pass and climbed to my assigned cruising altitude of 7,000 feet. There was a deeper note of sadness with this departure for I knew I would miss Clare more than ever before. The demands of flying over strange, mountainous terrain put these feelings in the back of my mind as I headed for Camaguey.

As predicted by the Jamaican Meteorological Office, the weather was beautiful and for the very first time on my entire trip I had a slight tailwind. On arrival at Camaguey I was greeted by the Pan Am staff like an old friend. They helped me clear Cuban immigration and customs in minimum time and soon I was on my way to Havana.

LOGBOOK ENTRY: May 19, 1954
Camaguey—Havana, 330 miles, flight time, 2.33 hours.

The uncertainty of weather forecasting was proven as I wrote in my logbook for this leg, "Cruise altitude, 2500 feet, dodging rain showers." The special forecast prepared for me by the Jamaican Meteorological Office called for clear weather and tailwinds all the way to Miami. However, a distinct change in the weather pattern occurred, resulting in a 180-degree shift in wind direction, once more presenting a headwind.

The clear sky soon gave way to clouds and rain showers that were not serious enough to cause problems en route. Immediately on my entering the traffic pattern at Havana the tower gave me a green-light clearance to land. Remembering again to land beyond the black skidmarks at the approach end of the runway to avoid potholes caused by frequent airliner landings, I rolled to a stop and taxied back to the terminal. Among the crowd of people who came out to see the Love was a young man who introduced himself as the official airport photographer. He asked me to pose for a picture with a high-level government official. He promised to send me a copy.

I talked to the few Cubans who spoke English while the Love was being refueled. One of those standing near was the customs agent, who happened to glance at the gas bill as the attendant presented it to me. He immediately asked where I had landed en route (which would have been illegal since it was not on my flight plan). The Love had used only eight gallons of gas for a 330-mile flight, much less fuel than any standard licensed light aircraft would burn. Only by showing the agent the gas bills from all my previous flights was he convinced, allowing me to go on my way. I filed my flight plan with Havana Departure Control with specific instructions to notify Miami Approach Center of my intentions to land at Broward International Airport in Fort Lauderdale instead of Miami and to notify the customs and immigration office in Hollywood, Florida.

LOGBOOK ENTRY: May 19, 1954
Havana—Ft. Lauderdale, 265 miles, flying time, 1.83 hours.

Turning quickly after takeoff to avoid flying over the presidential palace of dictator Fulgencio Batista, I climbed to cruise altitude and leveled off on a northerly heading toward Key West. My logbook entry for this leg simply stated, "Cruise 2500 feet, landfall only 3 miles west of Key West." My plan had been to steer slightly west of a direct course to Miami to make sure I would be over land areas on approaching the coast of Florida. Venturing too far east of the Florida coastline could very easily result in my becoming lost over open water. As the colorful Miami Beach hotels appeared ahead I started my letdown in preparation for landing at Broward International Airport, Fort Lauderdale. Taxiing up to the small terminal building, happy with the successful conclusion of my last flight leg over open water and parking on the ramp, I was surprised there were no customs or immigration officials to meet me. Knowing they did not have an office at the airport I asked the receptionist at Chalk Airlines in the terminal building to notify the customs and immigration facility at Hollywood, Florida, of my arrival. I went out into the warm sun and sat by my racer waiting for the officials to arrive.

About 15 minutes later a government car drove up and the stern-faced immigration officer, F. W. Raggett, Sr., walked swiftly to me and, without even saying hello, pointed out that I had made an illegal entry into the United States. And further, he continued, unless I could provide a satisfactory explanation I could be subject to a $10,000 fine and up to six months in jail. Thoughts of being in a jail hundreds of miles from friends and legal counsel created more trauma than any other event during my flight to Jamaica. Trying desperately to remain calm, I informed Mr. Raggett that I had filed my flight plan in Havana in accordance with his telephoned instructions in December 1953. I even showed him his home phone number which I had had the foresight to write down on a small piece of paper, proof of my conversation with him before leaving Miami.

When he realized that I had followed his instructions, his anger began to cool. He agreed I had done my part but said that Miami Traffic Control had failed to notify his office as requested. By this time it was past his 4:30 P.M. quitting time so it was necessary for me to pay him a half day's extra pay, $9.84, for 15 minutes of his time. This was a bargain compared to the $10,000 fine he had threatened me with. During our subsequent conversation I learned he was a student pilot. After sharing some of our flying experiences we parted good friends.

LOGBOOK ENTRY: May 21, 1954
Ft Lauderdale—Jacksonville, 330 miles, flight time, 2.75 hours.

The weather outside was windy and cool. I went into the weather office for a briefing. It was bad news. A "norther" had come through the area, accompanied by winds at 25–35 knots resulting in a stiff headwind—my usual bad luck of not having typical southerlies, which I had hoped would provide a tailwind for my trip home. I took off on runway 31 and climbed through the turbulent air trying to find a smooth layer. My logbook simply stated, "Headwinds as usual, 20–25 knots." The duration of this flight was the longest of the entire round trip. The one advantage was that the visibility was razor-sharp clear and there were no problems finding Jacksonville Airport.

LOGBOOK ENTRY: May 21, 1954
Jacksonville—Charleston, SC, 210 miles, flight time, 1.75 hours.

The airport at Charleston, South Carolina, was the home base of Hawthorne Flying Service, owned by my friend and famed world-champion aerobatic pilot Bevo Howard, whom I had the pleasure of meeting at the 1951 National Air Races in Detroit. Unfortunately, he was not in his office when I arrived. My logbook entry provides a brief impression of my visit, "Southern hospitality at Hawthorne Flying Service."

LOGBOOK ENTRY: May 21, 1954
Charleston—Raleigh, NC, 230 miles, flight time, 2.16 hours.

This was to be the last flight of the day. I had the customary problem of answering all the bystanders' questions before I could take off. Good weather, other than headwinds, was still holding out so I had no navigational problems on my flight to Raleigh. The logbook entry was short: "Landed 20 minutes before sunset."

LOGBOOK ENTRY: May 22, 1954
Raleigh—Baltimore, 280 miles, flight time, 2.43 hours.

During my preflight inspection I found some minor damage requiring several hours of repair. When they were completed, I filed a VFR flight plan to Baltimore with a forecast of warm and clear spring weather. Uncle Les's brother Alan lived in Baltimore and I had promised to call him. My flight to Baltimore was uneventful, which I noted in my logbook: "Everything OK after late start due to repairs." Uncle Alan was not at home so I proceeded to New York City for a reunion with the Floissacs whom I had not seen since Carl and I visited them in 1950.

LOGBOOK ENTRY: May 22, 1954
Baltimore—Teterboro, NJ, 150 miles, flight time, 1.58 hours.

Civil Air Authority regulations required all aircraft landing at either LaGuardia or Idlewild airports to have a radio transmitter. Mine was not working so Teterboro, New Jersey, became my destination. The visibility was good all the way and my flight, other than being slowed down by strong headwinds, was uneventful. Taxiing up to the Atlantic Aviation hangar, I was treated as if I were a visiting celebrity. My pride showed in my logbook entry, "Amongst the aristocrats of Atlantic Aviation."

Arthur Godfrey (the well-known radio entertainer) kept his luxuriously equipped Douglas DC-3 in the same hangar. I gazed in envy at this fabulous airplane. Godfrey's mechanics provided solace when they told me that Arthur was equally envious of my homemade racer! Privately they agreed I would have no problems flying his DC-3, but Godfrey's skills were probably not sufficient to meet the challenge of Loving's Love. Our conversation ended abruptly when the Floissac family appeared en masse as a welcoming committee. I spent the following week at the Brooklyn home of Uncle Flo, Aunt Beryl, and their lively teenage daughter, Joan.

After several calls during the week to the LaGuardia weather station I finally received a favorable forecast for a flight to Pittsburgh and scheduled my departure for the morning of Sunday, May 30. I wanted an early start for two practical reasons. First, the morning winds out of the west are generally lighter than those in the afternoon, resulting in a lesser headwind component. Second, I did not want to fly into the late afternoon sun approaching smog-ridden Pittsburgh. But my plans went awry because I waited for the Floissacs to return from church and have their breakfast. Additional time was consumed waiting for family friends who wanted to accompany us to the airport. I called Atlantic Aviation before leaving Brooklyn so when we arrived at Teterboro's airport at midday, the mechanics had Loving's Love ready for flight. After hurried farewells I was finally airborne and headed west toward Harrisburg, Pennsylvania.

LOGBOOK ENTRY: May 30, 1954
Teterboro—Harrisburg, 170 miles, flight time, 1.58 hours.

Not trusting my flatland navigational skills over the rugged Appalachians, I elected to fly southwest to Philadelphia and follow the Pennsylvania Turnpike all the way to Pittsburgh; as my logbook reported, "Followed the turnpike from Philly." The highly visible double highway not only kept me from getting lost but also gave me much more peace of mind in case of an emergency landing. Without the miles of concrete highway below me available for an emergency landing I would be forced to use my parachute in case of engine failure over mountainous terrain. With comparative peace of mind I flew to Harrisburg where there was so little traffic I was on the ground and off again in record time.

LOGBOOK ENTRY: May 30, 1954
Harrisburg—Pittsburgh, PA, 172 miles, flight time, 1.75 hours.

My eyes were burning from looking through the smog into the western sun now low in the sky. As promised I flew over Henrene's house 30 miles east of Pittsburgh to announce my arrival. Her husband, Sydney Yuille, had painted a large SY on the top of his house to help me locate it among the surrounding hills. Completing a few circles while waggling my wings to the Yuille family below I headed west to Allegheny Airport and entered the usual left-hand pattern on downwind leg. All of a sudden an airplane went swiftly by headed in the opposite direction. One of us had to be wrong and being a stranger I assumed it was me. Looking around to make sure there was no other traffic I made a fast 180-degree turn to follow a right-hand pattern.

I landed with no further problems and wasted no time checking with the local flight operator to make sure a right-hand pattern was correct for the runway in use. This whole experience was recorded in my logbook: "Buzzed the airmarked (SY) Yuille home." My stay with the Yuille family lasted an entire week.

LOGBOOK ENTRY: June 6, 1954
Pittsburgh—Akron, OH, 87 miles, flight time, 1.16 hours.

This was one of the slowest legs of the entire trip due to strong headwinds and inattentive tower operators at Akron Airport who didn't see me until I had circled the field enough times to get dizzy. My original plan was to fly nonstop to Detroit but I had forgotten to call Bernadine and my office at Detroit City Airport before takeoff to tell them of my arrival. I confessed in my logbook, "Took off Pittsburgh without calling Bernadine, landed at Akron and called." On previous flights to Pittsburgh or Cleveland I always followed the Lake Erie shoreline to Toledo, thus avoiding flying over about 60 miles of open water. This time I decided to fly straight across Lake Erie; after flying 800 miles over open water I had full confidence in my dependable Continental engine. There were no doubts my faithful Loving's Love would carry me home so I could sleep in my own bed that night.

LOGBOOK ENTRY: June 6, 1954
Akron—Detroit, 165 miles, flight time, 1.50 hours.

The weather was so clear, the south shore of Ontario, Canada, was visible on reaching cruise altitude. My anticipation became almost unbearable as I approached the final landing of my dream flight to Jamaica. As the buildings of downtown Detroit came into view I decided to buzz my home office at Detroit City Airport before my scheduled landing at Wayne Major Airport. After passing over Windsor, Ontario, I crossed the Detroit River and started my letdown as runway 33 came into view. I could see heads turning as I flew a low pass down the runway with the tower's enthusiastic permission. Mission accomplished!

Now it was time to head west for the 20-mile flight to Wayne Major Airport for my last landing of this long journey on the same runway from which I had departed. Several of my flight students were on hand to greet me, including Bristoe Bryant, a local disk jockey and his wife, Alice, and Warren Quates who along with his brother Frank learned to fly at Wayne School of Aeronautics. As we were talking, the fuel truck arrived with the same attendant who had fueled the midget when I departed on December 1, 1953.

Like the cabdriver in Atlanta, he had been very skeptical when I told him I was flying my midget racer to Jamaica. Taking a good look at Loving's Love shining like new in the afternoon sun, he said with a sarcastic laugh, "Ha, I thought you said you were going to fly to Jamaica." I guess he assumed that if I did get back to Detroit the airplane would show highly visible signs of wear and tear after such a long and arduous trip. As proof of the validity of my flight I reached into the cockpit and retrieved all my gas bills for the entire trip and showed them to him. Like the biblical Thomas, "he believed" and after gassing up my airplane drove back to the airport office to tell his buddies about my unbelievable trip.

After confirming my arrival, Carl McKay flew over from Detroit City Airport in a borrowed airplane and flew me back to where planning for my flight had started—Detroit City Airport. Dick Paridee, my office manager, had the office open for business and our Piper J-3 N6822H was on the flight line ready to fly. Anxious to get back into the air, I flew 15 minutes with Carl McKay, just long enough to practice two takeoffs and landings. It took a little time to adjust to an airplane that in normal cruise flight was slower than the landing speed of my racer.

Most of my flying friends and favorite waitresses were on hand when I entered Nick Manteris's airport restaurant for my first dinner there in six months. It was difficult to eat while trying to answer all the questions regarding every aspect of the flight. Weariness finally overcame me; I apologized for leaving early and headed for home. Going to bed that night I had mixed emotions, happy to be safe at home in my own bed, but already lonely for the Barnett family in Jamaica. Sleep was long in coming as the many exciting memories of Jamaica flooded my mind. Unbidden thoughts came, focusing on my growing affection for Clare and recalling the many pleasant hours we had spent getting to know each other. As drowsiness began to overcome my tired body, a warm, comfortable feeling that Clare was thinking of me as well lulled me into a deep, satisfying sleep.

CHAPTER SIXTEEN

CHANGING COURSE

In many ways the summer of 1954 was the "beginning of the rest of my life." It was during that time I first gave thought to making a fundamental change in the direction of my career. Motivation was provided by my warm relationship with Clare; I began to dream of marriage. Although we never discussed such a commitment during our many hours of conversation on the Barnett verandah, I decided to plan my future based on such a possibility.

One major objective was to establish new career goals that would provide financial security. My initial concern was the slowly diminishing volume of business at Wayne School of Aeronautics as the number of veterans entitled to GI educational benefits declined. Also, the United States was experiencing a postwar depression that reduced the number of non-GI students who were financially able to enroll. If those trends continued, the economic future of Wayne School of Aeronautics was doubtful.

As a bachelor I was able to live on a limited income which for me was more than compensated for by the daily opportunity to experience the never-ending joy of flying. But with thoughts of marrying Clare I definitely needed to choose a career that would provide a more substantial and stable income for the future. Since aeronautical engineering had always been a major interest, second only to flying for me, I decided to re-enroll at Wayne State University to resume my studies that had been interrupted when I went to Alabama in December 1945 to buy my Vultee BT-13. My first step was to visit the WSU registration office and obtain enrollment information for the aeronautical engineering department.

With Dick Paridee doing his usual good job of managing the office and "Jackie" Johnson handling the chores of chief flight instructor (CFI), I felt free to attend the second annual Experimental Aircraft Association (EAA) Fly-in scheduled for August 7–8, 1954, in Milwaukee. I had joined the EAA shortly after meeting Paul Poberezny in November 1953 and was now receiving their monthly magazine, the *Experimenter.* Now, for the first time, I learned of other people involved in designing and building homebuilt aircraft and looked forward to sharing my airplane-building experiences with them. My first task, before planning my flight to Milwaukee, was to inspect and prepare my midget racer for its annual relicense by the CAA. In spite of the rigors of the 4,800-mile round trip to Jamaica the Love passed the CAA inspection with flying colors. My first flight in the racer after the inspection and since arriving home from Jamaica was on August 6. After a happy 30-minute reunion in the air I was satisfied with its readiness for my next cross-country flight. The next morning, I took off for Milwaukee with a planned enroute refueling stop in South Bend. I arrived at Milwaukee Airport at 11 A.M., in time to see the scheduled afternoon air show. My arrival was described by Paul Poberezny in the August 1954 issue of the *Experimenter:*

> Most interesting arrival of the morning was that of Neal Loving and his little racer, "Loving's Love." The workmanship and design of this unique airplane drew many compliments from the members and was admired by all. Later in the day Neal demonstrated very conclusively that his airplane is a top performer in the air as well as being a marvel of workmanship on the ground. Here is truly a fine example of homebuilding at its best—both pilot and airplane. I'm sure that all who were at the meet will agree on this.

All the EAA members gathered Sunday morning at the main tent for a business meeting and awarding of trophies. I was both surprised and gratified to be given the Most Outstanding Design award by Paul Poberezny for my Loving's Love. To be given this prestigious award by my peers, especially since I was the only black entrant, was an honor I had not even dreamed of. The only problem was that the trophy was so large the little luggage compartment in the racer wasn't big enough to hold it. Arrangements were made for another participant to bring it home for me.

The second annual EAA fly-in in 1954 attracted a total of 28 airplanes and 500 attendees. In sharp contrast, the 39th annual EAA fly-in held in 1991 at Oshkosh, Wisconsin, was attended by 820,000 EAA members and spectators and 12,000 airplanes. The national EAA fly-in had grown to become the world's largest aviation event.

As the summer of 1954 progressed Clare and I maintained a steady flow of correspondence. Normally, very few Jamaican letters were delivered to the Detroit City Airport office, so when Clare's letters arrived the secretaries showed more than casual interest.

News of this potential romance also reached my long-time friends at Nick Manteris's airport restaurant; the waitresses wanted me to verify the latest gossip. To satisfy their interest I showed my favorite snapshot, one that I took of Clare on Easter Sunday wearing a beautiful white dress, kneeling in front of a cluster of brilliant red triple poinsettias. This picture tended to confirm rumors that my status as a 38-year-old bachelor was about to change.

When registration for fall classes at Wayne State University was announced in the local newspapers, I immediately made plans to enter on a part-time basis. After reviewing the course curriculum, I enrolled in two mathematics classes totaling six credit hours. This sounded like an easy workload until I was advised that a minimum of two hours of study per week was generally required for each credit hour. This meant my six hours of classtime plus twelve study hours would use up nearly half of my workweek.

In my case the general estimate of required study time turned out to be unrealistically low. What I had assumed to be a part-time study program was becoming more and more like a full-time job. Shortly after classes started I was notified by the admissions office that I would have to take an entrance examination even though I had received an accredited diploma from Cass Technical High School in January 1934. My enrollment at Wayne State 20 years later evidently exceeded the statute of limitations.

By mid-October I found myself in far more difficulty than I had dreamed of, especially in establishing good study habits. While trying to concentrate on algebraic equations and calculus, my mind frequently wandered off to thoughts of Clare and plans for our future. These distractions increased the hours needed to complete my class assignments and to prepare for the many "blue book" exams. In the midst of all this mental turmoil I received notice of the date of the entrance exam.

Dropping everything else, I spent several nights cramming in preparation for this crucial test. I was extremely tired on exam morning but my nerves were so tense I felt wide awake throughout the test period. Several days later my counselor called me into her office to discuss my test scores. She was extremely pleased with my overall performance, particularly in language arts and social studies. With an encouraging smile she strongly recommended I select liberal arts as my major. Noting on my application that I had chosen aeronautical engineering, she suggested I change my mind. "After all," she said, "you probably have no talent for aeronautical engineering anyway." Undaunted, I reiterated my choice. She gave me a scornful look for not accepting her counsel but filled out the forms as requested. I didn't bother to tell her about the success of Loving's Love; I was sure she would not believe me.

As my classwork continued, my confidence increased until I began to feel my goal to earn a degree in aeronautical engineering could be attained. If I succeeded, there was reasonable assurance of steady employment at a professional level, which would remove one of the principal obstacles that had kept me from asking Clare to marry me. Now with the financial security problem potentially resolved, I proposed to Clare in a letter airmailed to her in mid-November.

It seemed forever before her letter arrived agreeing to become my wife. I joyfully announced the good news to my relatives and friends, many of whom thought I was destined for permanent bachelorhood. When I told Red Rapp about my engagement, he immediately offered his assistance in the purchase of a suitable ring. Through his watch repair business he was familiar with most of the jewelry supply houses in Detroit. With his expert help I selected a suitable diamond engagement ring. Wanting Clare to wear it before the upcoming Christmas season, I airmailed it to her without delay along with a letter expressing my great happiness at her decision to become my wife.

Anxious to hear her voice and how she felt about the ring, I placed a long-distance telephone call to her on Christmas Day 1954 for our first conversation since my departure from Kingston in May. It was the best Christmas gift of the season.

My application for entry into the aeronautical engineering department was accepted in the spring of 1955. An appointment was made for me to see the head of the department, Professor A. A. Locke. In spite of his high academic position, he had the facility to make even nervous students feel comfortable in his presence. As I began to relax he gave me his views on my chances of obtaining a degree. Noting I had been out of school for 21 years he expressed his belief that, in reality, I did not have an adequate high school background. He used statistics to reinforce his argument: "Neal, two out of every three students flunk out of engineering school before graduation, and all are recent high school graduates with good high school transcripts." He added, "When a professor prefaces his lecture with the words, 'of course you remember this from your high school math or physics,' you are going to be at a serious disadvantage."

Just as I was getting the sinking feeling that I would not be allowed to continue my classes in the engineering department, he assured me I was free to do so. He was only doing his job as my advisor, he told me, and wished me luck as I expressed my desire to continue to work toward my degree. But his words were to haunt me during the many lectures I attended before graduation, finding myself precisely in the position he had described.

My classes were scheduled to end in early June. Clare and I were planning our marriage for the middle of June. She arranged for the ceremony to be held at the Holy Trinity Cathedral in Kingston, followed by a reception at the Barnett home. We were then to leave on our honeymoon at a place of her choice. Clare selected Torre Garda, a small tourist lodge (eight guests) located near Blue Mountain Peak about 4,000 feet above sea level. The trip to Torre Garda required a two-hour drive from Kingston to the town of Mavis Bank, followed by a long hike or horseback ride up steep, narrow mountain paths. There were no telephones or radios in this secluded area, to assure privacy, peace, and quiet. It appeared to be the perfect place for a honeymoon.

The farmers in the Torre Garda area grew flowers and vegetables of higher quality than those grown at sea level, due to the cooler temperatures and more frequent rains at the higher elevation. But it was a long and tedious journey for them to take their produce down to Mavis Bank by mule or horseback, where it was trucked to the Kingston markets. This journey usually took several hours, whereas an airplane could make the trip in 15 minutes.

To solve this problem the farmers decided to build an airstrip by leveling off the top of a nearby mountain. Borrowing a bulldozer, they managed to create an 800-foot strip, far too short for safe everyday use. Starting at a lower level, they began to cut new runway, which they hoped would be at least 1,000 feet long. Unfortunately, the bulldozer was called away after making only a few cuts, which reduced the length of the remaining original strip to only 740 feet. When Earsly and Carl learned of this new airstrip they decided, unilaterally, to fly Clare and me there for our honeymoon.

The Barnetts wasted no time in making practice approaches to the tiny Torre Garda airstrip. Earsly was the first to touch down on the runway but took off without stopping. Carl made a full-stop landing a few days later, the first to do so. With Carl's successful landing they were sure they could fly Clare and me, one at a time, to Torre Garda in VP-JAZ. I was less than enthusiastic about landing on such a short runway at 4,000 feet elevation. The less-dense air would result in our actual landing speed being about 8 percent higher than at sea level. But Carl insisted we had to do it for the good of Jamaican aviation. However, all of this flight activity was illegal, for the CAD had not approved the strip for use.

After determining the date of my last final exam I wrote to Clare to set my date of departure from Detroit. After discussing arrangements with her parents and church officials, she set our wedding date for Thursday morning, June 16, 1955, at 9 A.M.

When two of my flight students, Warren Quates and William "Bill" Lane, heard of my impending marriage they asked to be invited. Not only did they want to share this event with me, they also wanted to enjoy the beauty of Jamaica and its people they had heard me speak so much about. Bill had the distinction of being the first black flight-line attendant hired at Detroit City Airport.

We made plans to drive to Miami in Bill's car and take a Pan Am flight to Kingston. My cousin Bernadine also decided to see her long-time bachelor cousin get married and made similar reservations for an airline flight from Detroit to Kingston, arriving the day after our Pan Am flight. We promised to greet her at the airport on her arrival.

Our drive to Miami was a long, all-night affair with only a brief stop in Tuskegee for a visit with Bill's sister to break the monotony. On arriving in Miami we sought the advice of a black cabdriver who recommended the Elizabeth Hotel. After a much-needed night of rest we took a cab to the airport and boarded our Pan Am flight to Kingston with an intermediate stop in Havana.

As our Convair 240 airliner arrived at Havana's Rancho Boyeros Airport, the stewardess announced that passengers could go into the terminal for 20 minutes. Having been there the year before in my midget racer on my way home from Jamaica, I planned to stay on board but Bill and Warren insisted I go with them. While we were sightseeing in the terminal a young Cuban came up and spoke. "Hello, Mr. Loving, don't you remember me? I am the airport photographer who took the picture of you and your racer last year." I reminded him he had promised to send me a copy of the picture which I never received. Telling me to wait a minute he dashed off, returning minutes later with the negative. If my friends had not coaxed me into accompanying them into the airport terminal I would have missed receiving this treasured memento, my only picture of the Love in Havana.

As we started our descent over the north coast of Jamaica, I was able to point out to Bill and Warren prominent landmarks that I had flown over many times in the midget and VP-JAZ. Our flight arrived on time at Palisadoes Airport and the Barnett family was there in full force, waving to us from the "waving gallery." We headed for the customs and immigrations area. After the usual lengthy interrogations and inspections we were given our tourist permits and allowed to enter the passenger lounge in the terminal.

The Barnetts gave us a warm welcome but my eyes were centered on Clare as she came up. We embraced for the first time since we were engaged. She was the same Clare, of course, but now that she was to be my wife in just a few days, I was seeing her in a wonderfully different light. As much as we wanted to make up for the loneliness of our months apart, last-minute preparations for our wedding kept us from spending much time together. Bill and Warren were new to Jamaica so I showed them the sights and scenes of Kingston. It was a thrill for me to be able to take them to places of interest not seen by many tourists.

The day before the wedding Carl and I went out to the airport for what I thought was a local flight in VP-JAZ. But he really wanted to fly to the Torre Garda airstrip and pick up some beautiful orchids for our wedding. As I climbed into the passenger's (rear) seat of the cockpit Carl quickly informed me that he wanted me to fly VP-JAZ into Torre Garda. Protesting, I reminded him I did not have the benefit of practice flights. Carl remained adamant. Without further argument I took the front seat. As soon as we were airborne he directed me to the airstrip, a 20-minute flight. On seeing the tiny airstrip surrounded by rugged mountains and deep valleys I was amazed that any pilot in his right mind would even consider landing there. Carl was more confident than I was during my final approach to the 740-foot runway. Holding considerable power at an airspeed just above stall, I barely cleared the precipice that marked the beginning of the runway and quickly cut the power. VP-JAZ dropped sharply onto the runway, stopping just past midfield. I don't know who was more surprised, Carl or me. The gardeners had Clare's flamboyantly beautiful orchids ready for us which we loaded into the luggage compartment and took off for the return flight to Palisadoes Airport. This flight proved the practicality of the airstrip—if only it could be lengthened as needed for safe everyday use.

Clare and I were married in a quiet ceremony that was reported in the Kingston daily newspaper:

U.S. Flyer Weds Miss C. Barnett

Mr. Neal V. Loving, aeroplane pilot of Detroit, Michigan, married Miss Clare Therese Barnett, only daughter of Mr. and Mrs. Leslie A. Barnett, of Eden Gardens, Saint Andrew, at Holy Trinity Cathedral on Thursday morning, June 16. The ceremony was performed by Monsignor Gladstone Wilson. For her wedding gown, the bride chose chantilly lace with a three tier train of slipper satin. Her gown was designed and made by her mother. . . .

Our marriage set another precedent. Clare was Roman Catholic but I was not and in that pre–Vatican II era, the priest usually performed such marriages at a side altar or in the rectory. But Monsignor Wilson married us at the main altar, a signal honor indeed. This somewhat mollified my cousin Bernadine, who wanted me to convert to Catholicism before marriage so that Clare could have a nuptial mass. Several years later, even though Clare graciously refrained from trying to influence me, I decided to join her in her faith.

The wedding reception was held in the Barnett home replete with delicious Jamaican food, wedding cake, and traditional champagne toasts to the bride and groom by friends and family. Staying just long enough to meet our social obligations, Clare, Carl, and I slipped out as quietly as possible to change clothes and drive to the airport. It was agreed Carl would fly me to Torre Garda first so I could take 8mm color movies of his subsequent arrival with Clare. Sitting comfortably in the back seat, I relaxed as we climbed over the formidable mountain range, thinking of how fortunate Clare and I were to be able to spend our honeymoon in such an idyllic tropical setting.

Arriving at the Torre Garda airstrip, Carl's first approach was clearly too high and fast. We went around for a second attempt. This approach also was well above the correct glide path; he gunned the engine for a third try. This time Carl succeeded in touching down at the beginning of the airstrip but was going too fast to stop before reaching the precipice at the far end. It was soon evident we had slowed too much to be able to take off again.

Carl's only choice left was to lock the brakes, rapidly slowing us down. Losing elevator control, we sat helplessly as the tail began to rise uncontrollably. The nose came down and the spinning propeller struck the ground, sending up a shower of dirt, rocks, and pieces of broken propeller. The nose of the airplane continued to slide along the rocky ground accompanied by sounds of metal grinding as the engine cowl and carburetor crumpled into a shapeless mass.

When Carl shut off the engine, the sudden silence accentuated the noise of debris falling off the wings of our beautiful VP-JAZ, her battered nose resting on the rough, rocky ground. Sitting there until all was silent, Carl angrily began a string of Jamaican-American expletives followed by profuse apologies for ruining my honeymoon.

Climbing awkwardly out of the fuselage, the Cub's tail high in the air, we were met by villagers who helped us lower the tail to the ground. The propeller was broken beyond repair. The lower engine cowling was bashed in, and the carburetor and air cleaner were severely damaged. With the help of onlookers we tied VP-JAZ down to prevent possible wind damage and discussed plans to repair and fly the disabled Cub back to her home port.

Mrs. Stedman, proprietor of Torre Garda, limped over on her bad leg to offer help. Our main concern was to contact Clare, still waiting expectantly at the airport, and arrange other means of transportation for her. Since there was no telephone service at Torre Garda, Mrs. Stedman suggested I write a telegram, which she would send off to Kingston by having two of her men run down the trail (faster than a horse) to the Mavis Bank telegraph office.

Clare was at the airport sitting in Carl's car anxiously waiting for his return, so she could not be reached. I addressed the telegram to Earsly at the Barnett home where some of the family members were still gathered. Not wanting to alarm anyone, my telegram read, "HAD A LITTLE ENGINE TROUBLE. PICK UP CLARE." Since everything that could and needed to be done had been accomplished, Carl left Torre Garda by horseback for Kingston. I sat on Torre Garda's spacious verandah and waited impatiently for Clare's arrival.

Although the wedding celebration was officially over, family members at the Barnett home in Kingston were concerned about Earsly's sudden and unexplained departure. On her return hours later, Earsly described the details of our accident.

Sunset comes quickly in Jamaica. In the brief twilight and following darkness, I sat in the darkened living room (no electricity) worrying about the hazards Clare faced as she came up the winding, narrow paths bordered by sharp dropoffs on a black moonless night. Mrs. Stedman, whose nervous pacing back and forth across the floor belied her words, offered unconvincing assurance there was no danger. After all, she had sent her two best men and horses down to Mavis Bank for Clare. I was also concerned about Clare becoming chilled by the cool mountain air, which I was sure she wasn't prepared for. After midnight we could hear the sound of horses in the distance. Lamps were lighted and placed on the verandah as we waited anxiously those last few moments. Soon, shadowy figures emerged from the darkness and Clare and I were reunited at last.

In spite of our carefully laid plans, the first day of our honeymoon was the only day we had to ourselves. Unaware that Carl and Earsly were planning to come up the next day, we blissfully enjoyed the peace and privacy we had dreamed of for months. It was a wonderful new experience to sit with my bride on the spacious verandah at 4,000 feet elevation and watch puffy cumulus clouds slowly approach, surround us momentarily, and then drift away. The scenic valleys and surrounding mountains were dotted with coconut and banana trees among colorful tropical bushes and flowers. It was another unbelievable—and most beautiful—dream come true.

In the meantime, Carl and Earsly were making plans to repair VP-JAZ, for Wings Jamaica, Ltd., was out of business until it was back on the flight line. After locating the necessary repair parts for the airplane they organized an airplane rescue party. In addition to Carl and Earsly, other members of the party included Bill Lane, Warren Quates, and Bernadine. They arrived by horseback and, due to the limited accommodations at Torre Garda, Mrs. Stedman moved out of her room to make room for her guests. It took several days for the repair work to be completed. In spite of our well-laid plans for privacy, Clare and I had ample company for our honeymoon.

Finally, VP-JAZ was ready to fly. Experienced pilot and Jamaican aviation pioneer Jackie Biscoe had the honor and distinct advantage of making the flight back to Kingston. The rest of us boarded our horses for the uncomfortable two-hour ride to Mavis Bank. For our peace of mind, each of us had a guide holding the reins as we followed the narrow trail bordered by a dropoff to the valley below. A few days later the following story appeared in the Kingston newspaper:

Loving Romance: Nearly a Tragedy
No Hitch in Wedding Reception

THE FLYING HONEYMOON of the Lovings, who were married here last week, almost ended in tragedy on Thursday last when the plane of the groom, legless American pilot, Neal Loving, came to a mishap on the private airstrip at Torre Garda up in the Blue Mountains. The mishap came shortly after the marriage of Mr. Loving to Miss Clare Barnett when his Piper Cub aircraft in which the Detroit airman had travelled to the mountain top hotel to await the arrival of his bride, nosed over on the airstrip in landing; with damage but fortunately causing no injury to either Mr. Loving or his brother-in-law, Mr. Carl Barnett who was at the controls. Mr. and Mrs. Loving had said their vows at the Holy Trinity Cathedral. Plans were made for separate flights to the mountain resort for the honeymoon. The flight went well but at the point of landing, nosed over. The propeller, oil tank and carburetor were damaged. As a result, the return flight for Mrs. Loving was abandoned and she travelled to the hotel by road and horseback.

Back in the familiar surroundings of the Barnett family home in Kingston, Clare and I spent much of our time discussing plans for our future in Detroit. She was especially looking forward to meeting Red and Helen Rapp as well as the Loving family and other friends. In the midst of our happiness we realized we had a problem that quickly put a damper on our plans. Clare was a Jamaican citizen and therefore could not accompany me back to Detroit. She would have to apply to the U.S. consulate in Kingston for a permanent visa to which she was entitled as the wife of a U.S. citizen. This required a mountain of government paperwork, including a certified copy of our marriage certificate which could only be obtained at the records office in Spanish Town. Also, numerous government forms had to be filled out, each requiring specific approvals.

The general time estimated to obtain a visa from the American consulate in Kingston ranged from weeks to months. The joy of our marriage was as exciting as ever, but the thought of being apart in the months to come was disappointing for both of us. Heartened by the sure knowledge of a joyful reunion in Detroit, we joined the Barnett family for a final round of goodbyes before leaving home for my departure from Palisadoes Airport. With more than the usual mixture of gladness and sadness, always experienced in leaving Jamaica, I joined Bill and Warren in boarding our Pan Am flight to Miami.

During the flight and the long drive to Detroit there was ample time to think of the strange vagaries of fate that had affected my life. With my marriage to Clare, long-time friend and business partner Earsly was now my sister-in-law; former flight student Carl Barnett was now my brother-in-law; and adding to my blessings, I now had Uncle Les and Aunt Jeanne as my new, loving "parents."

During the all-night drive to Detroit from Miami I established two goals that I was determined to accomplish by 1957. First, I planned to enroll at WSU on a full-time basis. This was necessary for on a part-time basis it would take me over 10 years to get my degree. With a wife and the possibility of having children to provide for, I could not afford to wait that long. Second, I planned to close the Wayne School of Aeronautics. The volume of business had diminished to the point where it had no market value other than physical assets, that is, airplanes, office equipment, parts inventory, and the like. This meant that Clare and I would have to subsist on my small government disability allowance until I graduated from Wayne State University. We had talked endlessly about these possibilities and she had agreed that the short-term sacrifices would be worth the long-term benefits of my degree in aeronautical engineering. I couldn't wait to get home and get started in this new direction in my life.

CHAPTER SEVENTEEN

NEW RESPONSIBILITIES

Completing the backlog of work accumulated at Wayne School of Aeronautics during my absence, I began planning for the fall semester at Wayne State University. In spite of my busy schedule I was lonesome for Clare. My airport friends laughed at my frequent visits to my office mailbox. In her first letter she wrote of the maze of paperwork and numerous approvals necessary to obtain her permanent visa. Remembering that a good friend of mine, Ruth McCrary, was employed as secretary in Michigan Senator McNamara's Washington office, I called for assistance. I told her of my Jamaican marriage and described Clare's visa problems. She agreed to write a letter to the U.S. consulate in Kingston for the senator's signature, asking what action had been taken on Clare's application for a visa. When the letter arrived, the consulate staff took greater and more immediate interest in processing Clare's application.

With pleasant memories of the 1954 EAA national fly-in still fresh in my mind, I made plans to attend the 1955 fly-in again scheduled to be held in Milwaukee. Packing my soft-sided luggage, made in Jamaica especially to fit Loving's Love, I took off from Wayne Major Airport on August 7 heading westward. My direct, nonstop flight to Milwaukee was completed in two hours despite headwinds and low ceilings in the Chicago area.

Shortly after my landing, Paul Poberezny and I were engaged in prolonged, enthusiastic "hangar talk," including details of my flight to Jamaica. He told me of the many requests received at EAA headquarters for detailed information on Loving's Love, including its construction plans. Many of the major aviation magazines in the United States, as well as France and England, had published articles and three-dimensional drawings of the Love, creating national and international interest. Paul strongly recommended I draw up a set of plans for the midget racer and offer them for sale. He also asked me to help organize a Detroit chapter of the EAA. I agreed to both commitments.

As usual, Loving's Love was a popular attraction during the 1955 fly-in. I spent many hours talking to EAA members about its performance and discussing my flight to Jamaica. The next day I flew to Chicago's O'Hare Airport, which at that time was a quiet general aviation facility and home of an Illinois Air National Guard fighter squadron. There I was met by my host for the next few days, Father Birney Smith, an Episcopal priest and former Detroiter, now assigned to a church in Evanston just north of Chicago. Father Birney was a student pilot at a local airport and was looking forward to my visit and a look at Loving's Love, the first racing aircraft he would have seen. My brief stay with Father Birney, his wife, Jetawyn, and their three children was spent socializing and talking airplanes. On August 9 I was driven to O'Hare for my return flight. The tower gave me the latest airport advisory and requested a low-level, high-speed pass in front of the tower before I departed the area. After making what I thought was a low-level flight slightly above the tower level I received a call on my radio, "You are looking good but the request was for a *low-level* pass." This time I flew down the flight line just above a row of parked Illinois National Guard F-86 jet fighters and well below the tower facility. After thanking me for my performance and waving enthusiastically as I rocked my wings in salute, they wished me tailwinds on my flight home. Today O'Hare International Airport is the world's busiest airport; such unorthodox maneuvers as I performed that day would never be permitted.

Returning home, I found Clare's letters more optimistic about obtaining her visa. Three weeks later she phoned with the news that the U.S. consulate had granted her a permanent visa. Ruth McCrary's assistance was instrumental in hurrying the U.S. consulate into taking necessary action. Clare planned to depart Kingston on September 8 for New York via Eastern Airlines and visit with her cousin Rena Livingston until my arrival. I decided to drive to New York so that we would have the car to get around the city.

Clare's call from New York came on Friday evening, and Saturday at 3 P.M. I was on my way to New York at the wheel of my 1950 Plymouth. This was before the freeway era so I had to pass through numerous towns, large and small, on narrow two-lane highways before reaching the Pennsylvania Turnpike. Stopping only to get gas and occasional rest, I continued to drive through the night. The monotony of turnpike driving, coupled with fatigue, caused me to doze off, allowing the Plymouth to slide off the road onto the unpaved shoulder. Suddenly awakened, I stayed reasonably alert for a few minutes before drifting off again. The bright morning sun kept me awake as I encountered the busy New York City traffic.

Armed only with Rena's address, I drove uncounted miles on strange streets, confused and unable to locate her home. Tired and frustrated, I stopped at several gas stations where helpful attendants gave me supposedly foolproof directions. Getting lost again and becoming more and more bewildered, I finally stopped a policeman. He gave me several sets of directions which I confessed I had already tried without success.

In exasperation he asked, "Can you read the name of the large hotel across the street?" On answering, "Yes I can," he suggested I call my wife, tell her where I was, and have her come and pick me up. Since neither Clare nor Rena could drive, I drove off again, bleary-eyed, until I finally reached Rena's home and a reunion with Clare at 7 A.M. Even the joy and excitement of being with Clare again could not overcome my body's demand for sleep. After reveling in Clare's presence for the first time in three months, I finally went to bed. With just a few hours of sleep I woke up full of energy, ready to enjoy the company of my new wife and cousin Rena. After Rena's lovely dinner we spent the rest of this joyous Sunday celebrating our reunion. Clare Therese Barnett Loving was now the new "Loving's Love"!

During the several days we spent with Rena we also visited the Floissacs, Clare's Aunt May Bradshaw and her daughter Alice. This was my first opportunity to tour New York City with Clare so we included some sightseeing during our short stay.

With family visits finished, we left New York and drove to Philadelphia for an overnight stay with Ivy Alves, Clare's maid-of-honor and long-time friend whom we had not seen since the wedding. We filled every minute of our visit with Jamaican "labrish." The next morning we headed for the Pennsylvania Turnpike and home. The Plymouth cruised away the miles as we reminisced about the events leading to our marriage and talked of our plans for the future.

For several years I had been renting a room from Alion and Fairy Tolbert on Lee Place near Harper Hospital and was considered a member of their family. On hearing of my marriage, they looked forward to welcoming Clare as if she were a long-lost cousin. Arriving in Detroit, we drove directly to the Tolberts' home where they welcomed her with hugs and family-like hospitality.

Fairy and her sister, Victoria Barlow, were slow-speaking Southerners in contrast to Clare, the fast-paced Jamaican, but the differences did not seem to inhibit their conversation during the hours spent getting to know each other. This relieved some of my inner concerns about taking Clare out of her luxurious Kingston home, staffed with two maids and a gardener, to live in the confines of a rented bedroom. Aided by the friendship of Fairy and Victoria, Clare took the change in stride.

Clare took over as office manager at Wayne School of Aeronautics when I enrolled for the fall 1955 semester at Wayne State University. She scheduled student flights and instructors, took care of the billings, and answered the telephone. I was pleased with the way she handled her duties and made new friends. Clare was a naturally shy, reserved person but adjusted readily to her new surroundings with a sense of humor, winning the respect of everyone.

Following Paul Poberezny's suggestion, I wasted no time in starting the long and tedious task of drawing up plans for my racer. Having lost my original drawings through a Canadian hustler, I had only a few sketches to work from. A smooth-talking, well-dressed man had come into my office at Wayne School of Aeronautics and expressed his desire to obtain a set of plans for the Love. He then made a tempting offer in which he would replace my pencil tracings with new drawings more suitable for commercial use in exchange for a set of plans for himself. With naive trust I gave him my tracings. Not hearing from him within the time period he promised, I made a few discreet inquiries of my friends in Windsor, Ontario. I soon learned that he was a scam artist and was using my plans, which had a Wayne Aircraft Company title block, to increase his credibility. He then sold fake stock in my own (now defunct) company, keeping the illegal proceeds for himself. When I contacted Canadian law enforcement officials in Windsor, they informed me that they knew of his activities but could not retrieve my plans unless I had a signed agreement with him, with a definite return date, which I did not have. Unfortunately, he never returned my plans.

I brought my old drawing board, left over from my Wayne Aircraft Company days, out to my office and started to work on the new plans in my spare time. I also teamed up with another amateur airplane builder in my area, Roger Perrault, to form EAA Chapter 13 (Detroit) and at the first meeting members voted Roger and me charter president and vice-president respectively. The fall of 1955 promised to be a busy one.

One of the pleasures I looked forward to after marrying Clare was introducing her to my relatives and friends. Fellow pilot King Walter Johnson commented on his first meeting with Clare, "You talk so fast it must be near Mach One!" With quick Jamaican wit she responded, "The problem with you is that you listen too slowly." My brothers and sister, as well as long-time friends Helen Rapp and Billie Lewis Means, adopted Clare as their sister. Billie was especially helpful when our small bedroom at the Tolberts became more and more confining. Using her influence with the Detroit Housing Commission, Billie helped us obtain a one-bedroom apartment in the federally funded Jeffries Housing Project near Wayne State University.

Another event I eagerly awaited was Clare's first experience with snowfall. As with most Jamaicans, her knowledge of winter came only from pictures of snow in movies and on Christmas cards. Winter arrived in late November and Clare eagerly went outside our office and swept the new snow from the wings of our Piper Cub. After finishing her work and making a few snowballs, she came inside with cold hands and feet. Although her face was reddened by the cold, Clare's bright eyes and smiling face were evidence of her enthusiasm for snowtime.

Clare's sense of humor was always a part of our lives. When I came home from school on my fortieth birthday on February 4, 1956, she met me at the door with birthday hugs and kisses. The flavorful aroma of dinner permeated our apartment. The meal was delicious and for this special celebration we opened a bottle of our favorite wine. But I saw no evidence of the traditional birthday cake. Leaving the kitchen for a moment, she returned with the cake. On seeing it I had to burst out laughing. Instead of candles, she had placed a cardboard cone on top of the cake with a 40-watt electric light bulb in the center! Aunt Jeanne would have been proud of her.

One day, after spending several hours in preparation at the student union, I headed for my last class of the day, English composition. Stepping off the curb in front of the student union my left artificial leg suddenly slipped off and I fell to the ground with my left stump taking the brunt of the force. Curious bystanders watched as I struggled to put my leg on again. Blood was seeping through my stump socks and I was in considerable pain, but after getting my leg back on again I decided to attend my English class anyway. It was only a one-hour class and I figured I could last through the period. I managed to walk to class with difficulty but within minutes the pain became unbearable due to swelling of my stump within the rigid confines of my artificial leg. When I explained this to my instructor, he ordered me to go home but not before questioning my sanity.

On taking my legs off I realized I would be out of school for several weeks. A fellow student, Harry Gibson, agreed to contact all my teachers and bring my class notes and homework to my apartment. Since I was bedridden and did not have a wheelchair, Clare had to let Harry into our apartment every morning. Wednesday morning, however, was her assigned day to use the basement laundry facilities, so she could not meet Harry as usual. She wrote a note and placed it on the front door of our apartment. It simply read:

Dear Harry,
The door is unlocked. Please go straight to the bedroom.

Clare

Looking around furtively to see if anyone had noticed, Harry snatched the note off the door and hurried down the hall to my bedroom. We thought the note was quite humorous for its unintentional implications. But Clare explained it to us very simply, "If I meant what you two are thinking I would have said, 'please *come* to the bedroom.'" We could see the difference but still thought it was funny.

One of my former flight students, Sammy Massenberg, a USAF colonel and B-29 pilot, was shot down over North Korea and imprisoned for months. On his release, he was assigned to Wright Field at Wright-Patterson Air Force Base near Dayton. While stationed there he invited Clare and me to pay a visit.

I had been 12 years old when I read an article in the September 1928 issue of *Western Flying* (which I still have) about the opening of Wright Field. It was to be the largest aeronautical research facility in the world. I envied Sammy; working there would be a dream come true. During the first scheduled vacation break we made the 220-mile drive to Wright-Patterson AFB.

While Clare enjoyed the company of Sammy's wife and family, he took me on a tour of the research facilities at Wright Field. I was impressed by its immense physical size and the thousands of military and civilian employees (about 35,000). One particular facility made a lasting impression. It was Building 65, a huge facility housing the Structural Test Division which had the responsibility for flight-load and fatigue testing of all USAF aircraft prior to their being committed to full production.

During my visit tests were being conducted on a full-size Convair B-58, the USAF's first supersonic bomber. Structural loads were combined with heat generated by thousands of infrared lamps to simulate supersonic heating (enough electrical energy to supply a small city). I left Building 65 convinced this was the place I wanted to work when I graduated from WSU. As a constant source of inspiration, Sammy gave me a standard federal employee application form and wrote on a piece of paper my probable GS level and starting salary. This would be the carrot that kept me going when my classwork and exams became more and more difficult. I put the note in my bedroom dresser drawer for quick access. Whenever I failed a subject (it happened three times) I would read the form again to raise my sagging spirits. This, along with Clare's constant support, provided the means to keep me working toward my degree. My overall progress and grade average remained satisfactory. I closed Wayne School of Aeronautics permanently at the end of the 1957 flying season and sold the assets to Woody Coche, the flight school operator next door. I was now able work full-time at my WSU studies.

This loss of income was partially compensated for by Professor Locke's decision to hire me as laboratory assistant in charge of the aeronautical engineering laboratory. The small salary was helpful (we ate a lot of hot dogs and beans) but the additional workload had serious negative effects. The lab work, plus emotional strains caused by difficult courses and exams (knowing full well my financial future depended on graduation), resulted in severe digestive problems. Upset stomach conditions became so frequent that I asked the WSU medical office for assistance. On reviewing my problem, the doctor concluded that it was caused by eating dinner while under emotional stress. He offered two solutions; either a prescription tranquilizer or relaxing with a glass of wine at least an hour before dinner. After warning me he had given a similar choice to a chronic alcoholic, he recommended the latter. I chose the wine and my digestive system returned to normal. Although school pressures are now far behind me, I still find a glass of wine a pleasant prelude to my evening meal.

During the summer of 1958 the EAA announced its Roadable Airplane Competition under the direction of Harry Zeisloft. The rules were deceptively simple, one of which required that the wings be folded in such a manner that the airplane could be stored inside a standard one-car garage. With the wings folded, the overall width could not exceed eight feet to meet highway towing regulations. Another requirement was that it be towable at highway speeds up to 45 MPH. Lesser details were also spelled out.

First prize was $5,000, a considerable sum in 1958. I was halfway through Aero Design Course 512 in the spring of 1959 before I decided to enter the competition. When I asked Professor Locke if I could change my design goals at mid-semester his answer was simple: "If you can complete a full semester's work in the remaining half semester, then go ahead."

Full of enthusiasm, I started the design work on my fourth airplane, WR-2. In its final configuration it was an all-wood, high-wing airplane with pilot and passenger sitting side by side ahead of the wing, and the Continental 85-HP engine mounted in a pusher installation. For the first time I planned to use a tricycle gear with a steerable nosewheel.

Clare and I decided the wings and rakishly swept tail were to be painted a bright red, the lower fuselage glossy black, and mid-fuselage contrasting white. The wings were designed to be folded back, and made ready for auto tow in seven minutes by one person, unassisted. I completed the course requirements on schedule with an A grade. With Professor Locke's blessing, I started construction of my new airplane in the aero lab the summer of 1959.

It was about this time that Clare and I were advised by our doctors that we would not be able to bear children. We began to consider adopting a child through the Detroit Catholic Social Services as recommended by our good friend Van Wallace. After our initial inquiry we were invited to attend a meeting of prospective adoptive parents by the social workers in charge of the program.

As the requirements for adoptive parents were spelled out we became painfully aware of our deficiencies. We were too old, did not own our own home, did not have adequate living space, hadn't been married long enough, and had insufficient income. As we started to leave, one of the social workers asked us to stay for further discussion. We found out that white infants were in great demand and the supply was short, hence strict arbitrary requirements were drawn up to aid in the selection process. Our hopes were raised when the worker said, "There are black babies available for adoption and very little demand for them." Assuring us that the important standards for adoption were not diminished for black babies despite their availability, they told us our chances of adoption were very good.

In February 1959 we received a call from the agency inviting us to come to their nursery and meet a boy we might consider adopting. We were told not to bring any baby clothes to eliminate any feeling of obligation on our part, in case we decided against adopting the baby. When we were introduced to the beautiful, curly-headed boy of six months we instantly fell in love with him and expressed our desire to bring him home. The staff gave us a few basic baby necessities and we drove home, proud parents of our first child, Paul Leslie Loving (Leslie for his grandfather, Uncle Les). It was Friday afternoon when we brought Paul home. Over the weekend we introduced him to all our relatives and friends. He went from lap to lap, smiling at everyone like the 22-pound cherub he was. Paul did not cry until Monday morning when Clare withheld his breakfast to make sure his vocal cords were in working order. They were!

My roadable WR-2, designated N112Y by the Federal Aviation Agency (FAA—successor to the CAA), was completed in the spring of 1960, and I won the American Institute of Aeronautics and Astronautics (AIAA) student award for my design. I could not have completed this enormous task in such a short time without Clare's continuous support. Every day she came over to the aero lab and performed many important tasks while little Paul alternately played and slept in his playpen. Her most tedious and important job was making 26 "ribs" for the wing, each one made of $\frac{1}{4}$-inch-square spruce strips held together with glue, tiny $\frac{1}{4}$-inch rib nails, and $\frac{1}{16}$-inch plywood gusset plates about the size of a postage stamp. This task was quite different from her household chores but she accomplished it with professional quality.

With great excitement, we rolled N112Y out to the parking lot of the engineering building in May 1960 for engine startup and brake tests, with good results. However, the initial taxi tests at Detroit City Airport were very disappointing. Some of the compromises I had made to ensure ease of construction were causing structural and aerodynamic control problems. With the competition due to start at the 1960 National EAA Fly-in at Rockford, Illinois, in late July, I worked feverishly to solve my problems. As the fly-in date neared it was clear I was not going to be able to complete the 50 hours of flying time required of all entrants. But wanting to attend the fly-in anyway so that Clare could enjoy the experience, I borrowed a low-bed trailer from my friend Lee Rivard to tow the WR-2 to Rockford.

On Sunday morning, about two weeks before we were to leave for Rockford, Clare and I received a phone call from Bud and Toni Harwood in Rockford inviting us to be their houseguests. We were surprised and flattered that a white couple who were total strangers would be kind enough to make such an offer to guests who were black. We gratefully accepted and were pleased with the warmth of their reception when we arrived in Rockford. They had a lovely home with a large garage where Bud had built his award-winning homebuilt airplane, a Wittman Tailwind N111N, truly a masterpiece of craftsmanship with superb flight characteristics. It was typical of Bud, I discovered, to be very modest in spite of the trophies he had received attesting to his skills.

Four airplanes were entered in the Roadable Design Competition in 1960 but the judges determined none met minimum requirements. Each of us received $125 for appearing and we were invited to reenter in 1962.

The cover of the *American Modeler* magazine, January 1961 issue, featured a full-color picture of N112Y, with the wings folded back, hooked up to a car ready for tow. Other magazines also carried articles, pictures, and sketches. While I was enjoying this favorable publicity, Toni Harwood called to let us know that Bud had died of natural causes. Clare and I cherished our pleasant memories of his wonderful hospitality more than ever. We still stay in contact with Toni.

Despite having failed a total of three courses, my honor point average was high enough to assure graduation from WSU in June 1961, provided I did not fail a required course during the last semester. During the spring of 1961, recruiters from all the major aerospace companies converged on the campus to interview prospective engineering graduates. I waited patiently until mid-May for the arrival of Charles Mayrand, the recruiter from Wright-Patterson AFB. It must have been a satisfactory interview for Mr. Mayrand told me I would definitely receive a job offer by mail. When it arrived, Clare and I were overjoyed by the terms of the offer. Because of my previous aviation experience, I was offered a starting position at the GS-7 level instead of the customary GS-5 for new graduates.

With a secure financial future now almost a certainty, Clare and I decided to go back to the Catholic Social Services and apply for a baby sister for Paul. Several weeks later, we were introduced to our future daughter, Michelle Stephanie, age about 2 years. We brought her home for a visit with Paul and other members of our family before returning her to the agency. We agreed to take permanent custody of Michelle when I was settled in my job and we had established our new home.

At the time I was nearing graduation, Colonel Massenberg left Wright-Patterson so I began to look for another contact at the base. I remembered reading about Ambrose "Ben" Nutt in the *Michigan Chronicle,* Detroit's black weekly newspaper. Ben, a former Detroiter and graduate of the University of Michigan's aeronautical engineering department, was one of the first black engineering graduates to be hired at the base in the early 1940s. Although we had never met, I called his home in Yellow Springs, Ohio, and asked him to share some of his knowledge and experience with me. He agreed and invited Clare and me to spend the night at his home on my next visit to the base, an invitation we were happy to accept. We made our visit a few days later. Ben drove me to Wright Field and gave me a tour of my new workplace, the flight dynamics laboratory. I had the opportunity to meet project engineers who would be my coworkers and view some of their work.

On arriving back in Yellow Springs (pop. 4,000), we drove by a new, bilevel house that was for sale. Looking at it again the next morning we decided it was just what we were looking for. We contacted the realtor and made a deposit. Driving home I was alternately happy with my new career and scared at the thought of flunking one of my courses. My job offer at the base was clearly contingent on my obtaining an engineering degree. Every assignment and exam from then until the end of the semester was like climbing Mount Everest.

After completing final exams, I gave each of my professors a self-addressed postcard requesting my grades be mailed as soon as possible. I was particularly concerned about my course in metallurgical engineering. My semester grades had not been very good. After taking the final exam I waited impatiently for my grade card. Finally, I went to the professor's office for a direct answer. He explained his strict policy of not giving out grades unofficially, but I was able to convince him my only interest was knowing if I passed the course, not my grade. He grudgingly admitted that I had passed, in spite of my poor semester performance. It was a surprise when I received a *B* for the course, the highest grade in the class. Months later, on receiving my official transcript, I found my scholastic standing was 39th in a graduating class of 86 engineering students. I learned also that at the age of 45 I was the oldest full-time engineering graduate in WSU history.

There were almost 1,800 graduates at the June 22, 1961, ceremony held at the huge, newly opened Cobo Hall in downtown Detroit. My fellow graduates appeared so capable and intelligent (I did not yet know my class standing) that I worried I would not be able to match their performance in the workplace. But with a job firmly in hand, I was determined to work hard to be competitive. After the graduation ceremonies, Clare held a party at our apartment for family and friends. Listening to a conversation, I heard a member of my family say, "Neal is sure lucky to get such a high-class, well-paying job." I thought of the seven years of emotional stress, sleepless nights, hours of study and exams—lucky? It was clear he was not familiar with the saying "Success is 99 percent perspiration and 1 percent inspiration."

Shortly after graduation Professor Locke invited me to his office for an informal chat. As I walked in and saw his eyes beaming through his horn-rimmed glasses, it was apparent we were both happy that I had reached my goal of becoming an aeronautical engineer. During our talk he recalled the discouraging comments he had made during our first conference. He admitted that of all the factors he mentioned to make his point he had left out the most important one: determination.

My high school transcript unfortunately made no mention of this characteristic. Professor Locke now realized the high rate of young engineering dropouts he had quoted was largely due to lack of determination, not scholastic skills.

With my handicap, and a wife and child to support, I had no alternative other than to persevere. I left his office with an invitation for Clare and me to spend a few days at his beautiful home facing the clean blue waters of Lake St. Clair. His wife, Dorothy, joined in issuing the invitation. We enjoyed our friends and the vacation.

My report date at Wright Field was August 15. Clare and I had time for a short vacation in Jamaica. Before leaving for Kingston, we drove from Detroit to Yellow Springs to sign the bank mortgage for our new home. While there I measured all the rooms and took color pictures so we could plan our room arrangements. Back in Detroit, we had a few days to shop for furniture and appliances before our departure for Jamaica.

Finally the great day arrived and Clare and I, with our toddler son Paul, now almost 3 years old, boarded a TWA flight for New York, stopping there briefly before flying on to Kingston. This was our first visit to Jamaica in six years.

Most of the New York branch of the Barnett family met us at the brand-new futuristic TWA terminal, where they spent most of their time getting acquainted with Paul. I had already learned that parents, on many occasions, play "second fiddle" to their children, especially a child as lovable as Paul. Soon our boarding call came and we walked through the jetway to a Pan Am Boeing 707, our first ride on a jetliner. In a little over three hours we were descending through a cloud layer and passing over the distinctive plaza of Spanish Town. Minutes later we were making our final approach over the waters of Kingston Harbour, gently touching down on the runway at Palisadoes Airport.

During our three-week vacation we tried our best to make up for the years we had been away from Jamaica. Earsly and Carl, Aunt Jeanne and Uncle Les, Felix and his wife, Sheila, and many others crowded our days with family activities, and most important, loving affection. Of course, baby Paul was the center of attention when he wasn't sleeping. Now that the pressure of graduation was over and my financial situation secure, I was able to fully relax for the first time since 1954. Our Jamaican vacation soon came to an end and we departed with the usual mixed emotions, sorry to leave our Jamaican family, yet looking forward to living in our new home and enjoying a rewarding, exciting career at Wright-Patterson AFB.

Home again in Detroit, we began the arduous task of packing our furniture for shipment to Yellow Springs. When finished we drove son Paul up to Red and Helen Rapp's home in Memphis, Michigan, where he would stay until Clare and I were settled in our new home. We made the four-hour drive to Yellow Springs on August 4 where the temperature was a scorching 100° F. Both of us were very tired and hungry, so we just set up our beds and rested while waiting for the plumber to finish installing our kitchen gas range. One of our new neighbors was kind enough to bring a pitcher of iced tea to quench our thirst during that hot, sultry afternoon. This act of thoughtfulness convinced us that we would enjoy living in Yellow Springs. After a week of moving furniture into the various rooms and hanging pictures on the walls, our house was in order. On Thursday morning, August 15, 1961, I drove to Wright Field, 12 miles away, and reported for work.

CHAPTER EIGHTEEN

FULFILLING DREAMS

H eading west along the quiet, two-lane Dayton–Yellow Springs Road leading to Wright Field, I found it hard to contain my excitement and anticipation. For the first time in my life I had professional status, assigned to work at the world's largest aeronautical research facility, Wright-Patterson Air Force Base (WPAFB), with a workforce of over 30,000 military and civilian employees. As I entered the gates of the giant, sprawling WPAFB at Area B, my bright mood changed to concern about my ability to meet the challenges of my new career. I was a 45-year-old, physically handicapped graduate with no formal engineering experience about to enter the world of advanced aeronautical research. Putting on an air of confidence I obtained a visitor's badge at the reception center and was directed to Building 12, the employment office for professional employees, and the office of Robert H. Schmidt, college relations representative, Civilian Personnel Division. He had written to me to offer me the position and was the first person to welcome me as the newest aeronautical engineer at WPAFB.

After the preliminary paperwork was completed Mr. Schmidt gave me my WPAFB identification credentials and a short briefing on my job status. He had circulated my résumé among various research agencies on base and now many were asking to interview me for positions in their engineering facilities. Mr. Schmidt advised me to take as much time as needed to find a position that satisfied my technical interests. During the next few days I met many supervisors and engineers who seemed to be anxious for me to work for them. It was quite a unique experience to have prospective employers asking me to work for them, instead of the other way around. One branch chief even came to my home to convince me I should work with him on his research projects. After a week of interviewing I entered the office of Denver W. Mullins, chief of the Special Loads Research Unit of the Structures Division, Flight Dynamics Laboratory.

Denver was a young, blond, Southern gentleman from Birmingham. His soft Alabama accent might have frightened me away from even considering working for him, given my own prejudices against Southern whites. His enthusiasm, scientific knowledge, and innate courtesy, however, made me listen intently as he told me about his latest project, measuring turbulence in thunderstorms using a converted Douglas B-66 jet bomber as a flight test vehicle. After the technical discussion was over he reached into his lower desk drawer and pulled out some magazines containing articles on Loving's Love and my latest design, the folding wing WR-2. We then talked of our mutual interest in aviation and discovered we were both active licensed pilots. There was no doubt about my decision now. I would work for Denver Mullins, 15 years my junior.

Arriving home I told Clare of my decision to work for a white supervisory engineer from Alabama, despite my fear of white Southerners. After an in-depth discussion about my interview with Denver, she agreed I had made the right decision. It also ended my own racial stereotypes and fears that were based on unhappy past experiences.

The next day I reported to Denver's office and met my coworkers, research engineer Larry Phillips and illustrator Tom Lyle. They were both very friendly and helpful. My desk was ready, complete with telephone, office supplies, and a desk nameplate made especially for me by Tom Lyle. During the first few months I attended many orientation meetings and read volumes of dull government regulations but was not allowed access to classified information. Issuance of my required secret clearance took months of investigative procedures by the security office. Meanwhile, Denver, realizing I had time on my hands, very thoughtfully invited me to work on any of my private projects in my spare time. With this golden opportunity I began to plan a new design, WR-3, to replace WR-2, which I had unsuccessfully entered in the 1960 EAA Roadable Design Competition. I was not satisfied with the results of a test program I was now conducting at Springfield Municipal Airport (five miles from Yellow Springs) and the modifications to correct the deficiencies promised to be a long and difficult task. It was also possible that the WR-2 could not be made to meet reasonable standards of safety and performance.

One beautiful early fall day, I walked out in front of Building 45 (where I was assigned) and looked down the hill at the runways and buildings of Wright Field. I was overwhelmed when I realized that another of my impossible dreams had come true. This exhilaration, however, was soon gone, replaced by my earlier concerns about meeting the performance standards of the skilled scientists who would be my coworkers. I developed such anxiety that my stomach began to churn as it had while I was taking important exams at WSU. Rushing to the nearest men's restroom, I began to vomit violently.

My anxieties gradually diminished with the unfailing encouragement, support, and especially the sense of humor of my young supervisor, Denver Mullins. As soon as my security clearance was issued we drove over to Area C, Patterson Field, where his converted Douglas B-66 jet bomber was undergoing modifications in preparation for flights into thunderstorms to measure turbulence. I shared his excitement and enthusiasm as he inspected the turbulence-measuring system of this swept-wing bomber. During our drive back to Wright Field, he leaned toward me and, speaking in hushed, confidential tones, said he had information he wanted me to keep secret. Being new to the world of classified information and judging by his serious tone of voice I was sure this data was important to national security. Tingling with excitement I heard Denver whisper, "If the government only knew how little they had to pay us to do what we are doing, they would cut our salary in half!" Our mutual love of airplanes and all things aviation made us kindred souls.

The Roadable Design Competition was scheduled for the annual EAA fly-in in late July 1962 at Oshkosh, Wisconsin. Now I had to decide whether to continue my test program with WR-2 or build a new airplane. With unwarranted optimism, I decided to start a new project, the WR-3, with the hope of having it ready for the EAA fly-in competition only eight months away. This was a daunting goal for I would soon be working full-time and traveling extensively as project engineer for a new research program of my own. However, I did have the distinct advantage of having the space to build my airplane at home. The upper level of our bilevel home in Yellow Springs was completely finished, with living and dining room, kitchen, two bedrooms, and bath, providing ample living space. The lower level was totally unfinished with only the outer walls of two-by-fours enclosing the living space. I put up a temporary wall enclosing a family room and a utility room for Clare, leaving the other half of the lower level as a shop to build my airplane. Having completed the basic design work at the office I began construction of WR-3. Keeping the engine and salvageable parts, I scrapped the remains of the WR-2.

Armistice Day, November 11, 1961, was my second paid government holiday. Clare and I took this opportunity to drive to Detroit to pick up our new daughter, Michelle Stephanie, who had just turned 3 on October 17. At the appointed hour we arrived at the Catholic Social Services office where our bright-eyed, charming little girl was waiting for us. Giving us a welcoming hug and saying goodbye to her social worker, she walked happily out of the office with her new family. We took her on a round of visits with her Detroit relatives before leaving for Yellow Springs. We had talked to Paul at length, prior to our trip, regarding his baby sister and especially how he was to share his toys with her. On arriving home Paul immediately took Michelle to his playroom where they got along fine until she picked up one of his favorite toys, sparking their first fight. However, they grew to love each other very much and always put up a united front when confronted by what they considered, at times, their "tyrannical" parents.

Construction proceeded rapidly on the WR-3, a completely different configuration from WR-2 while still retaining the wing-fold mechanism. It was a low-wing, open-cockpit airplane seating two people in tandem, powered by the 85-HP Continental engine from the dismantled N112Y. The materials were all wood and fabric and I went back to a conventional two-wheel landing gear.

As work progressed, I applied to the FAA for a registration number and was assigned N553A. In spite of working every night until 3 A.M., my planned schedule was not being met. However, I continued to work and managed to complete all the major component parts by early June. I then moved it out of the house and started final assembly in the carport. My usual practice was not to work on Sundays. But being behind schedule, I decided to work Sunday evening, July 16, to install instruments in the cockpit. Standing up in the rear cockpit to connect an instrument line, I lost my balance and fell to the ground, cutting a deep gash in my right hand. A neighbor drove me to a nearby hospital where my hand was sutured and bandaged. The doctor ordered me not to use my hand for a month. The EAA fly-in would be over by that time. I had a one-car garage built behind the carport and stored N553A until once again I had spare time to resume work.

Shortly after I received my secret clearance, Denver gave me the task of initiating a high-altitude clear air turbulence project to measure atmospheric turbulence from 50,000 to 70,000 feet altitude in support of the USAF aerospace plane (now the X-30) program. The objective was to develop a manned vehicle capable of taking off from a typical USAF base runway like an airplane, fly into orbit, and land at the point of departure. The X-30 mission would require supersonic flight at the 50,000- to 70,000-foot altitude level. Atmospheric turbulence was known to exist at these altitudes but no accurate, measured flight data was available suitable for establishing structural design criteria for such high-performance aircraft.

I proceeded to write a statement of work defining the project's scope and objectives, which was incorporated into a request for proposal by the contracting office and sent to prospective bidders. The contract was won by the Lockheed-California Company of Burbank, California. Walter Crooks was the project engineer. It was now contractually the High Altitude Clear Air Turbulence (HICAT) Project, which would eventually receive widespread recognition in the United States, Europe, Australia, and the Soviet Union.

The only airplane capable of meeting the high-altitude requirements was the Lockheed U-2, a highly classified airplane very difficult to requisition for militarily nonstrategic projects such as HICAT. One day I received a request to attend a highly classified meeting at a secret location on base. They gave me no information on the agenda or the reason for my being invited. On arriving at the designated conference room I was impressed by the high rank of both the military and civilian attendees. The highest ranking officer opened the meeting by introducing me and then asked that I give a thorough, detailed briefing on my HICAT project. The purpose of the meeting was to determine if the technical merits of HICAT warranted the assignment of a U-2. Completely surprised by this request, and with no time for preparation, I gave a complete review of the details of the instrumentation system and meteorological planning for the HICAT project. I was very pleased when I later received a call on a secure base phone from the U-2 office telling me they had assigned one of their aircraft, serial number 66722, to my project for the required period of time. This was my first important milestone as project engineer for HICAT.

Preparations were underway to install the $750,000 gust-measuring system in our assigned U-2, based at Edwards Air Force Base near Lancaster, California. As HICAT project engineer it was necessary for me to visit both of these facilities. My first TDY (Temporary Duty) to Los Angeles started March 4, 1963, at Dayton Airport when I boarded a TWA Lockheed Constellation bound for Chicago. There I changed to a TWA Boeing 707 for a nonstop flight to Los Angeles. As I sat in this luxurious jet airliner it was difficult to believe I was being paid not only my regular salary but all trip expenses as well. For me, this was more like a paid vacation than a job.

On arriving in Los Angeles I was met by my old friend from my Detroit City Airport and BT-13 days, King Walter Johnson, now living in Los Angeles with his family. His short course on how to drive safely on the notorious Los Angeles freeways gave me enough courage to rent a car for my local business travel.

My first official visit was to the Lockheed-California facility in Burbank where I met Walter Crooks, Lockheed's project engineer for HICAT, and Pat Underwood, electronics engineer. After Walter and

Pat gave an overview of the program, arrangements were made for me to fly to Edwards AFB in a small twin-engine airplane used to transport Lockheed personnel. Walter introduced me to the pilot, who gave me the privilege of sitting in the copilot's seat during the short flight. Soon after taking off from smog-ridden Burbank Airport we cleared the mountain range and started our descent into the crystal-clear air of Antelope Valley. The vast expanse of desolate, brown desert was dotted with rectangular plots of beautiful, green irrigated farmland. Also clearly visible from the air were the original shorelines of several huge, very flat, dry lake beds. This area was perfect for emergency landings, which were quite common during test flights of high-performance experimental aircraft. As we taxied up to the hangar I saw the HICAT U-2 for the first time. It was painted a sinister dull black with only the white tail number, 66722, for contrast. Walter, Pat, and I were briefed by Col. Harry Andonian, chief of the U-2 section, and Ray Mumford, a civilian employee in charge of maintenance. I felt privileged to work with these skilled professionals who treated me as a social and professional equal without regard for my race or handicap. My efforts to earn a degree were now paying rich rewards.

After the HICAT U-2 successfully completed the initial flight testing of the instrumentation system at Edwards in February 1964, we scheduled the first operational gust-measuring flights out of Patrick Air Force Base, Florida. Pat Underwood preceded the rest of the HICAT team to Patrick so he could set up his special highway trailer containing electronic equipment for printing and analyzing raw data recorded on each flight. Soon after his arrival Pat called from Melbourne, Florida, not far from Patrick AFB, offering to make motel reservations for me. Accepting his offer, I suggested he mention my race when talking to the motel reservations clerk. Being a native Californian he couldn't understand why, but I insisted. Of course, he was given a practical lesson in racial prejudice in the South. After several futile tries at making reservations at local motels (always mentioning my professional status) Pat finally found a room for me in a second-rate motel. Aware of his innocence in racial matters, I politely refrained from saying "I told you so."

Upon completing a week of gust-measuring flights at Patrick AFB as planned by our Lockheed research meteorologist, Dr. William Hildreth, we selected Ramey AFB, Puerto Rico, as our next base for research flights. This operation was to last five weeks so I bought a round-trip airline ticket for Clare so we could spend these weeks together.

I arrived in San Juan via a Pan Am flight and rented a car to drive to Ramey AFB, 70 miles west of San Juan. Clare was scheduled to arrive in San Juan three days later so I had time to arrange suitable housing for the two of us at Ramey AFB officers quarters.

Returning to San Juan Airport to meet Clare, I found a comfortable seat on the observation deck and leisurely watched the airliners take off and land. While a Pan Am Boeing 707 was in the final boarding process a fire broke out on the left wing. Pandemonium ensued as passengers scrambled to safety amid the smoke and flames. With red lights flashing and sirens wailing, the fire crews came to the stricken 707 and applied fire-retardant foam. The fire was soon extinguished but not before the left tires burned out, causing the jetliner to lean awkwardly like a wounded bird. Fire damage was also clearly evident in the left wing flap area. For no particular reason, I made a mental note of the tail number, N759PA. On our drive back to Ramey AFB I told Clare all about the incident after exchanging family news, especially about Paul and Michelle.

With five weeks of work and pleasure completed, we drove back to San Juan Airport for departure. Hearing the boarding call, we hurried to the designated gate to our Pan Am 707. Walking by the left wing I noticed that shiny new flaps and other components had been installed. Looking up at the tail I saw the number—N759PA! After we were comfortable in our seats I told Clare the news. Full of confidence she said if I didn't walk off the airplane neither would she. I kept my uneasiness to myself.

Detroit Chapter 13 of the Experimental Aircraft Association held its second annual awards dinner at the Detroit Arsenal Officers Club on February 8, 1964. Paul Poberezny was the honored guest and speaker.

As founding vice-president, I received a special award. During my dinner conversation with Paul, I offered to donate Loving's Love to the newly opened EAA Museum located in Hales Corners, a suburb of Milwaukee. Paul was very pleased with my offer and promised it would have a good home. Two months after arriving home from Puerto Rico, I began to prepare the Love for her final flight to the museum. The following comments describe my feelings:

LOGBOOK ENTRY: October 16, 1964
Springfield, Ohio—Warsaw, Indiana—Milwaukee, Wisconsin.
Total flying time: 2.50 hours

Loving's Love purred its way to Milwaukee for this last flight as though it were brand-new. In fact, the FAA had just relicensed it and I spent considerable time polishing it back to nearly new condition for its final destination, the EAA Air Education Museum. My decision to donate the Love was based on my busy work schedule, which precluded my being able to maintain or fly my racer as necessary for continued safe flight in this high-performance aircraft. Shutting off the engine for the last time brought an end to a chapter of my life filled with challenge, fear, joy, and excitement. Paul was there to assist me as I climbed out of the cockpit for the last time. Countering my sense of loss was the hope that while on display at the museum, Loving's Love would provide inspiration and pleasure to others. The last entry in my logbook for N351C under Pilot Remarks was simply, "Last flight—Paul Poberezny on hand to greet me."

As the HICAT Project progressed, it became evident that the aerospace industry was depending on my project to provide the critical data needed to establish gust load structural design criteria for the Supersonic Transport (SST). SSTs were now under development in the United States as well as Britain, France, and the Soviet Union, and these data were needed for certification. I was invited to give technical papers at various symposia and seminars attended by U.S. and foreign officials. My first opportunity to travel overseas came when Richard "Dick"

Hoener, chief of the Structures Division, came into my office in mid-May 1965. He asked if I was interested in attending as an observer an Advisory Group for Aeronautical Research and Development (AGARD) meeting sponsored by the North American Treaty Organization (NATO). The meeting was scheduled for Paris, June 6–15, 1965, and I was invited to discuss HICAT data and instrumentation. I accepted with unabashed enthusiasm and wasted no time in preparing a foreign travel request and my presentation. Due to the short notice of my travel request I had to stop in Washington, D.C., to pick up my diplomatic passport before proceeding to New York for a TWA flight to Paris.

Sitting in the luxurious cabin of the Boeing 707 flying at nearly 600 MPH I couldn't help thinking of my boyhood hero, Charles Lindbergh, making the first nonstop flight to Paris in 1927. On seeing the Eiffel Tower on our approach to Orly Field I was sure that Lindbergh could not have been more thrilled than I on arriving in this famous metropolis of Europe.

In addition to my AGARD discussions I had an appointment to meet with Y. Sillard, Direction des Transports, Ariens. Since Mr. Sillard's understanding of English was no better than my limited command of French he invited his secretary, Mademoiselle Filladeaux, to act as translator during our technical discussions. Mr. Sillard invited her to accompany us to lunch at a sidewalk café on the Champs Élysées. At her suggestion I ordered frog legs and wine as a change from my usual hamburger and french fries. During our conversation I complimented her on her excellent command of the English language. "I spent two years in Detroit, Michigan, teaching French at a Catholic high school," she responded. We spent the rest of the lunch hour discussing her experiences teaching at a school that was only a few miles from my home. What a coincidence!

The longest TDY of my career was a survey of airport facilities in the South Pacific which might serve as bases suitable for HICAT U-2 operations. A four-engine Douglas C-118 (military version of the DC-6) and two flight crews were assigned to the flight in addition to our HICAT staff of fifteen people. In command of our flight was Col. Harry Andonian, who also had the responsibility for determining the suitability of the airports on our itinerary for U-2 operations. It was my task to brief local officials and research scientists on HICAT objectives and obtain their financial and technical support.

We departed Edwards AFB on January 6, 1966, and our itinerary included Hickam Field, Hawaii; Pago Pago, Samoa; Nandi, Fiji; Christchurch, New Zealand; Melbourne, Canberra, Sydney, Darwin, Australia; Manila, Philippine Islands; Kadena AFB, Okinawa; Tokyo; Wake Island; Eniwetok, in Micronesia; Hickam Field, Hawaii; and back to Edwards. Most memorable of my many briefings were for Major General Rowland, PACAF chief of staff at Hickam Field in Hawaii, and A. M. Morris, minister of external affairs for the Australian government in Canberra. I particularly remember white-haired, dignified Mr. Morris assembling his staff in a beautiful walnut-paneled room for the briefing. With a kind look, he reminded me that I was talking to politicians, not scientists, and to speak in words they could understand. The briefing was a success, resulting in the HICAT U-2 being stationed at Laverton Field near Melbourne. Originally I had some apprehensions about going to Australia since they had an exclusion act that prohibited entry by blacks and Asians. But my program had the approval of the U.S. State Department and the secretary of state, Dean Rusk, personally signed my diplomatic passport. The exclusion act was repealed two years later in 1968.

Having very little spare time when we arrived in Sydney, Australia, Walter Crooks, Pat Underwood, and I rented a cab and asked the driver to take us to places and scenes of interest. We drove over the famous Queen's Bridge and toured Sydney's new futuristic opera house with its soaring arched roofs then nearing completion. As we rode around town on this weekday I noticed many children playing in the streets. Since it was January, I was sure they were supposed to be in school. The cabbie just laughed when I asked him about it. "Blimey, governor, they are on summer vacation y'know!" I had completely forgotten I was on the other side of the equator and the seasons were reversed. When I arrived at Dayton Airport on a cold, blustery January 29, I had traveled over 28,000 miles in 24 days and crossed the equator twice.

By now my international status earned me an invitation to present a technical paper entitled "Turbulence in the Stratosphere" at the International Union of Geodosy and Geophysics (IUGG) Conference in

Lucerne, Switzerland, on October 5, 1967. Now that I was scheduled to be in Europe I received additional invitations to meet with members of the French-Anglo-United States Supersonic Transport (FAUSST) in Paris and London. Seizing this golden opportunity to take Clare on her first trip to Europe, I asked the WPAFB travel office to make duplicate airline reservations for her. Clare's initial reaction was skeptical. "I won't believe it until I step off the airliner in Zurich." For me it was a dream trip, spending nine days with Clare in Lucerne, and seven days respectively in London and Paris, for a total of twenty-three days.

When I went to the travel office to pick up Clare's ticket the young woman at the counter suggested I cut my visit to twenty-one days which, she said, would save me hundreds of dollars. Without giving it a second thought I told her I had no intention of shortening this wonderful trip with my wife just to save money. The travel clerk and I had developed a mutual sense of humor during my many visits to her office and she asked in a voice loud enough to be heard by everyone in the office, "Are you sure this is your *wife* you are taking with you?"

As we stepped off the TWA Boeing 707 in Zurich on the misty morning of September 27, I turned to Clare and asked, "Do you believe it now?" Looking at the beautiful Swiss landscape she replied, "No, I won't believe this has really happened until we are home and the pictures we have taken are developed." We took a cab to downtown Zurich where we boarded a train to Lucerne. On arrival we found our hotel, the Waldstotterhof, across the street from the station. Our stay in Lucerne, a picture postcard of a city, was the highlight of our trip. During my HICAT presentation to the IUGG I met members of the Russian delegation, including Dr. N. K. Vinnechenko who was involved in research similar to mine for application to the Russian SST. He spoke almost perfect English. We conversed at length about our respective research activities and agreed to write each other, but I had doubts I could obtain official permission to do so. I was surprised that the AF Foreign Technology Division at WPAFB encouraged me to initiate correspondence as long as it was in accordance with their guidelines. We went on to become personal friends by exchanging letters and holiday cards.

N553A was rolled out of the garage for her first public appearance on Memorial Day, May 30, 1967. Sitting in our driveway resplendent with bright, shiny red wings and dazzling white fuselage with red trim she attracted considerable attention from the neighbors and passersby. Eugene Brazier, my supervisor, and several of my coworkers were on hand for the informal ceremony. But months of small detail assembly work remained to be finished before it was ready for flight. Meanwhile, my fears associated with the potential dangers of WR-3's first test flight were the same as those I experienced before testing Loving's Love with one important exception. This time I was jeopardizing the security and future of my family. In spite of her deep concerns, Clare was both understanding and supportive of my plans to test-fly N553A.

The momentous day for the first flight of my new roadable WR-3 came on April 26, 1968, at Springfield Municipal Airport, about five miles northeast of Yellow Springs. With Clare and Chet Swinehart of the FAA watching from the ramp in front of the terminal building, I taxied out for takeoff from runway 24 on a cool, cloudy, misty Thursday morning.

Pulling my goggles over my eyes I opened the throttle and N553A fairly leaped down the runway and into the air under perfect control. Leveling off at 2,500 feet I began to relax from my first-flight jitters and went through my preplanned test maneuvers. I was pleasantly surprised that my airplane flew hands-off in perfect balance, with well-harmonized control responses. All engine parameters were in the normal range. After 35 minutes of trouble-free flying, I began to feel the damp, cold air seep through my flying clothes, so I headed back to the airport for my first landing. After a surprisingly smooth touchdown I taxied up to the terminal building and shut the engine off.

As I raised my goggles Mr. Swinehart reached into the cockpit to congratulate me on my successful test flight. Not having talked to him about the flight I wondered just how he knew it was successful except that I didn't crash. "I have developed the Swinehart Rule," he explained, "which has never failed. If the pilot taxies up with his lips compressed and the pupils of his eyes mere slits, the flight was a disaster. But if his teeth are showing in a big smile and his eyes are bright, the flight was clearly a success." My shining eyes and teeth met the Swinehart Rule for success. After I had successfully completed 50 hours of test flying as required by the FAA, Clare became the first passenger on Labor Day, followed by Paul and Michelle.

This milestone was accomplished six years after the 1962 EAA Roadable Design Competition was over. Over the next 23 years I completed 696 hours of safe, enjoyable flying. The WR-3 still attracts surprised smiles and stares when I pull it out of the garage, tow it with my Ford Escort to the local auto gas station for a fill-up, and then out to the airport for the joy of exhilarating flight!

In 1968 the U.S. Civil Service initiated an annual award program to recognize outstanding handicapped civil service employees. For my work in 1967 I was named the Outstanding Handicapped Employee of the entire U.S. Air Force.

Ten finalists were invited to attend the first annual presentation of the Outstanding Federal Employee of the Year Award on March 25, 1969, in Washington, D.C. Clare received special invitational travel orders from the secretary of the Air Force. I was somewhat jealous since her per diem was almost twice that of mine. After all, I asked myself, was Clare being honored or me? The award ceremony was held in the commerce department auditorium and first prize was won by Katherine Niemeyer, employed by the Veterans Administration in East Orange, New Jersey.

Each finalist received his or her individual award from the vice-president of the United States, Spiro Agnew. We were then driven by bus to the Mayflower Hotel where a special luncheon had been arranged for the awardees. Sitting next to me on the bus was the chaplain for the event, Rev. Neal T. Jones, pastor of Columbia Baptist Church, Falls Church, Virginia. In his rich Virginian accent he explained why I did not win the final award. "As each finalist was called to the center of the stage they were carrying canes or crutches, using walkers or riding in a wheelchair. But you walked across the stage as though you weren't handicapped at all," he observed. "The least you could have done was *limp* a little bit!"

In the fall of 1970, a Pan Am Boeing 747 took off from John F. Kennedy Airport in New York bound for London with Sen. Jacob Javits from New York among the passengers on board. While climbing to cruise altitude the Boeing 747 encountered severe turbulence in clear air while passing over Nantucket Island. Injuries suffered by some crew members and passengers caused the pilot to return to New York without delay. The news media made headlines out of the fact that a modern, high-technology jumbo jet airliner equipped with the latest weather instrumentation had encountered severe turbulence without visual or radar warning. Senator Javits's presence on board added to the furor generated by this incident. It reminded me of the concerns I expressed in the title of a technical paper I presented at the second annual American Institute of Aeronautics and Astronautics/American Meteorological Society meeting in Los Angeles in 1966 entitled "Clear Air Turbulence (CAT)—A Menace to the Aerial Highway."

The FAA decided to convene a worldwide symposium on clear air turbulence to review current data and define research necessary to prevent future CAT incidents. The FAA Turbulence Symposium, held in Washington, D.C., March 22–24, 1971, was the largest symposium ever devoted strictly to aeronautical problems due to CAT and was attended by over 900 representatives from every airline in the free world. I was invited to give a technical paper entitled "Highlights of CAT Test Programs." Quoting from my trip report, "My paper was apparently well received and was even reported with a headline and article in the *Wall Street Journal*." The article, in part, was as follows:

More Research Urged on Dangers of Air Turbulence
An Air Force civilian flight safety expert said yesterday clear air turbulence (CAT), unseen violent disturbances in clear skies, menaces even the largest planes flying.

Neal V. Loving of the Flight Dynamics Laboratory at Wright-Patterson Base, Ohio, said CAT is still such a mystery that additional research is essential.

This was followed by seven paragraphs containing my additional comments and recommendations.

Several months later, while I was en route to Los Angeles in a TWA Boeing 727, the captain announced that due to unusual jet stream activities at our assigned altitude we might be required to make an unscheduled fuel stop at Los Vegas, Nevada. The anticipated conditions did not occur and we made our flight into Los Angeles without incident. My return flight three days later was on a TWA Lockheed L-1011 jumbo jet. Shortly after reaching cruise altitude the captain left the cockpit and spoke pleasantly to passengers on his way to the restroom. I called to him as he passed by and asked about the unusual atmospheric conditions prevalent during my flight out to Los Angeles. Sensing my question predicated more than a casual knowledge of meteorology, he asked me to come to the cockpit 10 minutes later. I hesitantly knocked on the cockpit door, which was opened quickly by the captain. Inviting me to sit in the jump seat behind him, he asked my name and background, and expressed surprise I was the Neal Loving whose CAT research he had read about in the *Wall Street Journal.* During our discussion on atmospheric turbulence and its problems the copilot leaned over, introduced himself as a member of the Seattle chapter of the EAA, and said he was pleased to meet the designer, builder, and pilot of Loving's Love.

Getting up to go to the restroom, he invited me to take his seat. I looked questioningly at the captain; without hesitation he waved me into the copilot's seat. Turning the controls over to me he suggested I fly it for a while. I couldn't believe I was at the controls of a huge Lockheed L-1011 with 250 innocent souls on board flying 600 MPH at 40,000 feet! At first I was scared to move the controls for fear I would upset a passenger's coffee. But the captain assured me my experience in handling the delicate controls of a racer was ample qualification to fly an airliner. I stayed at the controls performing gentle maneuvers, not returning to my seat until we entered the Indianapolis Approach Control area. If the FAA ever knew that a certain TWA captain had allowed a black, double-amputee passenger to fly his jetliner filled with passengers he would be grounded forever. But wherever that captain may be, I want to thank him for making another impossible dream come true.

In April of 1974 my area of research changed from atmospheric turbulence to advanced composites. My supervisor was now Havard Wood who, for reasons I never determined, was nicknamed Jack. He had interviewed me during my first week at WPAFB in 1961 but I decided in favor of Denver Mullins. But now he intrigued me with the possibilities of replacing conventional metal materials used in aircraft structural components with advanced composites. This new material consisted of tiny strands of strong carbon fibers (about the diameter of human hair) bonded together by epoxy resins under heat and pressure. The layers of composite tapes (resembling black electrical tape) were laid up in varying layer orientations like plywood for specific design requirements. Significant weight savings were possible with this new material with the added benefits of no corrosion or rust.

For my first assignment Jack appointed me project engineer on a contract with McDonnell-Douglas of St. Louis to develop a composite speed brake for the USAF's newest fighter, the F-15 Eagle. The project was a success and all subsequent production F-15s were equipped with this speed brake. I followed this project with a $17.5-million contract with General Dynamics/Fort Worth to develop composite wings and inlet ducts for their latest fighter, the F-16 Falcon. On my first trip to the plant I was taken on a tour of their research facilities, especially those dedicated to my project.

This involved so much walking that for the first time in my life I was unable to function due to extreme pain resulting from blisters forming on my stumps. I was taken to the company doctor, Dr. Keyes, who prescribed pain pills and a prolonged rest from walking. We then had a long talk about aviation pioneers during which I discovered he was related to the Keyes brothers who held the world endurance record for refueled flight during the thirties. He forwarded his medical recommendations to Jack Wood, who banned me from all further travel until I was fitted with a new set of artificial legs. I objected strenuously. I felt my responsibilities as project engineer required my being on-site regularly at General Dynamics to check project progress. But Jack was adamant. Several months passed before I was sufficiently adjusted to my new legs to wear them to my office for the first time. My initial pain and physical discomfort were forgotten when I was greeted and cheered by my coworkers. Several months later, due to General Dynamics's previous decision to use only metallic components on the F-16, my contract was canceled prior to completion.

Carl Barnett celebrated his March 22, 1975, birthday by taking Earsly out the evening before for a quiet dinner for two at a popular Kingston restaurant. This was a welcome respite from the daily dawn-to-dusk airport activities at their flight school and charter service, Wings Jamaica, Ltd. Earsly had earned her FAA commercial pilot rating before leaving Detroit and had gone on to become the first certified flight instructor in Jamaica. She was also kept busy by their two sons, Mark and Chris. This happy birthday celebration was to be their last evening together.

Early the next morning, as Carl was about to take a charter flight to Grand Cayman Islands, Earsly complained of a headache. This was a very rare thing for her, so Carl advised her to stay in bed and offered to stay home in case he was needed. Earsly was adamant that he make the charter flight, insisting the headache was a minor problem that could be solved with simple remedies.

After Carl's departure, Earsly's condition worsened rapidly and a doctor was called to the house. In spite of medical treatment she slipped into a coma and was rushed to the hospital. She died later that afternoon of a cerebral hemorrhage without regaining consciousness.

As Carl was calling Kingston Approach Control he was advised of an emergency at home. On arriving he found his family had gathered and was advised that Earsly had passed away as quietly as she had lived. Her death left a grieving family and a void in the Jamaican aviation community. Fred Wilmot, aviation writer and good friend, wrote movingly of Earsly's achievements and her outstanding personality in an article entitled "I Remember Earsly." The following are the first and last paragraphs of an article he wrote for the July 1975 issue of the Jamaica Defence Force Air Wing publication, "The Altimeter."

The unfortunate and sudden death of Earsly Barnett recently brought to an end in Jamaica the career of a personality which more than any other on the island stood for aviation. Earsly was a rare and talented person. As an instructor she launched more fledgling pilots into airborne careers than any other person has in Jamaica's aviation history. She occupies and will continue to occupy a special place in the hearts and memories of hundreds of fliers and persons connected with aviation in Jamaica. . . .

One doesn't know, and no one has ever told, where it is that we take off for when we leave this place. But, wherever she is flying today, I am sure she is flying carefully and well, and perhaps, as the poem says, reaching out and touching the face of God.

My last research project, the advanced composite wing/fuselage program, was a five-year, $17.5-million contract with the Northrop Company, Hawthorne, California, to develop valid long-term design criteria for composite structures of newly developing USAF aircraft. Northrop's project engineer for this important program was a young, capable, personable engineer from England (now a U.S. citizen), James Eves, who was assisted by a fellow British scientist, Dr. Robin Whitehead. I initiated the program in 1979 and was directly responsible for coordinating the efforts of the Northrop engineers in setting up and approving the design and test procedures for the composite wing/fuselage components.

Two years later, satisfied that the program was on its way to success, I fulfilled my desire to retire at age 65 after completing 20 years of government service. During those 20 years I had made 138 trips for the USAF to places on the globe I never dreamed of seeing, received twenty-four awards (including the Meritorious Civilian Service Award), and presented fifteen technical papers at various symposia and technical meetings. I officially retired on January 9, 1982, with my retirement party the following month. This event was highlighted by the surprise attendance of Red and Helen Rapp from Memphis, Michigan, and Carl Barnett, who traveled all the way from Jamaica.

I was very flattered when Col. Ralph A. Custer, chief of Structures Division, wrote me the day before my retirement:

You have been the driving force in the successful effort to establish a productive relationship and management interface with the Aeronautical Systems Division to develop and apply Advanced Composite structures for use in Air Force systems. Your extra-ordinary initiative in this effort, and your expert technical management have directly contributed to the successful achievement in transitioning Advance Composite structures to Air Force aircraft.

Your leadership, knowledge, and technical ability will stand as a major record of excellence against which future engineers will be measured. Your high standards have contributed to a stronger National Defense and a better Air Force.

In reading those words I had difficulty believing they were directed to a black, double-amputee engineer from the ghettos of Detroit. The last of my impossible dreams had come true.

CHAPTER NINETEEN

REFLECTIONS

Sometimes a moment lasts a lifetime." These words aptly describe the moment I looked up into the sky and saw the DH-4 pass overhead on that hot summer day in Detroit back in 1926.

That special moment, a true gift, has continued to live with me to this day. But as I reflect on it, I cannot take credit for any inspiration it provided. According to my *Winston College Dictionary,* a gift is defined as "something given or bestowed." I would be less than human if I did not give thanks to God for the gift of my continual love of aviation which has brought so much joy and satisfaction to my life. Similarly, I would be less than human if I did not want to share that gift with others. Ever since teaching my first model airplane class at the Detroit YMCA in 1936 I have been privileged to share my enthusiasm and skills with other people, young and old. Some members of my 1936–40 YMCA classes still keep in touch to remind me how I have touched their lives.

Maceo Williams was 9 years old when I met him in 1936. He now drives a 42-wheel truck, is an FAA-rated private pilot, and is engaged in helping black teenagers learn how to fly under the sponsorship of the Negro Airmen International (NAI) chapter in Detroit. Grim Clemons went on to become the first black hired in the engineering department at General Motors Technical Center. Emile Sandelin owns a successful travel agency, traveling all over the world in support of his business. He still cherishes a trophy he won at my YMCA 1940 annual model airplane exhibit.

Leroy Mitchell, after studying in various art schools, followed my example and graduated from Wayne State University with a B.S. in education, specializing in fine art and social science. He is a talented artist, teacher, lecturer, and author and has lived in Ghana, Africa, teaching at the Achimota School, and lectured at the Faculty of Art, University of Science and Technology, Kumasi.

Col. Samuel Massenberg (USAF, Ret.), now Dr. Massenberg, Ph.D., is presently the director of Minority University Research and Education Programs Division at NASA Headquarters in Washington, D.C. Sammy Harmon, the young man who borrowed my crutches back in 1945, is now Dr. Samuel Harmon, Ph.D., who for many years headed a mathematics and computer facility in Ann Arbor, Michigan. More recently, he has held high-level posts in Nairobi, Kenya, and is currently working and living in Swaziland, South Africa.

These are only a few of the young men whose lives I hope I have favorably influenced. I am very proud of them all.

Over the years I have been invited to give motivational talks from elementary schools to universities. I always stress that no human being is perfect, that we are all handicapped in some way. It can be due to race, gender, physical handicap, illness, an inferiority complex, or nationality—the list is endless. The difference between the success or failure we experience as human beings is chiefly determined by how each of us deals with our own special weaknesses.

During a lecture at Wittenberg University in Springfield, Ohio, I stressed over and over again that we all have our own obstacles to overcome. My lecture was so well received that I was asked to come back the following year. When my second lecture was over I was informed that the students wanted me to have lunch with them at the student union. A young, white, female student volunteered to be my guide. During our walk to the cafeteria she confided she had heard me speak the year before and it changed her life. "I always wanted to be an aeronautical engineer but my conservative, well-meaning parents insisted there were no opportunities for women in technical fields so

I enrolled in a liberal arts college. After hearing your lecture I was inspired to apply for admission to the aeronautics college at Purdue University and I have been notified of my acceptance." Her story made my day!

One of my principal concerns is for the future of black youth in the United States. With black athletes and entertainment figures dominating our television programs, magazines, and newspapers, black children have a limited number of role models. As a result, these individuals are glamorized almost to the virtual exclusion of blacks who are making significant contributions to the fields of science, technology, economics, and military service.

This point was driven home to me in the summer of 1991 when I was invited to give a seminar on leadership to black high school youths at Wilberforce University, Ohio. General Colin Powell was an international hero at that time for his outstanding leadership during Operation Desert Storm. I used him as an example of outstanding success in a field not associated with sports or entertainment.

Later I walked over to the lunchroom with the seminar director who appeared to be discouraged. He told me I had wasted much of my time talking about General Powell. Seminar personnel had tested student knowledge of current events and famous people of the day and found that fewer than 30 percent had even heard of General Powell. I was not surprised by the students' lack of knowledge, which was indicative of what educators see as the general decline in the U.S. educational system. In this case, however, I thought that it was ironic that black youth, who are often described as lacking good role models, were unaware of General Powell and his extraordinary accomplishments. But I continue to praise Powell and other blacks of his caliber in my talks to raise black awareness of our many role-model black citizens who have achieved outstanding success in the worlds of commerce, science, and technology.

Occasional success is sufficient reward. At a talk I gave November 7, 1991, at the Nataki Talibah Schoolhouse, a private black elementary school in my hometown of Detroit, Clare and I were warmly welcomed by both the students and staff. We were particularly impressed by the attentiveness of the students. One of them honored me with a guided tour of the school. It gave me renewed hope that with the guidance and direction of dedicated parents and teachers our black youth will achieve success in the world of tomorrow.

Shortly after arriving home I received a letter from every student in the two class assemblies I had addressed. The following is typical:

Dear Mr. Loving,
My name is Jeffrey McCall and I don't know if you remember me, but I am the student who asked about your occupation. I'm in the 6th grade and I want to become a basketball player when I grow up. When you were talking about what a student should want to be when they grow up, it made me think. "I may not be a basketball player. Then I have to go to law school or get my real estate license." That really made me think. Mr. Loving, the school is really glad you came.
Thank you and come again.
Sincerely,
Jeff McCall

Another special goal in my life is to provide an active role model for handicapped people of all ages. I know full well the mental trauma that accompanies the loss of a limb. Even after the bright promise of being fitted with my new prostheses, I experienced periods of despair. The pain levels I endured during the weeks of adjustment were, at times, almost unbearable. When I finally resumed my preaccident level of aviation activity it became clear that pain was to be my constant companion. Walking and standing on busy days caused blisters to form, adding to my misery. There were times when I was tempted to sit in my wheelchair in comparative comfort. But my deep love of aviation motivated me to make full use of my artificial limbs so that I could live up to the title of the book, *Reach for the Sky,* a biography of Douglas Bader. This famous British Spitfire pilot of World War II was a double amputee, like me, and understandably became my favorite role model.

Fortunately, the publicity I have received as the only black double amputee to design, build, and qualify a racing airplane has helped promote a positive image for others with a similar handicap. I always let my audiences and interviewers know I am happy to discuss and publicize my disability rather than hide it.

Sometimes I am too successful in proving I am not handicapped. Youngsters have come up and asked to feel my legs to see if they are really made of wood (as the boys did in Cuba). The bright smile of discovery on their faces provides continuing inspiration for me (if not for them).

On Labor Day, 1983, I was riding my new three-speed bicycle headed north toward Ellis Park on Polecat Road, a narrow two-lane road just north of Yellow Springs. The park is popular for picnicking and its well-stocked pond draws many fishermen. Riding along the right side of the road, I waved in response to a middle-aged couple who were enjoying a walk to the park. On approaching the park entrance for a left turn, I saw a car coming up behind me. I pulled over to the center line so he could pass me on my right as customary, losing sight of him momentarily as I started my turn. Just as I straightened out and headed for the park entrance I was startled to see his car coming toward me from the left at a very high speed—estimated at 60 to 65 MPH. His car struck the front wheel of my bicycle at a right angle, passing within inches of my face. Losing control of his car, he bounced off a telephone pole and careened to a stop about a quarter mile down the road. Although the force was sufficient to demolish the front wheel of my bicycle, I was still sitting upright and had not lost my balance. Even with both hands on the handlebars, I did not feel the slightest tremor. Despite my engineering knowledge of vehicle crash dynamics, my survival without any personal injury was unexplainable. The couple to whom I had waved rushed to my side and offered assistance. The husband, a volunteer fireman, prepared to administer first aid before calling the firehouse for assistance. Fortunately I had no need for either service. But it is the words of his wife I shall never forget. "When I saw that car heading toward you I closed my eyes for I was sure you were going to be killed. When I heard the car crash I was sure the worst had happened. I opened my eyes and there you were, sitting on your bicycle as though nothing had happened. I don't know who you are but I am sure the Lord must have something for you to accomplish on this earth and He is not letting you die until it is finished."

During the ensuing years, and while planning and writing this autobiography, her words have frequently come to mind. Did the Lord really perform a miracle so I could accomplish this task? It would be presumptuous of me to think so. You the reader can decide for yourself.

PLANE SPECIFICATIONS

LOVING GLIDER NLG-1 (NX15750)

Wing span	30.0 ft.
Overall length	20.5 ft.
Height	7.75 ft.
Wing area	148.0 sq. ft.
Wing chord	5.0 ft.
Aspect ratio	6.0
Center of gravity (gross weight)	24.0%
Weight	
Empty	260.0 lbs.
Pilot	150.0 lbs.
Gross	410.0 lbs.
Wing loading	2.8 lbs./sq. ft.
Airfoil section	Goettingen 387

PERFORMANCE (Calculated)

Glide speed (max glide ratio)	38.5 MPH
Glide speed (minimum sink)	32.0 MPH
Stall speed	28.0 MPH

NLG-1 was a single-place, wire-braced, high-wing monoplane of all-wood construction, fabric covered. The design was basically a primary glider modified with an enclosed cockpit. The landing gear was a single-curved, hardwood skid. The entire plane was cream-colored with a brown stripe at the nose. It was never flown due to ground damage sustained while on exhibit at the St. Antoine YMCA in Detroit in 1937. Potential weight and balance problems were also identified.

Wing span	25.25 ft
Overall length	16.60 ft.
Height	7.10 ft.
Wing area	87.00 sq. ft.
Aspect ratio	7.12
Wing chord	3.50 ft.
Wing airfoil	Goettingen 387
Center of gravity (gross weight)	24.2%
Weight	
Empty	160 lbs.
Pilot	135 lbs.
Gross	295 lbs.
Wing loading	3.4 lbs./sq. ft.

PERFORMANCE (Calculated)

Glide speed (max glide ratio)	34.6 MPH
Glide speed (minimum sink)	30.5 MPH
Stall speed	25.0 MPH
Sinking speed	3.17 ft./sec.
Glide ratio	15 : 1

The S-1 was a single-place, strut-braced, high-wing monoplane of all-wood construction, fabric covered. The design was in the utility glider category. The landing gear was a single 10×2.75 tire and wheel. The wings, upper fuselage, and horizontal tail were blue and the lower fuselage and rudder yellow. On its last flight, July 30, 1944, it had accumulated a total of 27 flights using auto tow. The glider was damaged beyond repair on that flight.

The S-2, a production version, was basically the same design with the wing span extended to 29.1 feet and an enlarged cockpit (see Fig. 1). This airplane, designed for the military and civilian market, was never completed.

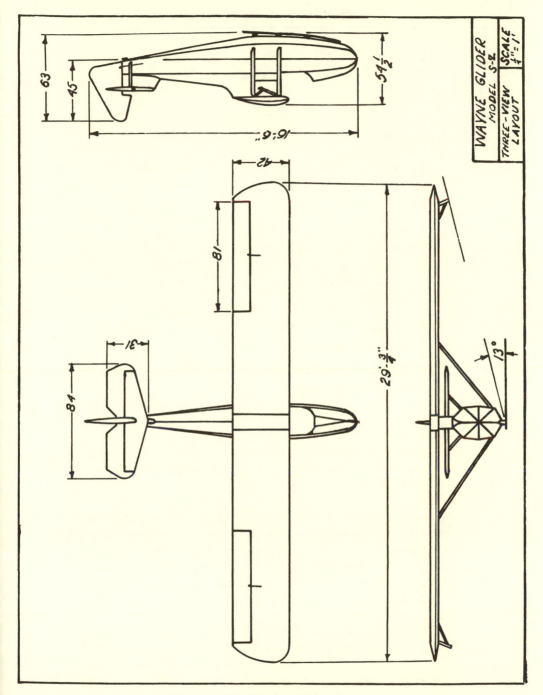

Figure 1 - The Wayne glider, model S-2.

Wing span	20.0 ft.
Overall length	17.2 ft.
Height	4.4 ft.
Wing area	66.0 sq. ft.
Aspect ratio	6.06
Root chord	4.125 ft.
Tip chord	2.125 ft.
Root airfoil	NACA 2412
Tip airfoil	NACA 2409
Center of gravity (gross weight)	23.8% of MAC
Weight	
Empty	631.5 lbs.
15 gal. gasoline	90.0 lbs.
4 qts. oil	7.5 lbs.
Baggage	10.0 lbs.
Pilot and parachute	170.0 lbs.
Useful load	277.5 lbs.
Gross	909.0 lbs.
Wing loading	13.46 lbs./sq. ft.
Power loading (115 HP	
at 3,800 RPM)	7.73 lbs./HP

PERFORMANCE (Sea Level)

RPM	True airspeed
1,500	90 MPH
2,400	165
2,700	181
3,000	192
3,200	198

The above figures were obtained using a McCauley Met-L-Prop Design No. 1R92/Am6066, which turned about 2,325 RPM static. This propeller was used for all cross-country flights. The racing design 1R94/6054 allowed the engine to reach over 3,800 RPM in level flight resulting in a top speed of approximately 215–225 MPH. The climb performance was similarly improved. The Continental C-85-FJ used in "Loving's Love" is normally rated at 85 HP, turning a maximum of 2,575 RPM (see Fig. 2).

N351C was a single-place sport/racer designed to meet the standards established for the midget-racing category by the PRPA and the NAA. It was of all-wood construction with plywood and fabric covering. Wings and forward fuselage were metallic maroon and remaining portions were cream. The racing number, 64, was painted white with gold trim. Later the colors were changed to two-tone blue and white. "Loving's Love" had 269 hours and 35 minutes accumulated flying time at the time it was retired to the EAA Air Education Museum in October 1964.

Planes Worth Modeling

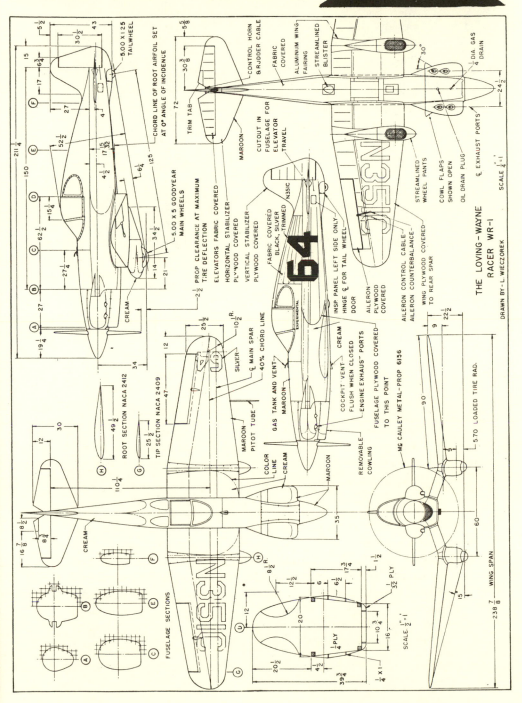

Figure 2 - The Loving-Wayne racer, WR-1. (Reprinted courtesy of *Model Airplane News*, September 1958.)

Wing span	24.90 ft.
Overall length	19.87 ft.
Height	5.51 ft.
Wing area	101.7 sq. ft.
Aspect ratio	6.05
Root chord	4.25 ft.
Wing airfoil	NACA 4309
Center of gravity location	
Empty	23.00%
Gross weight	25.10%
Weight	
Empty	687.50 lbs.
15 gal. gasoline	90.00 lbs.
4 qts. oil	7.50 lbs.
Pilot	170.00 lbs.
Passenger	170.00 lbs.
Baggage	20.00 lbs.
Useful load	457.50 lbs.
Gross weight	1,145.00 lbs.
Wing loading	11.25 lbs./sq. ft.
Power loading	13.45 lbs./HP

PERFORMANCE (Sea Level, Calculated)

Top speed	119.00 MPH
Cruise speed @ 70% power	110.00 MPH
Stall speed	52.50 MPH
Maximum rate of climb	845.00 ft./min.
Maximum range (still air,	
no reserve)	528.00 miles

Roadable WR-2 was a high-wing, strut-braced, fabric-covered monoplane of all-wood construction. Pilot and passenger sat side by side in a staggered seat arrangement. A tricycle-type landing gear was installed. The Continental C-85 was mounted in a pusher configuration. The wings and upper fuselage were red with the lower fuselage painted white. Initial taxi and lift-off tests were conducted at Detroit City Airport and Willow Run Airport. These tests indicated serious aerodynamic control and weight and balance problems. N112Y was dismantled at Springfield Municipal Airport, October 1961.

Wing span	24.83 ft.
Overall length	19.75 ft
Height	6.5 ft.
Width (wings folded)	8.0 ft.
Wing area	105.0 sq. ft.
Aspect ratio	6.0
Wing chord	4.25 ft.
Center of gravity (gross weight)	24.6%
Weight	
Empty	785.0 lbs.
15 gal. gasoline	90.0 lbs.
4 qts. oil	7.5 lbs.
Baggage	10.0 lbs.
Pilot	170.0 lbs.
Passenger	170.0 lbs.
Useful load	447.5 lbs.
Gross weight	1,232.5 lbs.
Wing loading	11.7 lbs./sq. ft.
Power loading	14.5 lbs./HP

PERFORMANCE (Sea Level)

Maximum speed (2,575 RPM)	115.0 MPH
Cruise speed (2,450 RPM)	105.0 MPH
Rate of climb	
Solo	650.0 ft./min.
With passenger	450.0 ft./min.
Range (no reserve, no wind)	315.0 miles

Performance was obtained with a Univair/Flottorp propeller, 72A46, at sea level, standard conditions, at gross weight. Maximum tow speed on level highway was 55 MPH.

WR-3 was a two-place, open-cockpit, tandem-seated, strut-braced, low-wing monoplane of all-wood construction, fabric covered (see Fig. 3). The landing gear was a standard two-wheel configuration with a steerable tailwheel. Wings, nose, and tail were red with all remaining surfaces white.

Total accumulated flight time from first flight on April 26, 1968, to October 18, 1991, was 696.84 hours. In June 1992 the local FAA medical examiner denied my application for a pilot's medical certificate for medical reasons. After reviewing the results of my examination, the FAA Medical Center in Oklahoma permanently revoked my pilot's medical certificate in a letter dated October 17, 1992. Thus my flying career spanning over 54 years was formally ended.

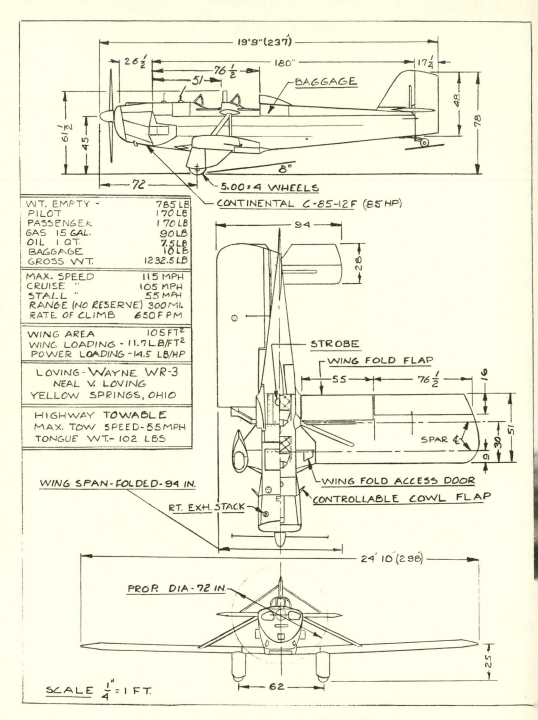

WT. EMPTY - 785 LB
PILOT 170 LB
PASSENGER 170 LB
GAS 15 GAL. 90 LB
OIL 1 QT. 7.5 LB
BAGGAGE 10 LB
GROSS WT. 1232.5 LB

MAX. SPEED 115 MPH
CRUISE " 105 MPH
STALL " 55 MPH
RANGE (NO RESERVE) 300 MI.
RATE OF CLIMB 650 FPM

WING AREA 105 FT²
WING LOADING - 11.7 LB/FT²
POWER LOADING - 14.5 LB/HP

LOVING-WAYNE WR-3
NEAL V. LOVING
YELLOW SPRINGS, OHIO

HIGHWAY TOWABLE
MAX. TOW SPEED - 55 MPH
TONGUE WT. - 102 LBS

19'9" (237)
26½   51   76½   180   17¼
BAGGAGE
61½   45   72   48   78
8°
5.00 x 4 WHEELS
CONTINENTAL C-85-12F (85 HP)

94   28
STROBE
WING FOLD FLAP
55   76½   16
SPAR ℄   51   30   9
WING FOLD ACCESS DOOR
CONTROLLABLE COWL FLAP
WING SPAN-FOLDED-94 IN.
RT. EXH. STACK

24' 10" (298)
PROP. DIA - 72 IN.
25
62
SCALE ¼" = 1 FT.

Figure 3 - The Loving Roadable, WR-3.

CARIBBEAN FLIGHT LOG

"LOVING'S LOVE" (N351C)

FROM DETROIT, MICHIGAN TO KINGSTON,
JAMAICA, WEST INDIES, DECEMBER 1–10, 1953

Flight Leg	Miles	Fuel	Cost	Time
Detroit—Cincinnati, Ohio	220	8.0 gal.	$ 2.80	1:55
Cincinnati—Lexington, Ky.	103	4.5	1.53	:55
Lexington—Knoxville, Tenn.	163	8.0	2.96	1:50
Knoxville—Chattanooga, Tenn.	90	3.6	1.31	:45
added 1 qt. oil			0.40	
Chattanooga—Atlanta, Ga.	120	4.0	1.48	:50
Atlanta—Macon, Ga.	98	3.7	1.37	:45
Macon—Jacksonville, Fla.	190	7.7	2.85	1:45
Jacksonville—Ft. Lauderdale, Fla.	330	10.3	3.81	2:30
Ft. Lauderdale—Havana, Cuba	265	9.0	4.07	1:55
Havana—Camaguey, Cuba	330	10.0	4.83	2:20
Camaguey—Kingston, Jamaica	250	8.8	3.50	2:05
Total	2,159	77.6	$30.91	17:35

FROM KINGSTON, JAMAICA, TO DETROIT, MAY 19–JUNE 4, 1954

Flight Leg	Miles	Fuel	Cost	Time
Kingston—Camaguey, Cuba	250	8.0 gal.	$ 3.62	2:00
Camaguey—Havana, Cuba	330	8.0	3.62	2:20
Havana—Ft. Lauderdale, Fla.	265	9.0	3.33	2:10
added 1 qt. oil			0.40	
Ft. Lauderdale— Jacksonville, Fla.	330	11.7	4.33	2:45
Jacksonville—Charleston, S.C.	210	7.5	2.40	1:45
Charleston—Raleigh, N.C.	230	9.0	3.06	2:05
Raleigh—Baltimore, Md.	280	10.0	3.51	2:25
Baltimore—Teterboro, N.J.	150	6.0	1.14	1:35
added 1 qt. oil			0.45	
Teterboro—Harrisburg, Pa.	170	6.0	2.43	1:35
Harrisburg—Pittsburgh, Pa.	172	7.2	2.79	1:45
Pittsburgh—Akron, Ohio	87	6.0	2.17	1:10
Akron—Detroit	165	7.0	2.45	1:30
Total	2,639	95.4	$35.70	23:05